IN SEARCH OF GOLD

Elizabeth N. Conger
Holeski Collection

Horace S. Conger
Holeski Collection

IN SEARCH OF

GOLD

The Alaska Journals of HORACE S. CONGER 1898~1899

Carolyn Jean Holeski
and
Marlene Conger Holeski

The Alaska Geographic Society

Anchorage, Alaska

EB

Cover: Photograph No. 51, "Up the River from Saw Mill Bluff," by Neil D. Benedict from his manuscript, "The Valdes and Copper River Trail," 1899, an unpublished manuscript in the Alaska Historical Library, Juneau.

Library of Congress cataloging in publication data:
Conger, Horace Samuel, 1863-1941.
    In search of gold.
    (Alaska Historical Commission studies in history;
no. 28)
    Bibliography: p.
    1.Copper River Region (Alaska) — Description and
travel. 2. Copper River Region (Alaska) — Gold discoveries. 3. Alaska — Description and travel — 1896-1959.
4. Conger, Horace Samuel, 1863-1941. I. Holeski,
Carolyn Jean. II. Holeski, Marlene Conger. III. Title.
IV. Series.
F912.C7C78 1983   979.8'3   83-10036
    ISBN 0-88240-239-0

Published with assistance from the Alaska Historical Commission; however, all statements herein, whether of fact or opinion, are the responsibility of the author.

Design by Jon.Hersh
Layout by Pamela Adams

The Alaska Geographic Society
Box 4-EEE, Anchorage, Alaska 99509

Printed in U.S.A.

iv

1-16-76

For Tom,
who shared his great-grandfather's
spirit and love of adventure.

Acknowledgments

Morgan B. Sherwood, noted Alaskan historian and professor of history at the University of California, Davis, for encouragement, guidance, and valuable suggestions.

The University of California, Davis, for the support provided by a President's Undergraduate Fellowship Award.

Hortense Conger Hill, for permission to use her father's diary, letters, and photographs in this book.

Zelma Doig, Phyllis De Muth, and Verda Carey, librarians at the Alaska Historical Library at Juneau for help in obtaining obscure reference materials.

The Alaska Historical Commission, especially William S. Hanable, Executive Director, for reading the manuscript and supporting its publication.

C.J.H. and M.C.H.

Contents

Prologue

Gold was first reported in Alaska during the Russian occupation, about the time of the rush to the California gold fields. A Russian mining engineer found "colors" in the gravels of the Kenai River on the Kenai Peninsula in 1848, but he never found the source of the gold, and the report generated no excitement. Few attempts at prospecting by the Russians are known. It is generally believed that they suppressed information about the mineral wealth of Alaska, fearing an influx of American and English prospectors and the ruination of their lucrative fur trade.[1]

A series of placer gold discoveries in British Columbia began luring prospectors northward from California and other western mining communities in the late 1850s. When production from these deposits slackened, the miners scattered in search of new gold fields. In 1880 prospectors discovered rich placers at the head of what later was called Gold Creek in Southeastern Alaska. The resulting stampede led to the founding of Juneau and to the major lode gold discoveries in that vicinity. By 1883 Juneau was the center of mining activity in Alaska.[2]

Meanwhile, gold seekers had begun crossing the coastal mountains at the head of Lynn Canal, near Juneau, into the remote interior. They trickled over the 3,739-foot Chilkoot Pass, on the Alaska-British Columbia border, to the lakes and streams which lead to the Yukon River. The Tlingit Indians living along this section of the coast had long opposed the entry of whites into that country for fear of losing their trade monopoly with the interior Indians. But assured that white men were seeking only mineral wealth, the Indians opened the pass in 1880. Previously, white men reached the Interior of Alaska by way of a long all-water route, sailing by ocean steamer to Saint Michael, near the mouth of the Yukon River, and traveling up the Yukon in flat-bottomed river boats. A major disadvantage of the Saint Michael route was that it was available only when the Bering Sea and Yukon River were free of ice — usually between late June and mid-September. Though the Dyea Trail across Chilkoot Pass was more laborious than the Saint Michael route, it was less expensive and was open the year around, making it an attractive alternative route for prospectors.[3]

The first important discoveries of gold in Interior Alaska were made in the Yukon drainage basin. In 1886 prospectors discovered the auriferous gravels of the Fortymile River, and by 1893 more than 300 men were at work on the creeks of this district, located along Alaska's eastern boundary. News of a richer strike lured many of these prospectors north to Birch Creek, another tributary of the Yukon, in 1894. The town of Circle became the headquarters of the Birch Creek district, and its population grew to 1,500 before it was nearly depopulated during the winter of 1896-97 by news that large amounts of coarse gold had been discovered in the Yukon Territory of Canada, not far from present-day Dawson.[4]

The Canadian strike was destined to attract tens of thousands of gold seekers to the Far North. George Carmack, a white man who was married to an Indian woman, staked the Discovery Claim on Rabbit Creek, a tributary of the Klondike River, in August of 1896. Rich deposits of the precious yellow metal were soon located in nearby creeks, and by the end of November 500 claims were staked in the district. Carmack renamed Rabbit Creek "Bonanza Creek." This was an appropriate name, for Bonanza proved to be the richest creek in the Klondike district and one of the richest placer streams discovered worldwide.[5]

News of the Klondike was brought Outside early in 1897. On March 14 the *Seattle Post-Intelligencer* quoted from a letter written in the gold fields in January: "I may as well tell you," wrote W.F. Cornell, "that in my 42 years' experience on the

Pacific coast so much gold has never been found in the same extent of country. In fact, you may believe anything you hear; it can hardly be exaggerated.''⁶

Experienced miners and persons who received reliable reports of the strike by mail composed the vanguard of the rush to the Far North in the spring of 1897; however, the big stampede did not begin until the first heavy cargoes of Klondike gold reached West Coast ports in mid-July. The *Excelsior* arrived in San Francisco on July 14, and the *Portland* docked in Seattle three days later. The golden treasure on these two ships confirmed the early reports of the richness of the Klondike discovery and caused a dynamic public reaction.⁷

The following excerpts from a newspaper story, datelined Seattle, July 17, 1897, describe the excitement that existed in that city after the *Portland's* arrival.

> *It is safe to say that never in the history of the Northwest has there been such excitement as has prevailed in this city all day long and which is raging to-night. It is due to the arrival . . . of the steamer* Portland, *carrying sixty-eight men from the Clondyke gold fields, every one of whom brings down a fortune.*
>
> *There have been so many stories sent out from Alaska of great strikes which later proved to be without foundation that people were reaching that period where they refused to credit them. But when the big Portland ran alongside the ocean dock at 8 o'clock this morning and those sixty-eight men . . . walked down the gangplank struggling to hold up the weight of gold which was stacked high on their shoulders, the thousands of people who stood on the dock to receive them were suddenly seized with Clondyke fever, and to-night Clondyke is on the lips of every man, woman and child of this city.*
>
> *One could not enter the ticket offices of the companies running steamers between here and Alaska without waiting at least an hour. How the steamers are*

going to accomodate all who propose to go north is a mystery. One steamer is expected to sail to-morrow. There will not be standing room on it.

It is claimed that these people who are going north are making a mistake. Conservative men who have been in the country . . . admit that all of the fields in the vicinity of the Clondyke have been taken, but every river in Alaska is, in their judgment, filled with gold, which can be secured if the men are willing to risk the hardships.[8]

Because the Klondike discovery was made while the U.S. was suffering the effects of a long economic depression, largely caused by the scarcity of gold for coinage and the payment of foreign debts, word of the new El Dorado spread from Seattle and San Francisco across the land like wildfire. Though most people did not know precisely where the new placer field was, Klondike became the main topic of conversation wherever people gathered. Day after day, newspapers carried illustrated front-page accounts of the wonders of the Klondike, inciting thousands of gold-crazed people to make plans for the long journey to the Far North.[9]

Obtaining accurate information about routes and transportation to the new gold fields was not an easy task. The general public had expressed little interest in Alaska prior to the Klondike discovery; thus, the government was unprepared for the flood of inquiries it received about the remote territory in the summer of 1897. The supply of Coast Survey maps and charts was exhausted before August, and the demand for information became so great that newspapers began printing the advice of returning miners and others who claimed first-hand knowledge of the country. Low water levels halted traffic on the Yukon in late August, eliminating the Saint Michael route. Two weeks later unusually heavy rains obliterated the trails over the coastal mountains at the head of Lynn Canal,[10] stalling hundreds of other gold seekers. At the time, these were the only established routes to the placer fields of Interior Alaska and the adjacent Yukon Territory (which

The Excelsior, *July 29, 1897*

together were indiscriminately called the "Klondike" region). Consequently, in the fall of 1897, gold seekers became increasingly receptive to the vague reports of new, untested routes being circulated in newspapers, transportation company pamphlets, and hastily researched guidebooks. In their eagerness to reach the Klondike, gold seekers did not stop to question the reliability of these publications. As a result, inaccurate information and even deliberate fabrications were read and accepted as fact. Several thousand people who headed for the Copper River region of Alaska were the victims of such misinformation.[11]

In early August of 1897, newspapers reported the discovery of a "new route" to the Klondike via the Copper River. A civil engineer claimed that he had found a "short and easy" route which started from the mouth of the Copper and followed up this stream and its main tributary, the Chitina, to a pass in the mountains which led to the White River, a tributary of the Yukon. At

Entrance to Miles Canyon, Copper River.

this time, little was known about the Copper River region, which is located in Southcentral Alaska. Existing knowledge was confined primarily to Russian records, information obtained from the Natives, and an obscure government report of the first American to ascend and explore the Copper River, Lt. Henry T. Allen, Second U.S. Cavalry. Allen successfully ascended the Copper nearly as far as its headwaters in 1885, but the difficulties he encountered showed that this was not a feasible route to the interior.[12]

Allen found the Copper to be a mud-laden, turbulent stream which often flows in multiple, tortuous channels. It heads on a glacier on the north slope of the Wrangell Mountains, and on its 250-mile course to the Gulf of Alaska it first trends in a northwesterly direction, then makes a big bend to the southeast, half encircling the Wrangells before cutting through the Chugach Mountains in a deep narrow valley. About 30 miles from the

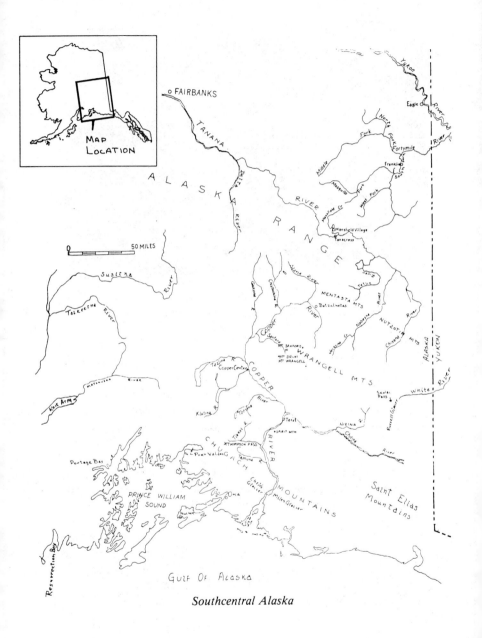

Southcentral Alaska

Looking north up the Copper from mouth of Chitina River, 1899.

sea, the Copper emerges from the mountains and is flanked by two fast-receding glaciers, Miles and Childs. At the turn of the century treacherous rapids, caused by glacial debris, occurred along this stretch of the river, preventing upstream navigation except with lightweight canoes. Though it was possible to shoot these rapids going downstream, voyagers were in imminent danger from great icebergs and the huge waves these ice masses created when discharged by the glaciers. At the river's mouth is a 20-mile-wide delta, consisting of marshes and extensive mud flats. Soon after departing from the river's mouth in March, Allen was forced to portage. He employed sleds until soft snow compelled him to abandon his sledding and a large portion of his supplies. Later he alternately boated and portaged along his course but the initial loss of provisions caused his party to suffer great privations. Little mention was made of Lieutenant Allen's arduous experiences when the "new route" via Copper River was first announced. Instead, the possibility of a Copper River route renewed speculation about the mineral wealth of that region.[13]

Since the early days of the Russian occupation of Alaska, it was known that the Copper River Indians traded specimens of pure copper with the coastal Natives. The Russians believed the source of this metal was located at the headwaters of the Copper. They made several attempts to locate it but were foiled by the difficulty of ascending the Copper and the hostility of the Indians. In 1848 a Russian expedition led by Serebrennikov reached the highest known Russian position on the Copper River. Serebrennikov and his men never returned from their journey, however, and were presumed murdered by the Indians. What is definitely known of their journey was learned from Serebrennikov's notes, which were surrendered by the Natives later: the party ascended the Copper to the mouth of the Tazlina and made a side trip up this stream, where they met friendly but destitute Indians. Upon returning to the Copper, they headed upriver. What happened after this is uncertain; however, the last notation in Serebrennikov's record was the latitude 62°48′45″.[14]

Information gathered by Robert A. McKennan in 1929-30 for his ethnological study, *The Upper Tanana Indians,* suggests that Serebrennikov and his party probably met their end at Batzulnetas, an upper Copper River Indian village. McKennan directs attention to the fact that Serebrennikov's last latitudinal observation approximates that of Batzulnetas, and that the Indians of the upper Nabesna River have a legend that there was once a Russian camp at Batzulnetas. "According to the natives," said McKennan, "the Indians were treated with great cruelty, the women were taken into the camp for the entertainment of the Russians, and the Indian men were told to go into the hills and seek furs. They returned in the dead of night and slaughtered the garrison to the last man."[15]

Reports of hostile Natives and the lack of an easy access route discouraged American prospectors and explorers from entering the Copper River region for many years. In the spring of 1882 C.G. Holt, a trader from the Alaska Commercial

Company's post at Nuchek, on Hinchinbrook Island, ascended the Copper to the Indian village at Taral, near the mouth of the Chitina. He accompanied the Copper River Natives, who were returning from a coastal trading voyage, hoping to learn the location of the region's copper deposits. Holt returned to the coast in September, having ventured no farther than a couple of miles from Taral "due to some accident that crippled him." He described the Natives as "treacherous and thievish," and about four years later he was murdered by them.[16]

In 1884 the War Department instructed Lieutenant W.R. Abercrombie, Second U.S. Infantry, to ascertain the numbers, character, and disposition of the Indians living in the country drained by the Copper and Tanana rivers. Abercrombie began his ascent of the Copper River in June of 1884, but by late August, the difficulties he had encountered in traveling a short distance prompted him to try an alternate route which he had learned of from the Natives. They had informed him that an abandoned Indian trail started at Port Valdez and went over the mountains to a lake, the outlet of which supposedly ran into the Copper River below the mouth of the Chitina. On September 12, Abercrombie set out from Port Valdez to try the old Indian route, but he found the snow too soft to continue and soon returned to camp. Thus, another attempt to penetrate the Copper River country ended in failure.[17]

The following year Lt. Henry T. Allen made the first successful reconnaissance of the Copper River, described previously. His explorations included a side trip up the Chitina River to the winter house of Nicolai, the autocrat of the Indians of Taral and the Chitina River. From Nicolai, Allen learned of three massacres of Russians on the Copper River — one near the mouth of the river, another on the upper river, and one just below Taral. Nicolai was reluctant to talk about these slayings, but he finally told Allen the details of the Taral massacre, which had been carried out by his own people: "Three Russians and as many sleds drawn by natives were en route to Taral with merchandise. The natives were not allowed to sleep and were compelled to haul the

Russians, who slept on the sleds. At a preconcerted signal the head of each of them was crushed in with an ax.'' Nicolai claimed ignorance of the details of the other massacres, but Allen assumed that the one which occurred on the upper river was that of Serebrennikov's party.[18]

Lieutenant Allen was shown a vein of copper by Nicolai during the course of his exploration of the Copper River, but he reported finding few indications of gold; yet, in view of the gold fever sweeping the nation in the summer of 1897, it is not surprising that rumors began circulating that the yellow metal was also present in the Copper River region. In late August of 1897, West Coast promotors with "secret information" began seeking recruits for private prospecting trips to the Copper River. The promotor of one expedition was a wealthy California real estate man who claimed he had discovered gold on the Copper while serving in the Revenue Service (now the Coast Guard). On August 24, the *San Francisco Chronicle* reported that he had formed a company, secured a schooner called *La Ninfa,* and was quietly seeking 50 shareholders who would join in the ownership of the boat and supplies. He claimed he would lead his stockholders up the river in small steam launches and whaleboats to the location of the precious metal, but where this was, he declined to say.[19]

As *La Ninfa* and other ships which had been chartered to ascend the Copper River sat idle at their wharves, waiting for recruits, newspapers suddenly began printing stories about gold strikes in the Copper River region. According to prospectors who had allegedly returned from the region, the Copper River country was richer than the Klondike, mining experts were buying up claims in the region, and smelters and stamp mills would probably be erected at the mouth of the river by the following spring. These embroidered stories accomplished their purpose: promotors of private expeditions filled their empty passenger billets and set sail for the Copper River.[20]

Evidence suggests that the Pacific Steam Whaling Company concluded that it could profit from the rumored wealth of the

Copper River country by promoting the unexplored Indian route across Valdez Glacier (which Abercrombie had learned of from the Natives in 1884) and then establishing public transportation to that wilderness region. The statements attributed to Captain O.J. Humphrey, appearing in the *San Francisco Chronicle* on October 11, 1897, apparently were designed to lay the ground-work for this scheme. Humphrey was the superintendent of four canneries operated by the Pacific Steam Whaling Company in Alaska. He had worked for the company since 1889, spending most of his time at the Orca Cannery near the mouth of the Copper River. He had arrived in San Francisco with specimens of quartz which reportedly assayed $20 gold and $10 copper to the ton. He stated that there was a mountain on the shores of Prince William Sound which appeared to be composed "almost wholly of this quartz," and though the more accessible deposits had been taken up, he proclaimed that "the whole district is rich in minerals and particularly at the head of the Copper river." Humphrey correctly emphasized the futility of attempting an ascent of the Copper River, then declared that "even the Indians long ago abandoned the river route and now come down by the Valdes Pass," which he said was located on a dead glacier, 96 miles from the Copper River. "By this pass," said Humphrey, "the upper Yukon and Copper River countries may be reached without going out of American territory."[21] Ten days after Humphrey made these statements, the Pacific Steam Whaling Company announced its intention of entering the Alaskan passenger trade with the former revenue cutter *Wolcott,* which it had purchased in March. The *Wolcott* sailed for the Prince William Sound area with its first passengers on November 10, 1897.[22]

Humphrey's intimations, published on the front page of the *Seattle Post-Intelligencer* eight days later, show that the Whaling Company was trying to boost the popularity of the Valdez Glacier route by escalating the rumors about the Copper River region's wealth. According to Humphrey, telegraph and stage companies were organizing to operate in the Copper River district, and detailed plans of these ventures would soon be made public. He reiterated the hazards of attempting an ascent of the Copper and asserted that "the trail by Valdes is the only way to escape the difficulties of the trip and it is bound to attract many prospectors as soon as its advantages shall be known." Humphrey hinted of an important enterprise in the works by stating, "The Company will not dally with the St. Michael trade. We are satisfied with the prospects of the Copper River business. You may imagine there is more in sight than is on the surface, or we should not establish a line of steamers scheduled to leave Seattle every fifteen days. But some propositions that are developing are not yet ripe, and I cannot yet make them public."[23] By the end of November, the Pacific Steam Whaling Company had secured a large passenger vessel in New York, the *Valencia*, and had added the steamers *Excelsior* and *Alliance* to its Alaskan fleet.[24]

Meanwhile, the *San Francisco Chronicle* reported that another company (which it did not name) had begun vying for a portion of the Copper River trade. But unlike the Whaling Company, it made too many obvious misrepresentations about the region. Its alluring prospectus reportedly offered to take passengers up the Copper River and land them in the interior for $75. The river was "navigable for light draft steamers and small sailing vessels for about 250 miles," it said, and there were "small stations and Russian missions at different points." The prospectus also referred to the region's "comparatively mild" climate, the "good crops" that could be raised in the summer, and the "abundance of game." Had the company limited itself to its claim that the region was "richer by far than the Klondike," it probably would have escaped criticism, for at the time no one knew that this was a fictitious statement. However, Prof. George Davidson knew enough about the Copper River and its climate from his work with the Coast Survey (now the National Ocean Survey) to denounce the prospectus, calling its statements "the most infamous falsehoods ever published." He added that "anybody who will read Lieutenant Allen's report of his ascent of the Copper River . . . will find out that the river is not navigable for vessels of any kind whatever."[25]

To illustrate the scarcity of game and the lack of other sources of food in the Copper River region, Davidson quoted from the journal of Fred Fickett, who accompanied Lieutenant Allen up the Copper River in 1885. The following excerpts are taken from Fickett's journal.[26]

> April 13: *[Indians] had left a few scraps lying around, and these, that neither they nor their dogs would eat, we were forced by hunger to gather up and make a meal on. This is Lieutenant Allen's birthday, and he celebrated it by eating rotten moose meat.*

> April 17: *Rotten moose meat would be a delicacy now. So weak from hunger that we had to stop at noon to hunt. All so weak that we were dizzy, and would stagger like drunken men.*

> May 28.: *Had a little paste, rotten goose eggs and a little rice for supper. Each meal about one-fourth of what we needed.*

> May 29: *Party nearly played out for want of food. Can just crawl. Had to stop middle of p.m. to make a flapjack for each and a little beef tea.*

> May 30: *Arrived at an Indian house at 11 A.M. hungry. Decided to abandon boat. Indian gave us a dinner of boiled meat, from which he scraped the maggots by handfuls before cutting it up. It tasted good, maggots and all.*

By mid-November of 1897, returning prospectors began to dispute the statements of great gold finds in the Copper River region. In Seattle, W.M. Wheeler warned that "nobody ever found gold on Copper River. All the stories about gold being brought from there are lies. There may be some at the headwaters but that remains to be proved."[27] In San Francisco, Frank Mariner stated that " there are no gold deposits there that I have either seen or heard of." Speaking of the men who had arrived at the mouth of the Copper River on *La Ninfa*, Mariner said: "They went because the man who got up the expedition said that when he was on a government survey he had discovered gold on

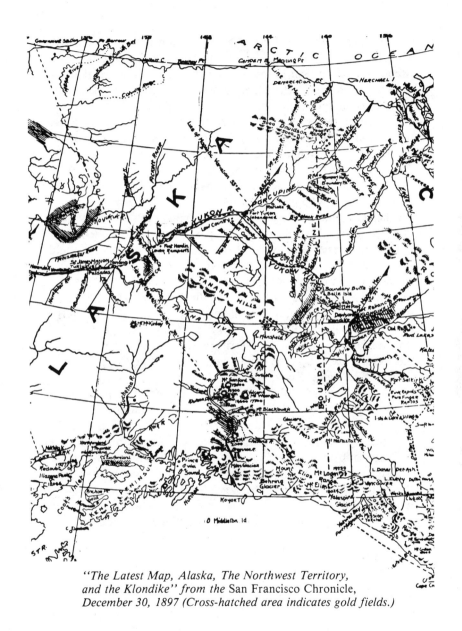

"The Latest Map, Alaska, The Northwest Territory, and the Klondike" from the San Francisco Chronicle, *December 30, 1897 (Cross-hatched area indicates gold fields.)*

the Copper river. No one else ever did, and the men from San Francisco found out that he knew nothing about the country."[28] Reports reaching San Francisco late in November stated that the promotor of the *Ninfa* expedition was "nearly hanged by the duped and indignant miners."[29]

Despite the warnings, rumors of gold in the Copper River region persisted, leading many fortune seekers to believe that the district was as rich as the Klondike and more accessible. By December nearly 200 prospectors had been lured to the mouth of the river and were stranded. Some of these gold seekers paid the Pacific Steam Whaling Company $10 each to transport them to the head of Valdez Inlet, on Prince William Sound, where Valdez Glacier reportedly offered an easy passageway across the mountains. But early December's weather had lacked the cold temperatures and snow necessary to fill the glacier's crevasses; therefore, no progress was made on this route until early 1898.[30]

In the closing days of 1897, the illusion of rich gold fields in the Copper River region was enhanced by a map published in the *San Francisco Chronicle*. It illustrated "the present gold fields" of Alaska and the Yukon Territory and included an extensive auriferous area adjacent to the west bank of the Copper River, north of the Tiekel River.[31]

An estimated 4,000 adventurers rushed to Port Valdez between February and June of 1898. Of this number, approximately 3,000 crossed Valdez Glacier to search for gold in the Copper River country. From all that had been published, their decision appeared logical: if the rumors of Copper River gold proved unfounded, they could proceed to the established gold fields of the upper Yukon by way of the "all-American route," which had been advertised as a short route over which they could travel without paying Canadian import duties on their outfits.[32]

Notes—

1. Frank A. Golder, "Mining in Alaska Before 1867," *Alaska and Its History,* ed. Morgan B. Sherwood (Seattle: University of Washington Press, 1967), pp. 150-51.

2. Alfred H. Brooks, *Blazing Alaska's Trails,* 2d ed. (1953; rpt. Fairbanks: Univ. of Alaska Press, 1973), pp. 298-304, 312; Total gold production from the Juneau district through 1959 was 6,883,556 ounces — 66,279 from placers and the remainder from lodes. See A.H. Koschmann and M.H. Bergendahl, *Principal Gold-Producing Districts of the United States* (Washington: Gov. Printing Office, 1968), pp. 20-21.

3. Hubert Howe Bancroft, *History of the Pacific States of North America: Alaska 1730-1885,* Vol. 28 (San Francisco: A.L. Bancroft and Co., 1886, pp. 737-38; Alfred H. Brooks, "The Yukon District," *Maps and Descriptions of Routes of Exploration in Alaska in 1898 With General Information Concerning the Territory,* Senate Documents, Vol. 13 [3737], 55th Congress, 3d sess. (Washington: Gov. Printing Office, 1899), p. 97.

4. The Fortymile district had uninterrupted output through 1959, totaling 400,000 ounces, all from placers. Total production of the Birch Creek district between 1894 and 1959 was 705,660 ounces, all placer gold. Koschmann and Bergendahl, *Principal Gold-Producing Districts,* pp. 23, 25, 27; Capt. W.P. Richardson, "The Mighty Yukon as Seen and Explored," *Compilation of Narratives of Explorations in Alaska* (Washington: Gov. Printing Office, 1900), p. 748; By October of 1897, the mining population in the vicinity of Circle was about 180. Capt. P.H. Ray's letter to the adjutant general, Circle City, Alaska, Oct. 6, 1897, Capt. P.H. Ray, "Alaska, 1897, Relief of the Destitute in Gold Fields," *Compilation of Narratives,* p. 531.

5. Brooks, *Blazing Alaska's Trails,* pp. 336-41.

6. "Gold But No Food," p. 6; Also see "Great Gold Find," *Seattle Post-Intelligencer,* Feb. 10, 1897, p. 8.

7. Brooks, *Blazing Alaska's Trails,* p. 343; Edwin Tappan Adney, *The Klondike Stampede of 1897-1898* (1900; rpt. Fairfield, Washington: Ye Galleon Press, 1968), p. 298; "Sacks of Gold from the Mines of Clondyke," *San Francisco Chronicle,* July 15, 1897, p. 1; "Gold! Gold! Gold! Gold!" *Seattle Post-Intelligencer,* Extra Edition, July 17, 1897, p. 1.

8. "Fortunes from the Clondyke," *San Francisco Chronicle,* July 18, 1897, p. 1.

9. Chicago Record, *Klondike: The Chicago Record's Book for Gold Seekers* (Chicago: Monarch Book Co., 1897), pp. 343-44; "Where Are the Yukon Mines," *San Francisco Chronicle,* July 19, 1897, p. 1; "Seattle is Clondyke Crazy," *San Francisco Chronicle,* July 17, 1897, p. 1.

10. In addition to the Dyea Trail across Chilkoot Pass, routes starting from the head of Lynn Canal included the Dalton Trail, established across Chilkat Pass in the early 1890s, and the White Pass Trail, opened in July of 1897. See Brooks,

Blazing Alaska's Trails, pp. 354, 368; "New Route to the Yukon," *San Francisco Chronicle,* July 16, 1897, p. 2.

11. "Demand for Alaska Maps," *San Francisco Chronicle,* July 27, 1897, p. 2; "Fleeing from the Shadow of Starvation at Dawson," *San Francisco Chronicle,* Sept. 14, 1897, p. 9; Capt. E.F. Glenn and Capt. W.R. Abercrombie, "Report of Capt. Abercrombie," *Reports of Explorations in the Territory of Alaska, 1898* (Washington: Gov. Printing Office, 1899), p. 341; Chicago Record, *Klondike: The Chicago Record's Book for Gold Seekers,* p. 519; A.C. Harris, *Alaska and the Klondike Gold Fields* (n.p. 1897), p. 159.

12. "The Copper River Route," *Seattle Post-Intelligencer,* Aug. 8, 1897, p. 16; "Report of Another Route to the Klondike," *San Francisco Chronicle,* Aug. 3, 1897, p. 2; Lt. Henry T. Allen, "Report of a Military Reconnaissance in Alaska, Made in 1885," *Compilation of Narratives,* pp. 409-94.

13. Alfred H. Brooks, *The Geography and Geology of Alaska: A Summary of Existing Knowledge* (Washington: Gov. Printing Office, 1906), pp. 54-56; F.C. Schrader, "A Reconnaissance of a Part of Prince William Sound and the Copper River District, Alaska in 1898," *Twentieth Annual Report of the USGS,* Part 7 (Washington: Gov. Printing Office, 1900), pp. 387, 398-400.

14. Clarence L. Andrews, "Alaska Under the Russians — Industry, Trade, and Social Life," *Washington Historical Quarterly,* 7 (Oct. 1916), 285-86; Bancroft, *History of . . . Alaska,* p. 191; Brooks, *Blazing Alaska's Trails,* pp. 235-36; Allen, "Report of a Military Reconnaissance," *Compilation of Narratives,* pp. 412-13, 487; Morgan B. Sherwood, *Exploration of Alaska 1865-1900* (New Haven: Yale Univ. Press, 1965), p. 106.

15. Robert A. McKennan, *The Upper Tanana Indians,* in Yale Univ. Publications in Anthropology, No. 55, ed. Irving Rouse (New Haven: Dept. of Anthropology, 1959), p. 27.

16. Allen, "Report of a Military Reconnaissance," *Compilation of Narratives,* p. 414.

17. Lt. W.R. Abercrombie, "Supplementary Expedition Into the Copper River Valley, Alaska 1884," *Compilation of Narratives,* pp. 383-91.

18. Allen, "Report of a Military Reconnaissance," *Compilation of Narratives,* p. 414.

19. Allen, "Report of a Military Reconnaissance," *Compilation of Narratives,* p. 487; "Will Seek Gold on Copper River," p. 2.

20. "To Prospect Copper River," *San Francisco Chronicle,* Aug. 30, 1897, p. 2; "Bound for Copper River," and "The Mines of Copper River," *San Francisco Chronicle,* Sept. 12, 1897, p. 14.

21. "Fifteen Stranded Hunters for Gold," p. 10; See also "Oil and Whalebone," *Seattle Post-Intelligencer,* March 11, 1897, p. 8.

22. "Rushing for Copper River," *San Francisco Chronicle,* Oct. 21, 1897, p. 10; "News of the Ocean and Waterfront," *San Francisco Chronicle,* Nov. 11, 1897, p. 10.

23. "New Route to the Yukon Over American Soil," Nov. 18, 1897, p. 1.

24. "News of the Ocean and Waterfront," *San Francisco Chronicle,* Nov. 30, 1897, p. 10, and Nov. 14, 1897, p. 30.

25. "Experts Denounce the Copper River Scheme," Oct. 20, 1897, p. 3; For more about George Davidson, see Morgan B. Sherwood, "George Davidson and the Acquisition of Alaska," *Alaska and Its History,* ed. Morgan B. Sherwood (Seattle: Univ. of Washington Press, 1967), pp. 253-70.

26. Allen, "Report of a Military Reconnaissance," *Compilation of Narratives,* pp. 430, 439.

27. "Cook Inlet Mines Just Opening Up," *Seattle Post-Intelligencer,* Nov. 13, 1897, pp. 1-2.

28. "No Gold Discoveries on the Copper River," *San Francisco Chronicle,* Nov. 17, 1897, p. 5.

29. "Petrified Bacon in La Ninfa's Menue," *San Francisco Chronicle,* Nov. 29, 1897, p. 10.

30. "More Gold than the Klondike," *Seattle Post-Intelligencer,* Nov. 21, 1897, p. 7; "Richness of Copper River," *Seattle Post-Intelligencer,* Dec. 10, 1897, p. 8; "From the Mouth of the Copper River," *Seattle Post-Intelligencer,* Dec. 18, 1897, p. 1; "Argonauts Stranded at Copper River," *San Francisco Chronicle,* Nov. 24, 1897, p. 2.

31. "The Latest Map, Alaska, The Northwest Territory, and the Klondike," Dec. 30, 1897, p. 12.

32. F.C. Schrader, "A Reconnaissance of a Part of Prince William Sound . . . 1898," *Twentieth Annual Report of the USGS,* p. 368; Glenn and Abercrombie, "Report of Capt. Abercrombie," *Reports of Explorations in the Territory of Alaska, 1898,* pp. 341-42.

Introduction

Horace Samuel Conger, a 34-year-old pharmacist from Minnesota, reacted to the exciting news of the Klondike gold discovery in a manner characteristic of thousands of others: he gave up a good position to seek his fortune in the wilderness regions of the Far North. In the following journal, Conger states that he was motivated by the opportunity to gain enough wealth to sustain himself and his family for the remainder of their lives; however, one may suspect that he also viewed the gold rush as a chance to regain the mobility of his earlier years.

Conger was born on a farm in Franklyn County, New York, on June 20, 1863. When he was 10, his father drowned in the St. Lawrence River, and one year later, his mother died. Conger was subsequently taken to live with relatives in Elyria, Ohio, and at age 16, he was sent to live with a bachelor uncle on a ranch in Utah. He received his education at the California State Normal School at San Jose, and afterward he returned to the ranch. After his uncle's death in 1889, Conger went East, visiting relatives in the state of New York and his brother, Leonard E., in Mora, Minnesota. Leonard persuaded Conger to leave the ranch and join him in the pharmaceutical business, which Conger did in 1892. Two years later he married Elizabeth N. Blank, a teacher in the Mora public schools, and the following year the brothers dissolved the partnership, with Horace opening a drugstore of his own at Kasota, Minnesota. In early 1898 Conger decided to sell his business to finance a trip to Alaska. During his 19-month absence, his wife and two children (Lila and Clifford) returned to Mora to be near relatives.

The following clipping from a Mora, Minnesota, newspaper announces Conger's intentions of becoming an Alaskan prospector.

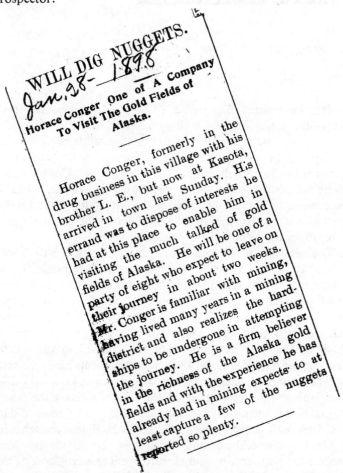

WILL DIG NUGGETS.

Jan, 28 — 1898

Horace Conger One of A Company To Visit The Gold Fields of Alaska.

Horace Conger, formerly in the drug business in this village with his brother L. E., but now at Kasota, arrived in town last Sunday. His errand was to dispose of interests he had at this place to enable him in visiting the much talked of gold fields of Alaska. He will be one of a party of eight who expect to leave on their journey in about two weeks. Mr. Conger is familiar with mining, having lived many years in a mining district and also realizes the hardships to be undergone in attempting the journey. He is a firm believer in the richness of the Alaska gold fields and with the experience he has already had in mining expects to at least capture a few of the nuggets reported so plenty.

The following pages have been compiled from Conger's original Alaskan diary and letters written to his wife. The diary consists of two standard diaries "published for the trade" and

Two of Horace S. Conger's diaries.

one notebook, each measuring about three by six inches. Editing included the following practices: corrections of obvious grammatical errors, misspellings, and punctuation; paragraph construction in the letters for easier reading; and the reduction of various inconsistencies in spelling (e.g., "to morrow," to-morrow," and "tomorrow" have been reduced to "tomorrow"). Repetitious and uninteresting material has been eliminated without comment; thus several diary entries have been omitted altogether. Obsolete spellings of Alaskan geographical place names have been retained as well as variations in the spellings of persons' names. Conger's letters to his wife have been inserted in the text of the diary in chronological order. Unless specified otherwise, brackets within the diary and letters denote supplemental information provided by the editors.

The diary contains the following information preceding the first diary entry. On the identification page Conger states his height as five feet, seven and one-half inches and his weight, on February 15, 1898, as 160 pounds. He also provides the names of his Alaskan prospecting party: M.J. Hessian, Neil Hessian, J.H. Buckley, M.A. Beatty, Frank Guyer, Le Roy Murfin, J.H. Reigel, R.V. Baasen, A. Wehrley, D. Wehrley, and John Corcoran. All were from Minnesota.

IN SEARCH OF GOLD

Dan Holeski

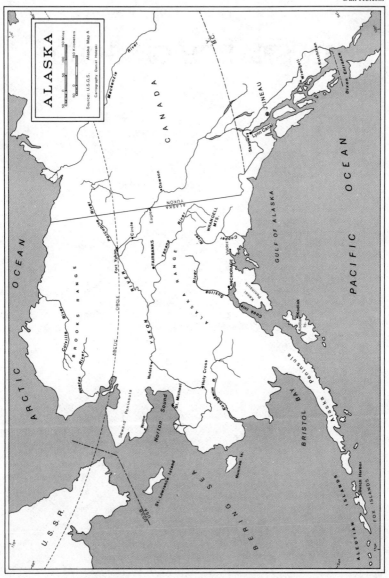

ALASKA

50 0 50 100 150 Miles
50 0 50 100 150 Kilometers

Source: U.S.G.S.   Alaska Map A
Cartography: Daniel Holeski

CANADA

Mackenzie River

JUNEAU

Skagway Lynn Canal

Wrangell
Ketchikan

Dixon Entrance

PACIFIC OCEAN

GULF OF ALASKA

Dawson

Porcupine River

YUKON
ALASKA

Eagle

Circle

FAIRBANKS

Tanana River

WRANGELL
MTS.

Copper River

Valdez

ANCHORAGE

Fort Yukon

CIRCLE

Koyukuk River

ARCTIC CIRCLE

ARCTIC OCEAN

Colville River

BROOKS RANGE

Noatak River

ALASKA RANGE

YUKON RIVER

Susitna River

Kenai Peninsula

Cook Inlet

Kodiak

Kodiak Isl.

Afognak Isl.

Seward Peninsula

Nome

Nulato

Norton Sound

St. Michael

Holy Cross

Koyukuk R.

Kuskokwim River

Nunivak Isl.

BERING SEA

BRISTOL BAY

Alaska Peninsula

St. Lawrence Island

U.S.S.R.

ALEUTIAN ISLANDS

FOX ISLANDS

Dutch Harbor

Chapter 1

Outfitting

The Klondike excitement, coming toward the end of a long economic depression in the United States, generated a welcome upturn of business, especially in West Coast cities, the outfitting centers of most stampeders. By August of 1897 woolen mills were having difficulty keeping pace with orders for heavy blankets and clothing, all marked "urgent," and demands for dried fruits and vegetables were inundating evaporated food companies.[1] Though "The Klondike" was an obscure and distant place, inexperienced miners found outfitting information widely available. This knowledge, gained by men prospecting in the Far North for more than a decade, was rushed into print in book and pamphlet form in late 1897 and was quickly bought up by gold-crazed people preparing to invade the new placer fields. The publications listed the supplies needed for prospecting and detailed the provisions and clothing necessary to survive an arctic winter. Similar advice was available in West Coast newspapers, which were crammed with the advertisements of Klondike outfitters and stories of life in the new mining camps. Experienced Alaskan miners recommended that gold seekers take provisions and clothing for two years plus several hundred dollars for expenses and the cost of a ticket home, should they fail in their endeavor.[2]

A complete Klondike outfit weighed between 1,500 and 2,000 pounds. It consisted of heavy woolen blankets and clothing; evaporated egg yolks, fruits, and vegetables; staples such as coffee, tea, beans, bacon, rice, sugar, flour, and rolled oats; a sled, tent, sheet iron stove, and tools; and a "medicine chest." The latter included quinine pills, compound cathartic pills, belladonna plasters, rubber adhesive plasters, tincture of iron, and a stock of antiscorbutics such as citric acid powder or lime juice capsules. Each lime juice capsule was advertised to contain the nutrients of a whole lime, and a box of 100 sold for one dollar.[3]

Conger's outfit contained most of the recommended supplies. Some of the individual items in his outfit and their cost are listed in the detailed records he kept on the memoranda pages of his diary, included in the appendix.

Tuesday, February 15, 1898
Left Kasota [Minnesota] for Alaska. Went to Minneapolis. Bought R.R. ticket to Tacoma for $36.00. Weather was fine. Stopped at the Pauly House. Met balance of the party there same evening.

Wednesday, February 16, 1898
Bargained for 1,500 lbs. bacon at $8.15 and 1,200 lbs. beans at $1.25 per C [hundred pounds].

Letter dated February 16, 1898, Minneapolis, Minnesota, Hotel Pauly
Dear Wife,
      Well, we are still here but expect to leave tomorrow. I bought $34.50 worth of clothing at Sommer's and picked out $38.00 worth more at Kennedy Bros. but will not take that as we found that we could buy cheaper in Tacoma. Will send you a list of all I take with me after I leave Tacoma and post the letter in Seattle. We will take 1,200 lbs. of bacon and 700 lbs. of beans from here. You have no idea what a job it is to select stuff for Alaska when you don't know what you want.
      Hope you are all well. Kiss the children for me. I am all excited and don't know what I am about half the time. It was a good thing I came up when I did for I never could have bought in so short a time. Keep well and may God bless you all.
Lovingly,
Horace

Thursday, February 17, 1898
Went to St. Paul. Bought half interest in rifle, $8.85; slicker suit, $2.25. Left for Minneapolis on the Milwaukee at 11:45 A.M. Left

C. A. PAULY, ⎱ MANAGERS
W. T. PAULY, ⎰

OPP. UNION DEPOT.

Minneapolis Minn. Feb. 16ᵗʰ 1898

Dear Wife
          Well: we are still here but expect to leave to morrow at 2:00 P.M. I bought $34,50 worth of clothing at Sommers; and picked out $38,00 worth more at Kennedy's Bros. but will not take that as we found out that we could buy cheaper in Tacoma. Will send you a list of all I take with me after I leave Tacoma and post the letter in Seattle. We will take 1200 lbs of bacon, and 700 lbs of beans from here. Saw Henry King to day. He is going down where Norman is. Guess he and Lucy are going to be married while there.

First page of a letter written by Horace S. Conger to his wife, Elizabeth.

Minneapolis at 2:10 P.M. for Tacoma. Had 7 dogs in same car as ourselves. Party of 26 from Wisconsin came on with 200 dogs.

157 lbs. bacon	$12.58
Hotel bill	2.20
Mattress on train	1.13

Friday, February 18, 1898
Thermometer: 20° below
Arrived at Simms, North Dakota at 8:15 A.M. Dogs still in car. Boys kicking like mules. Bad looking country. Entered the Bad Lands at Medora.[4] Limestone formation. Good grazing. Bought two cups and a coffee pot at Glendive. Removed dogs from our car at Billings. Tramp came on car and crawled under seat.

Saturday, February 19, 1898
Left Helena 7:15. Passed through Mullan Tunnel just before reaching Summit House. Had two engines ahead. Dogs got to fighting and one hurt so badly, he had to be killed. Arrived at Missoula 12:30. Large town at head of valley. Saw two deer on east side of Clark River. Just passed Heron, last town in Montana. Passed Lake Pend Oreille at Hope. Track follows lake shore for miles. Reached Spokane 6:10 P.M. City of 2,500. Stone pavements. Electric lights. Train 3 hours late.

Sunday, February 20, 1898
Passed through the Cascade Tunnel at 6:30 A.M. Tunnel 2 miles long. One hundred miles from Tacoma. Arrived at Tacoma 9:30 A.M. Put up at the Grand Central. Three nights and days from St. Paul. Bought balance of clothing from F.C. Merek's,[5] $27.10. [Included in the items Conger purchased here were a wire mask for mosquito protection and a paraffin bag to be used as a waterproof outer sack for provisions. See appendix.] Stores, most all open.

Letter dated February 20, 1898, Tacoma, Washington

Dear Lizzie,

Well, I have arrived here at last, safe and sound. It is raining just a little now. This morning at daylight we were in the Cascade Mountains where the snow was two feet deep. I thought we would take the boat [from] here but it seems that we will have to go to Seattle to do so. We had a fearful time on our trip in the way of accomodations. One of our party lost all his money in St. Paul but found it again. He also dropped his revolver off the train just before reaching here. Don't think he will find that.

I may change my mind and go to Cuba to help whip Spain. Wasn't it a fearful thing, the destruction of the *Maine?* [The battleship *Maine* was destroyed by an explosion in Havana Harbor on February 15 and the incident precipitated the Spanish American War.]

I have got with me $450.00, having spent the balance in the Twin Cities. I think I will have enough to outfit myself in good shape. I do hope I will make something for you and the dear little ones. Have thought of you all a good many times already. Don't know how it will be later on.

This town is all hustle and bustle. More Klondikers outfitting here than there are people in Kasota. If I had waited a week longer, could have got here for $20. They are cutting the R.R. rates. Expect there will be a big rush this coming week. [The Canadian Pacific Railroad began a railroad rate war with its American counterparts which resulted in lower fares.][6]

Will write you a long letter when I get on the boat and tell you all about my trip and what it cost me. Keep up courage and we will come out all right. Kiss dear little M. Clifford and Lila [his children] for me. Oh, how I would like to see them before I embark. Good by dear. Don't expect to hear from you again very soon.

Lovingly,
Horace

[The Tacoma *Daily Ledger* for February 21, 1898, noted the

arrival of Conger's party in that city in the following article, entitled "Twelve From Minnesota: Another Party of Klondikers Which Arrived in Tacoma Yesterday Morning."

Twelve strong and thrifty young men from Minnesota arrived in the city on the Northern Pacific yesterday morning and took up their residence at the Grand Central Hotel. They are on their way to the Copper River country and will embark on the steamer Excelsior which is expected to sail on the 25th inst.[7]

M.J. Hessian, who came here a week ahead of the party to make the transportation arrangements, said last evening, "We will buy our entire outfits in Tacoma with the exception of our bacon which we shipped from Minnesota. I have been here a week and made a careful investigation of the question of purchasing our outfits. I made comparisons of goods and prices in Tacoma and Seattle and in every instance I found that the prices were lower here and on nearly all of the needed articles they are lower than those which prevail in St. Paul and Minneapolis. We are buying our outfits of clothing tonight so as to get as much done as possible before Wednesday when the goods must be packed and ready for shipment.

"We will take a sufficient outfit to last us for two years. None of us have ever been in that country and we go without experienced miners or guides to assist us. We expect to do equally as well, however, as some of those who have gone ahead of us and we are well capable to withstand the rigors of the Northern climate."

The Minnesotans have seven of the finest dogs that have been seen on the way to the Alaska country. They are large strong St. Bernard, New Foundland and Chesapeake and have been thoroughly trained for the kind of work they will get after they are [dis]embarked from the steamer. The Minnesota party are: H.S. Conger, J.H. Buckley, Kasota; John Corcoran, A. Wehrley, D. Wehrley, Belle Plain; M.J. Hessian and Neil Hessian, St. Peter; L.R. Murphin, J.H. Riegel, Sleepy Eye; R.V. Baasen, New Ulm; M.A. Beatty, Tracy; Frank Guyer, Waseca.]

Monday, February 21, 1898
Bought hardware and saw it packed. Met Scharad, a furrier who used to hunt near Pine City in early days. Met a Mr. Woodward, brother of Mrs. O. Metcalf of Kasota. All the unmarried men are out painting the town red. Tacoma is very hilly.

Tuesday, February 22, 1898
Weather: Cloudy, rain
Had our pictures taken in our Alaskan costumes. [The Alaska costume ranged from a cowboy hat and corduroy or canvas suit to a thick cap and colorful mackinaw. A variety of high boots were worn. Conger probably wore the chamois suit and boots he had recently purchased — see appendix.][8] Bought medicine for the boys from Wynkoop-Vaughan Company. Bought hardware from Washington Hardware Company.

Wednesday, February 23, 1898
Weather: Clear
Saw steamer *Seattle* sail for Dyea. One thousand people on board. [The 1,411-ton *City of Seattle* was built in Philadelphia in 1890 and accommodated about 600 passengers. In 1897-98 she was operated by the Washington and Alaska Steamship Company on the Tacoma to Southeastern Alaska run.][9] Bought fur robe from Scharad. Paid $20.00. [The robes were made from a variety of animal skins and the better ones sold for about $100. They were used as sleeping blankets and for traveling in frigid weather.][10] Acknowledged contracts in Hudson and Holts law office. [The contracts referred to here were probably partnership agreements — see diary entry for June 10, 1898. Although Alaskan prospectors are sometimes depicted as loners, they often

organized cooperatively to seek discoveries, share costs, and increase their chances of survival in case of injury.] Received the first letter from Lizzie.

Thursday, February 24, 1898
Weather: Cloudy, rain
Groceries all packed. Bought from McLean, McMillan and Co. Total cost, $879.85 for 12 men. Met Dick Ballinger,[11] who has been on Copper River. "Proposition," "Old Man," are by-words used on this coast.

Letter dated February 25, 1898, Tacoma, Washington
Dear Wife,
    Today was the time the *Excelsior* was scheduled to sail but she will not go until tomorrow, and maybe not for a week. It is uncertain when the ocean steamers will sail exactly. We leave here this evening at 6 o'clock on the Aberdeen for Seattle with our goods, which amount to 8 tons. [The *City of Aberdeen* was built in 1891 and placed on the Seattle-Olympia run. The passenger fare in 1898 was 50¢ one way and 85¢ round trip. Her captain was fond of racing and he often used anything flammable in the cargo for fuel; thus, she was worn out by 1907. After being completely rebuilt, she was renamed *Vashon*.][12] The *Excelsior* sails from Seattle instead of here.
    Received your dear letter, also the socks and iodoform [a crystalline compound of iodine used as an antiseptic dressing.] Am glad you sent them. We all had our pictures taken in our suits and one will be sent to you, also a paper. Save the paper so that I can see it when I return. My clothing, R.R. fare, steamer fare [$70], and provisions amount to $292.60 [see appendix]. Will take with me $275 in cash so I will have enough to come home with if I don't find anything. People here speak very encouragingly of the Copper River country. Will write you again from Seattle if I can and give you an exact list of what I bought.
    Some of the boys have become dissatisfied already and I think there will be a split-up before we are a month on the way.

Left my (or your) valice at Merrick's clothing store. There is not anything in it to speak of and I had no use for it. Take good care of yourself and the darling little ones. Wish I could hear from you once more before I leave for Port Valdes but that will be impossible. You must write me at least once a month and I will get all the letters at one time. Will tell you where to address them when I reach the Alaska coast. Will now close, for I have got to help get the goods down to the dock. Good by dear and kiss the darlings for me.

Lovingly,
Horace

Friday, February 25, 1898
Weather: Pleasant
Left on the *Aberdeen* at 7:20 for Seattle. Arrived at City Dock 10 P.M. Put up at the New Western.

Saturday, February 26, 1898
Moved freight from City Dock to Arlington Dock. Had 8 tons and 153 lbs. exclusive of blankets and clothing. Terrible jam of people. Went to Third Avenue Theatre. Saw *The Ensign* [advertised by the *Seattle Post-Intelligencer* as "the glorious naval drama"].

Letter dated February 27, 1898, Seattle, Washington
Dear Wife,
Well, I am still on terra-firma but will leave this afternoon at 2 P.M. There will be 254 passengers on board, 16 of whom will land at Skagway, so we will have a chance to see that town. It is a hot one by all reports. A troop of U.S. soldiers left yesterday on the *Australia* for Skagway. She was the largest boat ever brought to this harbor. [Two companies of the Fourteenth Infantry sailed to Skagway on the *Australia* to subdue the lawlessness reported there. The 1,715-ton steamer accommodated 1,000 passengers and 2,000 tons of freight. Before being charted by the Pacific Coast Steamship Company in February of 1898 for the Alaska

trade, the *Australia* had operated for 10 years on the San Francisco to Honolulu run.][13]

If you see anyone who is going to Alaska, tell them to outfit here, as it will save them money in the end and prevent a whole lot of trouble. This is a mighty town, I can tell you. It reminds me somewhat of Chicago during the world's fair.

How are you darling, and the dear little babies? Have not looked at your pictures yet. Don't dare to for fear it will make me sick at heart. Will find out at the post office where to direct my letters. It will be either Orca or Port Valdes. I am keeping a diary of my trip so when I return we will look it over [the remainder of this letter is missing].

Sunday, February 27, 1898
Left Seattle for Alaska. Aboard ship opposite Port Townsend.

Notes—

1. "A Great Demand On The Woolen Mills," *San Francisco Chronicle,* Aug. 3, 1897, p. 2; "Dried Vegetables For The Yukon Trade," *San Francisco Chronicle,* July 28, 1897, p. 2.

2. See Chicago Record, *Klondike: The Chicago Record's Book For Gold Seekers* (Chicago: Monarch Book Co., 1897), pp. 43-53; 81; A.C. Harris, *Alaska and The Klondike Gold Fields* (n.p. 1897), pp. 173-75.

3. Advertisement, *San Francisco Chronicle,* Dec. 30, 1897, p. 7; Harris, pp. 173, 179; "The Klondikers' Outfit," *San Francisco Chronicle,* Dec. 30, 1897, p. 8; J.E. Spurr, "A Reconnaissance in Southwest Alaska in 1898," *Twentieth Annual Report of the USGS,* Part 7 (Washington: Gov. Printing Office, 1900), pp. 44-45.

4. "Mendora" in original. Similar misspellings of U.S. place names (e.g., Pend D Reille in next diary entry) have been corrected without comment.

5. Probably F.W. Merrick's, spelled correctly in letter of Feb. 25.

6. See "Northern Pacific Accepts the Challenge," and "The Soo Pacific Cuts Still Deeper," *San Francisco Chronicle,* Feb. 19, 1898, p. 10.

7. "instrument," archaic usage meaning present or current; thus February 25.

8. Pierre Berton, *The Klondike Fever* (New York: Knopf, 1958), p. 117; Alfred H. Brooks, *Blazing Alaska's Trails,* 2d ed. (1953; rpt. Fairbanks: Univ. of Alaska Press, 1973), p. 353; Harris, *Alaska and the Klondike Gold Fields,* p. 174.

9. Gordon Newell, *Pacific Steamboats* (New York: Bonanza, 1958),

p. 123; "Many Vessels Alaska Bound," *San Francisco Chronicle,* Feb. 16, 1898, p. 9; "More Steamers for the Alaska Run," *San Francisco Chronicle,* Aug. 3, 1897, p. 2; Advertisement, *Seattle Post-Intelligencer,* Feb. 26, 1898, p. 11.

10. Robert A. McKennan, *The Upper Tanana Indians,* in Yale Univ. Publications in Anthropology, No. 55 ed. Irving Rouse (New Haven: Dept. of Anthropology, 1959), p. 83; Harris, *Alaska and the Klondike Gold Fields* p. 175; J.C. Cantwell, *Report of the Operations of the U.S. Revenue Steamer Nunivak . . . Alaska 1899-1901* (Washington: Gov. Printing Office, 1902), p. 152.

11. Perhaps Richard Achilles Ballinger, a well-known Seattle attorney who codified the statutes of his state and who became an expert in mining law. He went on to become mayor of Seattle (1904-06) and Secretary of the Interior in the cabinet of President Theodore Roosevelt (1909-11). *Dictionary of American Biography,* s.v. "Ballinger, Richard Achilles."

12. Newell, *Pacific Steamboats,* p. 30.

13. "Big Steamers for Alaska," *Seattle Post-Intelligencer,* Feb. 25, 1898, p. 10; "The Australia at Seattle," *San Francisco Chronicle,* Feb. 25, 1898, p. 11; "Many Vessels Alaska Bound," *San Francisco Chronicle,* Feb. 16, 1898, p. 9; also *Seattle Post-Intelligencer,* Feb. 22, 1898, p. 8.

GULF OF ALASKA

VALDEZ
ORCA
COPPER RIVER

U.S.A.
CANADA
RIVER
WHITE

MT ST. ELIAS

NORTH

CHILKOOT PASS
DYEA SKAGWAY
CROSS SOUND
LYNN CANAL
JUNEAU

WRANGELL NARROWS

DIXON ENTRANCE
HECATE STRAIT
SKEENA RIVER

QUEEN
CHARLOTTE
SOUND
BELLABELLA

VANCOUVER
ISLAND

CAPE
FLATTERY

CANADA
U.S.A.

OLYMPIA SEATTLE
TACOMA

Southeast Alaska and coastal British Columbia

Chapter 2—

Aboard Ship

Two routes were available to ships heading for Port Valdez from Puget Sound during the gold rush. Ocean steamers with full cargoes usually took the "Outside Passage," turning west at Port Townsend, passing through Juan De Fuca Strait, and entering the open waters of the Pacific Ocean at Cape Flattery. Passenger vessels with stops in Southeast Alaska took the "Inside Passage" as far north as Juneau, then entered the open Pacific via Cross Sound. The Inside Passage is a scenic coastal waterway which extends 1,000 miles from Seattle, Washington, to Skagway, Alaska. For most of this distance, ships are protected from the swells of the Pacific by hundreds of islands, created by the partial submergence of the coastal mountains. The inland route was preferred by the many unseaworthy ships which voyaged north during the Klondike excitement; but it was avoided by heavily loaded cargo ships which were apt to run aground on the many uncharted reefs and submerged pinnacle rocks of the waterway. The comparative safety of the two routes in 1898-99 is illustrated by the fact that insurance rates for vessels plying the Inside Passage were double those of ships using the Outside route.[1]

Many shipwrecks occurred in 1898, at the height of the gold rush.[2] A principal cause of many of these accidents was a lack of adequate charts. Most of the charts of Alaskan waters in use in 1898 were based on the early surveys of Russian and British navigators. Although the Coast and Geodetic Survey began charting the more than 30,000 miles of Alaska's coastline soon after the U.S. purchase in 1867, only 9 percent of Alaska's waters had been accurately charted by 1918.[3]

Contributing to the casualties in Alaskan waters were the treacherous currents produced by the large tides in the North Pacific, inexperienced pilots, and a lack of navigational aids.

The steamer Excelsior *at Seattle, April 12, 1899.*

Because Alaskan waters had few buoys and no lighthouses until the early 1900s, the hundreds of ships which ventured north during the gold rush were forced to rely on the echo of their fog signals to find their way during the frequent periods of inclement weather. When disaster struck, ships were virtually helpless, for radio communications were still undeveloped.[4]

Conger traveled to Port Valdez by way of Juneau and the Inside Passage. He sailed aboard the steamer *Excelsior,* the ship which had brought the first cargo of Klondike gold to the States seven months earlier. The staunch little steamer was built in 1893 and traveled at nine knots fully loaded. In November of 1897, she had been purchased by the Pacific Steam Whaling Company, refitted to accommodate more passengers, and placed on the run from San Francisco to Prince William Sound.[5]

The departure of the *Excelsior* was described in the following excerpt from an article entitled "Four Within Ten Hours," appearing on page eight of the *Seattle Post-Intelligencer* of February 28, 1898.

CAPTAIN J F HIGGINS

A PORTION OF THE DINING ROOM

NEW BUNKS ERECTED IN THE STEERAGE

Scenes aboard the steamer Excelsior, *July 27, 1897.*

The steamer Excelsior *slipped away from the Arlington dock at 3:30 yesterday afternoon with 257 passengers aboard, all bound for Valdes, Alaska, from which point they will try to push-through to the head waters of the Copper and Tanana rivers. One hundred of the passengers came from San Francisco on the steamer, many of them purchasing their outfits here during the interval between arrival and departure. The other passengers were booked here but came from all parts of the country. Arlington dock was crowded with spectators, who gathered early and stayed until the steamer went out of sight around Magnolia bluff. Several times the police had to clear portions of the wharf that loading might proceed. The crowd was very curious and hard to keep back. As soon as loading had been completed the inspector ordered all the passengers on shore. There was much grumbling, but everyone finally got up the steep gang plank. They were counted carefully as they went back on board. The steamer had within two of the passenger limit. An Eastern youth named Pickens, who has been walking around the streets for several days in exceedingly heavy boots, a yellow Mackinaw suit and a big white Klondike hat, narrowly escaped falling into the bay. He started down the gang plank but was tripped up by the big revolver which he had purchased and landed in a heap at the other end. A drunken man insisted on going to Alaska on the* Excelsior *although he had no ticket and was without an outfit. He was finally steered to the Colman dock where the* Noyo *was loading. One of the passengers remembered just before the boat started out that he had forgotten to buy any cartridges for his revolver. He wanted the captain to hold the ship until he could purchase some. Six of the passengers were nearly left owing to the beer attraction of a neighboring saloon. As the boat left the dock the passengers gave three cheers for Seattle, as the best outfitting town on the coast. The last call that reached the wharf came from the throat of a big German, who cried, "The world is ours!"*

The Excelsior *carried the following passengers from Seattle* . . . [The names of the members of Conger's party were included in the second-class passenger list.]

Letter dated February 27, 1898, Aboard Ship

[This is an ongoing letter, continued on February 28, March 1, 2, and 3. Since the diary entries for this time period are largely repetitive, they have been omitted and the dissimilar information they contain inserted within the letters of the same dates.]

Dear Wife,

Left the Arlington dock at 3:30. The supper I had was enough to make one sick. Besides, I had to stand up to eat it. Have paid ten dollars extra for the privilege of eating in the first cabin.

February 28, 1898

Did not sleep much last night on account of the awful noise which the steering gear made. Have had my breakfast and am now sitting on top of the cabin basking in the sunshine. It is indeed lovely so far. Passed the steamer *Oregon* this forenoon. She has been to Skagway and Dyea. There are 254 passengers on board, two of whom are women. Most of them are going to Copper River, so you see, there are others.

Our boat is moving slowly, waiting for the tide to help us through the narrows [probably Seymour Narrows]. We are now on the east side of Vancouver Island. This would be a lovely trip in the summertime. My lungs feel quite sore today. Guess I have stayed on deck too much, as there is quite a breeze. There are Indian villages on either side of the strait. It is now 4 P.M. As we have supper at 5, will close for today.

March 1, 1898

It was a little rough last night, about 1 o'clock. [They were probably passing across Queen Charlotte Sound, a large stretch of the Inside Passage open to the swells of the Pacific.] This morning a stiff breeze is blowing from the north. Passed an Indian village (Bella Bella) on one of the small islands on our left. You can find it on the map, I think. Monuments could be seen back of nearly every house.

Noon: The boat is rocking badly. Some have gone to their berths sick and without their dinner. Expect I will get sick after we leave Juneau and reach the open sea. Passed steamer *Ellnyod* this afternoon just entering Hecate Strait. The scenery today has been magnificent. It is a series of waterfalls and cascades. The islands are covered with timber to the water's edge, and the higher ones are snow-capped. In places we passed between islands not more than one block apart with their peaks rearing 3 and 4 thousand feet high. Saw a whale today about ¼ mile from our boat. Some of the men fired at it, and you ought to have seen how it made the water fly. Passed several Indians in their skiffs, fishing.

March 2, 1898

We passed by the wrecked *Corona* this morning at one o'clock. She lay off our left one mile. I went up on deck to look at the spot but could see nothing, only the watch lights on her. She is all under water except her bow. [On January 23, 1898, the steamer *Corona* ran into a reef between Porcher and Kennedy islands, near the mouth of the Skeena River. All 238 passengers on board the Pacific Steamship Company vessel escaped to a nearby island in lifeboats, but two stowaways in the hold were drowned. The 220-foot-long ship, built in Philadelphia in 1888, sustained $30,000 in damage, but she was patched, pumped out, and floated on March 4, 1898. She was towed to San Francisco, renovated, and returned to service in September of that year. An investigation cleared the *Corona*'s pilot of blame for the accident; at the spot where she struck, the charts showed a depth of seven fathoms and no indication of rocks.][6]

We entered Dixon Entrance [another stretch of the Inside Passage which is open to the Pacific] this morning at 5 o'clock. I was up and on deck at that time. The sea was quite rough for two hours and I got a little sick. We met the following steamers today: *Tees* (going south),[7] *Alki,* and [*City of*] *Seattle,* which left Tacoma 3 days before we did. At noon we ran into a school of porpoises. They are about 5 feet long and look like a big codfish. They would jump out of the water 3 or 4 feet. Some of them were shot by those on board.

I can't write very much, as they are playing cards all around me. Some of the passengers in the steerage department made a big kick today because they get too much stew all the time and not enough dry food. Don't know how they came out. [Steerage passengers were quartered in the lower part of the ship and slept on triple-tiered bunks which were two feet wide and arranged in rows. They were not fed as well as the other passengers and no dining facilities were provided for them][8] Will close for tonight. With love and happy thoughts for you and the little ones.

Horace

March 3, 1898

· We anchored last night in 9 fathoms of water. Could not pass through the narrows in the night without danger of being wrecked. [This waterway was probably Wrangell Narrows, a 23-mile-long channel southwest of Petersburg. It is extremely narrow and winding and is filled with rocky reefs, islands, and strong currents. Today this passage is navigated with the aid of about 70 red, green, and white markers with flashing lights.]

Time changed one hour last night. Weighed anchor at 4:20 A.M. Met a tug towing a schooner at 8:30 this morning. At 10 A.M. met steamer *Alliance.* Our captain hailed her as she was direct from Valdes. Those on board said that Valdes Pass was open. Hope it will prove so when we reach there. It was very cold this morning with a stiff wind. Saw two glaciers and they looked mighty rugged.

I never noticed so many gray-headed men on the boat until this morning. I have taken particular notice of those on board, and I find young, old and gray, bald-headed, rich and poor, and one man with one arm. Men of all nations and colors. Am surprised to note the number who are going to Copper River.

At 3 this afternoon, steamer *Cottage City* caught up and passed us. She came around the horn. She is from Massachusetts and was bought by Claus Spreckles of San Francisco for passenger traffic on this coast. She was the fastest boat on the Atlantic Coast. We will reach Juneau this evening and I will finish and post this letter.

Horace

Letter dated March 4, 1898, Juneau, Alaska
Dear Lizzie,

We arrived here last night at 8 o'clock, and the captain said that we only had 15 minutes on shore, so I rushed uptown and posted the letter I had been writing while on my way from Seattle. I did not have time to finish it so will do so today. We will not leave here until tonight or tomorrow, as we have 40 tons of coal on board for steamer *Wolcott,* which runs between here and Dyea. [The *Oliver Wolcott* first served in Alaska in 1877 as a U.S. revenue cutter. On February 18, 1897, the government sold the 200-ton wooden-hulled ship at public auction, and in March she was sold at a good profit to the Pacific Steam Whaling Company of San Francisco.][9] If we did not wait here for the steamer to come down from Dyea, would have to chase up there after her. Would kind of like to go to Dyea and Skagway and see those towns, but in another sense, would not, for it would make 2 or 3 days later reaching Copper River. [Had Conger gone to Skagway, his Alaska trip might have ended abruptly, for the town was controlled by Soapy Smith and his band of thieves and swindlers. Through a variety of schemes, the gang robbed many unwary gold seekers of their money, and it was not until July of 1898, when a returning miner was robbed of his hard-earned gold, that the town rebelled and Smith was shot and killed.][10]

The Cottage City, *the latest Klondike steamer to meet mishap.*

Can find out nothing definite about the Copper River country. Most everybody gives it a black eye. Of course nobody has actually penetrated the interior so far as I can learn. I think we will reach that point if anybody does, for there are about two hundred of us well equipped for that purpose.

This is a town of 3,000 population situated at the base of a snow-capped mountain. Am surprised to see such a town in this far away place. Groceries, clothing, and outfitting are just as cheap here as in Minneapolis or Seattle and plenty of it. There are 3 drugstores (and well equipped ones too), 4 doctors, and 3 churches here. Was in one drugstore and they sell just the same here as they do in the East. Would like to live here for a year or so. Wages are $2.50 per day and board.

It is snowing a little just now, although it is not cold. The coldest it has been here this winter is 8° below zero. My head is swimming around from the effect of being on the boat so long. My trip from here to Copper River will be shorter but rougher. Wish I was safely there now.

I will mail you a *Mining Record* which is published here. All the Eastern periodicals published can be bought here. The steamer *Cottage City,* which passed us yesterday, was grounded on the rocks twice between here and Seattle. It was owing to their not having a good pilot. [The *San Francisco Chronicle* reported that because of her "green crew," the 1,885-ton vessel of the Pacific Coast Steamship Company entered Wallace Bight instead of Heikish Narrows, where she "touched lightly," causing a slight leak. Her pumps were adequate to handle the problem, but to satisfy the passengers, the captain decided to beach her in Swanson Bay, and there is where she suffered the most damage: an inexperienced quartermaster put the helm to starboard instead of to port, as ordered, and she struck a rock, knocking off her forefoot.][11]

Will now close dear. Kiss dear little Lila and M. Clifford for papa and consider one or two for yourself. Write to me at Port Valdes at least twice a month.

> Lovingly,
> your husband,
> H.S. Conger
>
> Address
> H.S. Conger
> Port Valdes, Alaska
> Care, Pacific Steam Whaling Co.
> Seattle, Washington

Friday, March 4, 1898
Thermometer: 26°
Went on board steamer *Cottage City.* Saw halibut weighing 150 lbs. Sent Lizzie a paper and map published here. Had concert down in the bull pen. Two violins, mandolin, guitar, and banjo. Steamer [*City of*] *Topeka* has arrived from Seattle. We leave tonight at 9:20 for Copper River. Captain Snow in command. Captain Donaldson goes on the *Wolcott.* The temperature, as shown in this book, was taken before sunrise.

Saturday, March 5, 1898
Weather: Cold wind; Thermometer: 38°
Sea very rough. Most everyone on board is sick. Buckley and Murfin are the only ones in our party who are not sick. Boat rocks like a cradle. Sensation similar to that experienced when going down in an elevator. Can see Mt. St. Elias in the distance. [This 18,008-foot mountain on the Alaska-Canada boundary was the first mainland landmark sighted by Vitus Bering on his voyage of discovery in 1741.]

Sunday, March 6, 1898
The same as yesterday. Sea still ruffled. I feel better. Ate a little dinner. Most everyone on board is holding down their bunks. Sun shines brightly although the sea is rough. Quite warm. It is just a week ago today since I left Seattle.

Monday, March 7, 1898
Rough and stormy. Most everyone on board is sick. 10 A.M.: Storm rages furiously. We are lost. Rocks in sight. Hopes nearly gone. The ship creaks and strains like a rickity barn. About nine o'clock at night, storm abated. Thank God. The moon shines and we can see our way. Reached Orca at 2 in the morning and am on my way to Valdes. [Orca was the site of a cannery owned by the Pacific Steam Whaling Company. It was located on the southeast shore of Orca Inlet, two and a half miles northeast of present-day Cordova. In 1898, Valdez was only a tent town. It was located at the head of the estuary of the same name in Prince William Sound. After the 1964 Good Friday earthquake, which severely damaged the town, it was relocated on firmer ground a few miles to the northwest.]

Letter dated March 8, 1898, Port Valdes, Alaska
Dear Lizzie,
Thank God I am once more on land. The trip from Juneau

here has been one fraught with awe and the most extreme danger. Last Monday a southwest storm struck us consisting of snow and sleet, which was blinding in the extreme. The sea was lashed into a foaming caldron. Waves 20 and 30 feet high. We were completely at the mercy of the water and elements. We were lost for 19 hours. Once during that time the cry came, "Rocks ahead." And sure enough, there they were, two hundred feet high, not over 300 yards from us. All steam was applied, and one of the steam pipes burst. I thought we were lost, sure enough. I thought of you and the little ones then and gave myself up to God. Would not go through the same thing again for all the wealth in Alaska.

Well, this is a bright day. Still wear the same clothes I did when I left home. There are about 130 men getting off here. Some are going to Portage Bay and some to Resurrection Bay,[12] but the majority are bound for Copper River. I hope and pray two years will find me on my way home with enough [wealth] to take us to Paris and to live on for the balance of our lives. There is a good deal of snow on the mountains around here, but it is not nearly as cold as I expected to see it. There are two women with us, but I don't know where they are going. They are from Boston. Guess they wish they had stayed at home, although they seem quite happy this morning.

Am glad there is a good party along. There are 36 dogs, 4 horses, and one jackass to be unloaded here. All the dogs came near being thrown overboard during the high seas of yesterday. Will now close, and if I have time, will write a few lines before the boat leaves here.

Landing at Valdes, noon March 8. Can land on the ice from our steamer without transferring to lighters. There are about 100 already on the landing to receive us. Snow to the water's edge. Quite a good deal of timber, although scrubby. Can see the glacier over which we pass. Snow is 18 inches on the level. It is not a bad proposition to look at so far. Am well pleased. Don't look for another letter for many months. One thing is sure: We have men enough to move quite an obstacle. Mountains are not very high here. Don't know how they will be farther inland. Good by

The Excelsior *unloading on the ice, March 9, 1898.*

darling for some time. Write whenever you can to your far away husband.

H.S. Conger

Tuesday, March 8, 1898

Our plunder is unloaded on the ice. Worked till 11 o'clock at night hauling it through the snow and slush over the ice for fear it would sink. About 900 camped here in the timber at the foot of the glacier. One man stole a sack of flour and I guess they hung him. [Though Congress had passed a bill in 1884 giving the District of Alaska its first form of civil government, law enforcement was almost nonexistent, especially in regions located far from the small population centers of Southeastern Alaska. Citizens in remote regions of Alaska settled disputes in public meetings commonly called "miners' meetings." Everyone was free to state their opinions in these forums, then by a majority vote of those present, the matter was concluded. With no jails for imprisonment, punishment was limited to hanging, banishment from the district, and fines.][13] Some of the boys have not come in yet. Am drying my clothes in the engine room on board ship.

Notes—

1. W.R. Abercrombie, "Report of Mr. Edward Gillette," *Copper River Exploring Expedition 1899* (Washington: Gov. Printing Office, 1900), p. 140.

2. Ethel Anderson Becker, *Klondike '98: Hegg's Album of the 1898 Gold Rush* (Portland, Oregon: Binfords and Mort, 1949), p. 6; Map of "Vessels Wrecked in Alaskan Waters," compiled by the Alaska Bureau, Seattle Chamber of Commerce and Commercial Club, 1918, map No. G4371, P57, located in Government Documents Section, Peter Shields Library, Univ. of California, Davis.

3. Supplementary information on map of "Vessels Wrecked in Alaskan Waters"; Alfred H. Brooks, *The Geography and Geology of Alaska: A Summary of Existing Knowledge* (Washington: Gov. Printing Office, 1906), pp. 22, 119.

4. Alfred H. Brooks, *Blazing Alaska's Trails,* 2d ed. (1953; rpt. Fairbanks: Univ. of Alaska Press, 1973), p. 427; C.L. Andrews, "Marine Disasters of the Alaska Route," *Washington Historical Quarterly,* 7 (Jan. 1916), 21, 29; Gordon Newell, *SOS North Pacific: Tales of Shipwrecks off the Washington, British Columbia, and Alaskan Coasts* (Portland, Oregon: Binfords and Mort, 1955), pp. 188-89.

5. See the following articles from the *San Francisco Chronicle:* "Ready to Sail to the Land of Golden Promise," July 27, 1897, p. 1; "News of the Ocean and Water Front," Nov. 23, 1897, p. 10; "News of the Ocean and Water Front," Dec. 3, 1897, p. 10; "Many Vessels Alaska Bound," Feb. 16, 1898, p. 9.

6. "Rescued from the Island," *Seattle Post-Intelligencer,* Jan. 31, 1898, p. 1; also see the following articles from the *San Francisco Chronicle:* "Steamship Corona On the Rocks," Jan. 29, 1898, p. 1; "Two Men Die in Corona's Hold," Feb. 11, 1898, p. 2; "Corona Off the Rocks," March 7, 1898, p. 3; "Terrible Suffering in Alaska," March 12, 1898, p. 1; "Ocean and Water Front," April 10,

1898, p. 30; "Corona's Master Is Not to Blame," June 8, 1898, p. 12; "Ocean and Water Front," Sept. 11, 1898, p. 30.

7. The *Tees* was owned by the Canadian Pacific Navigation Co. The all-steel vessel, worth over $100,000, was wrecked on March 25, 1899. See "Steamer Tees on the Rocks," *San Francisco Chronicle,* March 27, 1899, p. 5.

8. "Ready to Sail to the Land of Golden Promise," *San Francisco Chronicle,* July 27, 1897, p. 1.

9. Brooks, *Blazing Alaska's Trails,* p. 506; "The Wolcott to be Sold Today," *Seattle Post-Intelligencer,* Feb. 18, 1897, p. 8; "Bought Wolcott," *Seattle Post-Intelligencer,* March 26, 1897, p. 5.

10. David Wharton, *The Alaska Gold Rush* (Bloomington, Indiana: Indiana Univ. Press, 1972), p. 32.

11. "Corona Off the Rocks," *San Francisco Chronicle,* March 7, 1898, p. 3; "Many Vessels Alaska Bound," *San Francisco Chronicle,* Feb. 16, 1898, p. 9; "Accident to the Steamer Cottage City," *San Francisco Chronicle,* March 3, 1898, p. 3.

12. Several gold mining districts existed on the northern part of the Kenai Peninsula in 1898. Because ice prevented ships from reaching the upper part of Cook Inlet during the winter months, people used alternate routes to reach the mines. A 12-mile winter trail led from the head of Portage Bay (now called Passage Canal), on the northeastern coast of Kenai Peninsula, to tidewater on Turnagain Arm. Five miles of this route was over Portage Glacier. Another route led inland from Resurrection Bay, on the southeast coast of Kenai Peninsula. Prospectors reached Turnagain Arm by traveling over the ice of the various streams and crossing a low mountain pass. Brooks, *The Geography and Geology of Alaska,* p. 57; Brooks, *Blazing Alaska's Trails,* p. 169; Capt. Edwin F. Glenn and Capt. W.R. Abercrombie, *Reports of Explorations in the Territory of Alaska . . . 1898* (Washington: Gov. Printing Office, 1899), pp. 18, 34-35, 133-34.

13. Brooks, *Blazing Alaska's Trails,* pp. 508-09.

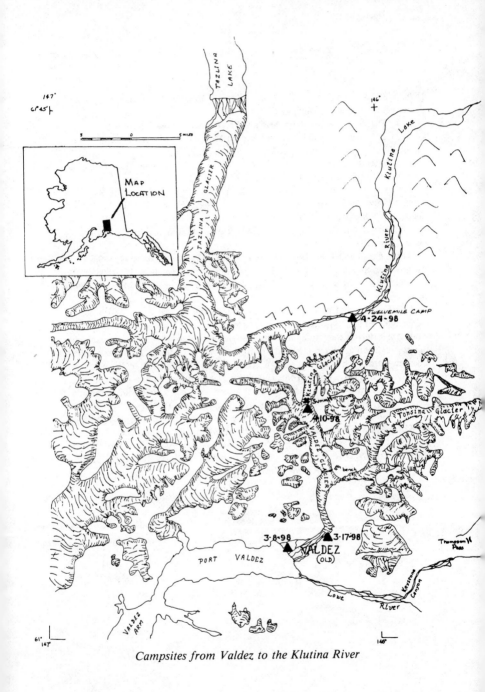

Campsites from Valdez to the Klutina River

Chapter 3—

Over Valdez Glacier

The Copper River basin is bounded on the south by a band of rugged mountains which rise abruptly from the shores of Prince William Sound and the Gulf of Alaska. Known as the Chugach Range, these mountains reach a general elevation of between 5,000 and 8,000 feet and extend inland as much as 80 miles. Near the sea, the range consists of a succession of jagged peaks and canyonlike valleys. In the winter of 1897-98 this terrain effectively isolated the Copper River basin from the coast. The canyon of the turbulent Copper River — the only break in this mountain barrier — held little value as an entry route, and the only visible gap in the snow-covered ridges at the head of Port Valdez was the valley occupied by Valdez Glacier. The 4,800-foot summit of Valdez Glacier was the lowest known pass in the Chugach Range leading to the Copper River country until Thompson Pass was discovered late in 1898.[1]

It appears that the information published about the route over Valdez Glacier in 1897 and early 1898 stemmed from knowledge obtained by Lieutenant W.R. Abercrombie in 1884. During Abercrombie's unsuccessful attempt to penetrate the Copper River valley, a Russian half-breed, commonly called a "Creole" in Alaska, informed him that the Indians "came down Copper River to the stream heading in the lake," then traveled up this stream "to the foot of the passage," where they left their boats and "packed their furs over to salt water." Abercrombie noted that "the portage lies between two mountains, the valley being filled with a large glacier."[2] Though Lieutenant Allen had explored and mapped the territory along his route of travel up the Copper River in 1885, the region between Port Valdez and the Copper River, through which the old Indian trail passed, remained unexplored in early 1898. Yet, the vague information about this route had been graphically represented on a number of maps which inaccurately portrayed the trail leading eastward

Foot of Valdez Glacier and mountains northeast of Valdez, 1898.

from the head of Port Valdez and reaching the Copper River in a short distance (see pages 31, 32 and 35).[3] The *Seattle Post-Intelligencer* concluded a front page description of the Valdez Glacier route on November 18, 1897, by saying, "The truth is that nothing is known of the country save what is gained from the Indians, whose reports, either because of stupidity or suspicious cunning, are very meager and unsatisfactory."

When the gold seekers began to realize that their northerly direction of travel across Valdez Glacier was in conflict with the easterly route indicated on their maps, a knowledgeable Indian woman confirmed that they were on the proper course. In earlier years, before the Copper River Indians stopped using the glacier

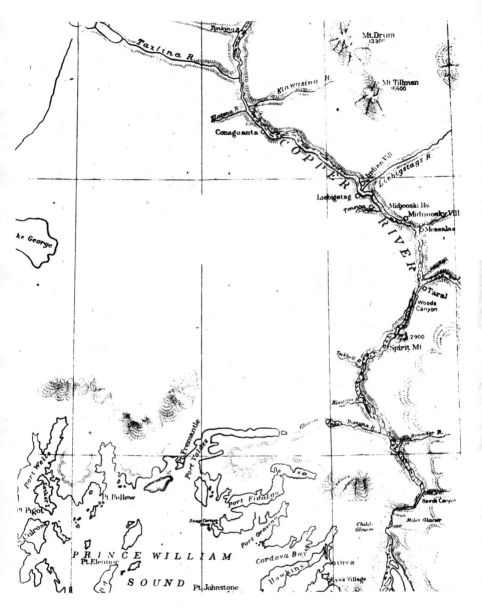

Prince William Sound and the Copper River, April 1898, USC&GS

THREE ALL-AMERICAN ROUTES
TO THE VALLEY OF THE YUKON.

Map Showing the Copper River Country, in Which Extensive
Explorations Are to Be Undertaken by the Government Reindeer Expedition.

"Three All-American Routes to the Valley of the Yukon,"
from the Seattle Post-Intelligencer, *March 18, 1898*

Camp Valdez

route, she had frozen her feet on the glacier and was subsequently abandoned by her people at Port Valdez. She was found by a white man, who took her in, and in 1898 she was still living with him on an island in Prince William Sound. The Indians abandoned the glacier route when a trading post was established in the vicinity of Cook Inlet.[4]

A few crude log cabins, the remnants of the Indians' former trading excursions over Valdez Glacier, existed on the beach at Port Valdez, about two miles east of the prospectors' camp. This site had become known as "Hangtown" as the result of two murders and a lynching that occurred there on January 2, 1898. Among the early arrivals that winter was a party of Eastern prospectors who had taken up residence there. In Seattle they had outfitted M.F. Tanner, a cowboy, for the benefit of his wilderness experience. On reaching Alaska, the Easterners realized that their arrangement with the arrogant cowboy was not going to work. One day, while loitering outside of their tent, Tanner overheard his partners discussing the prospect of cutting him out of the partnership. He became angry, rushed into the tent, and shot two of his partners to death. Two others escaped. Tanner was apprehended, judged guilty at a miners' meeting, and promptly hanged.[5]

The gold seekers at the forefront of the rush to Port Valdez discovered that traveling across the 25-mile length of Valdez Glacier with a degree of safety was possible only in late winter, after the abundant snowfall of this region filled its deep crevasses. The seaward side of the Chugach Range experiences a heavy amount of precipitation and moderate temperatures due to the Japan Current. In the Copper River valley, beyond the major influence of this warm ocean current, precipitation is less but extremes of temperature occur. In good weather conditions, a man without a load could climb the 19 miles to the summit of the glacier in less than two days. But usually, the upper reaches of the glacier are engulfed in storms or fog, and for prospectors transporting between one and two tons of supplies, the ascent took several weeks. Sledding down the six-mile inland slope of the glacier (later named Klutina Glacier) was comparatively easy, for it lacked the steep benches which made the ascent so difficult.[6]

Letter dated March 13, 1898, Camp I, Port Valdes, Alaska
My dear Wife,

Well, we have been here five days. This is an awful country. Nothing but snow and ice as far as the eye can see. Where we are now camped [on the beach] the snow is 7 ft. deep. Of course we do not dig down to the ground to pitch our tent. Will be here 3 days more and then will move our tents 5 miles farther up [to the foot of] the glacier. It is 16 miles over the glacier and not one stick of wood to be found in the whole distance. [Rough estimates of distances were obtained by word-of-mouth from leading parties.

Copper River region, a map enclosed in Conger's letter of June 30, 1898

Measurements made by a USGS geologist later in the season resulted in more accurate estimates — in this instance, 25 miles.][7] There are places where a man has to crawl on his hands and knees and can carry only 50 lbs. on his back. Other places where he has to hang on to a rope to keep from falling to his death. This is an awful proposition. The worst is yet to come but if we all live to get over the glacier and can find gold enough to do us the balance of our lives, all will be well.

A good many of our boys are lame. One is now sick abed with pain in the chest. There are lots of doctors, lawyers, and in fact all kinds of professions represented here. I am cooking for the party and I find it an awful task to do so for so many on our little stove. But at the same time, I am in camp all the day and am not exposed to the cold and storms. I have one man to help me cook. Bake bread twice a day. [Conger used a heavy sheet iron stove. This was the most common type on the glacier trail, measuring about 3 feet long, 15 inches wide, and 15 inches high. At one end was an opening for wood and at the opposite end, one for an oven.][8]

Today is Sunday and all the boys are in camp resting and writing. This is our first Sunday in Alaska. Got [out] the babies' and your pictures today for the first time since I left and took a long look at them. Oh, how I would like to see you, and I will, by and by, God willing. Do not advise anyone to come here, for the hardships are something almost unbearable. Should you see Turitin, tell him that he can consider his accident a providential circumstance and to not think of coming here for at least a year from now. There are about 700 people in camp, two of whom are women. I saw one woman yesterday wading through snow up to her knees, hauling a load of wood to camp. Wood is poor. Have to dry a good deal of it before it will burn.

When we got off of the boat we were landed on the ice about 1½ miles from land. Our goods were lowered over the side of the boat in two feet of snow and we had to haul them away at once to land for fear the ice would break off and float out to sea, which a hundred acres of it did the next day. We worked nearly all night

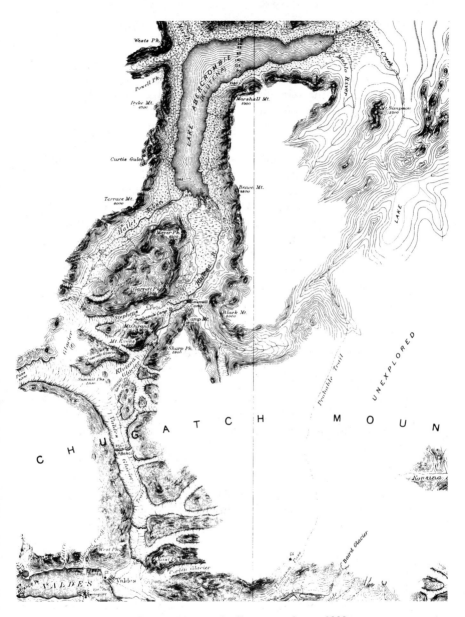

The Copper River and adjacent territory, 1898

midst a blinding snowstorm in order to move our stuff before morning. There were about 100 in the same fix as ourselves. I got wet through to the skin and some of my clothes are not dry yet. Clothes do not dry very fast here as the air is quite damp even when the sun shines, which it does not do. It is not cold, however. The coldest it has been was 15° above zero. Expect when we get on top of the glacier proper it will be cold and windy. Will stop writing now until after dinner, as it is 11 o'clock and I have got some evaporated potatoes cooking which need looking after.

Dinner over and dishes washed. Potatoes were no good; in fact they were decidedly obnoxious. Am baking bread and writing between bakes. One of the boys caught two codfish this forenoon which weigh 20 pounds. Will cook them for supper. Have just finished baking 8 loaves of bread and will bake the same number tomorrow and so on for each and every day we stay here.

Have often wondered how you are getting along and what you will do when your money plays out. Do hope you can collect all bills due. How are the dear little pets, anyhow? Don't suppose they realize what it is to be without a papa. Now Lizzie, I wish to say something about writing to me. It will cost me two dollars a month after we get over the glacier to get my mail, providing I get any, so we have all decided to have our mail sent to St. Cloud and forwarded from there in one bunch once a month. So when you write me, address St. Cloud, Minn., care of J.A. McDonald, who will put all the letters in one envelope and they will be received by us as one letter. Should a change of address occur, I will notify you. You must get your letters off so that they will reach St. Cloud on or before the 25th of each month. Now good by dear and write to me once a month without fail.

Your loving husband,
H.S. Conger

Tuesday, March 15, 1898
Thermometer: 22°
Still and cloudy. Roy is sawing wood. I am baking johnnycake. The rest of the boys have gone with loads up to the glacier. Most

Glacial river emerging from tunnel at foot of Valdez Glacier, 1898.

all of the trees here are balm of Gilead [balsam poplar]. Lots of kicking and growling in camp. It is snowing and melts as fast as it falls. Goes through my tent like a sieve.

Wednesday, March 16, 1898
Weather: Clear; Thermometer: 16°
Slept good last night. My cold still holds on. Can hear the crows cawing, which reminds me of New York. This is a lovely day. Baason let a revolver go off while in the tent. The bullet came within six inches of Buckley's head.

Thursday, March 17, 1898
Weather: Clear; Thermometer: 18°
Camp No. 2. Moved from Camp No. 1 today, distance 4½ miles [in a northeasterly direction]. There are 100 tents here at the foot of the glacier. Ate hardtack and dried beef for dinner.

Jackson, the mail carrier, at Lake Klutina.

Friday, March 18, 1898
Weather: Cloudy; Thermometer: 30°
The boys have commenced hauling our goods up the first bench
with block and tackle. [The benches were changes of elevation on
the glacier and most were steep inclines. The tops of the benches
were comparatively level terraces of varying distances. Five
benches marked the 19-mile slope to the 4,800-foot summit of
Valdez Glacier. The first three benches were located close together

near the foot of the glacier, and block and tackle was used to hoist the loaded sleds to the 830-foot level at the top of the third bench. In using the block and tackle method, prospectors anchored a post in the ice a distance up the slope equal to the length of their rope. One end of the rope was fastened to a loaded sled at the bottom of the incline, and the prospectors, holding the other end of the rope, would run down the slope, thus forcing the loaded sled up the incline. Then the men would reclimb the steep grade, backpacking a load of about 50 pounds, and repeat the process.][9] First accident happened today. Guyer got his fingers smashed. I bandaged them up. 1:30 — snowslide which made the earth tremble.

Saturday, March 19, 1898
Weather: Windy and clear; Thermometer: 30°
All our provisions are on top of the first bench. Snow is drifting badly. Some of the campers shot 22 ptarmigans. Noon: Jackson has come with first mail. None for me. [The postmaster at Orca had made arrangements with a "Squaw Man" (a term used to designate a white man who had married an Indian) named Jackson to carry the mail from Valdez into the interior.][10] Cooked beans, onions, potatoes, bread, oatmeal, and prunes today. Steamer *Valencia* unloaded at this port 600 souls. [This was the first trip to Alaska for the 1,198-ton vessel owned by the Pacific Steam Whaling Company, and it was an exciting one due to rebellious passengers and a terrible storm. Steerage passengers, dissatisfied with their food, threatened to take over the ship, but the captain deterred them with hoses attached to the hot water pipes coming from the ship's boiler. After entering the open sea, the heavily loaded *Valencia* ran into a storm, and the rolling of the ship caused livestock on board to suffer broken legs and other mutilations, necessitating their being killed and thrown overboard. Some of the passengers were so frightened during the storm that they sat on their bunks with guns, ready to shoot themselves should the vessel begin to sink.][11] Jangle in camp. Neil Hessian appointed captain. Mike dropping out.

Sunday, March 20, 1898
Weather: Cloudy; Thermometer: 30°
Mike Hessian is cook today. Roy is helping haul goods up 3rd
bench. There was a growling in camp across the way early this
morning. Man got shot in the foot while hunting.

Tuesday, March 22, 1898
Thermometer: 28°
Snowed 1 foot last night. Wind blows so today, one cannot see the
trail. Boys all in camp except Beatty and Reigel, who have
attempted to cross the glacier. Took everything out of the cooking
tent and leveled the snow. 4 P.M. — It is clearing off with some
wind. They have established a town site at Port Valdes. [The
townspeople voted to name their new tent-town after the adjacent
inlet. Port Valdez had been named by Lt. Salvador Fidalgo in
1790 to honor the Spanish admiral and minister of the navy,
Antonio Valdes y Basan. Prior to 1898, Valdez was just a lonely
wilderness locality, visited by occasional traders and adventurers;
yet it was sometimes referred to as "Copper City." See Conger's
map, page 37.][12]

Wednesday, March 23, 1898
Thermometer: 26°
Wind blew hard last night. Boys still in camp. Can't work. Snow
drifted too much. Lots [in Valdez] are $500 for front and $150 for
back. 9:30 — Roy shot accidentally through arm and hip. Now
under influence of morphine. Two doctors in attendance. Think
he will die. It was a 30-30 rifle bullet. Can hear a mandolin across
the way. One man was buried today. He was put into a sleeping
bag.[13] His name was Richard Updol from Minota, Minnesota.
[According to newspaper accounts, his name was T.H. Opdahl,
from Marshall, Minnesota.][14]

Thursday, March 24, 1898
Weather: Cloudy; Thermometer: 26°
Roy is a little worse this morning. Some of the boys have gone

after the heating stove. 9:20 A.M. — L.R. Murfin breathed his last. Poor boy was in great agony for 24 hours but died easy. His life was insured for $5,000 in favor of his father. Roy had $66.30 in his pocket. The body is laid out and five of the boys are digging his grave. I am in camp baking bread. Four of our party have gone 4½ miles lower down to procure a rough box [coffin]. This is a day of lamentations. Held inquest. Dr. Barrett appointed coroner.

Letter dated March 24, 1898, Camp No. 2, Port Valdes, Alaska
Dear Wife,

Since last writing you we have lost one of our party. He was shot accidentally yesterday morning. His name was Le Roy Murfin, from Sleepy Eye, Minnesota. The accident occurred in this manner: All of the boys were in camp that day, it being stormy, and were all in one tent, 10x12, except myself and M.J. Hessian. We were in the cooking tent. I had just finished baking bread and was sitting on a block when I heard the report of a gun and with it, a groan from within the tent. I rushed out and found that the bullet had passed through the elbow and into the body of Mr. Murfin. It was a 30-30 Winchester carbine bullet. It seems that some of the boys were oiling their guns to prevent them from rusting and one of the party went out of one tent and into another to get his gun out of the case. As there were several guns in the pile, he was pulling them out of the case to find out which one was his. Somehow or other, the gun was loaded and went off. No one knows just how it happened. There were only two guns in the outfit which had been fired. Mine has never been

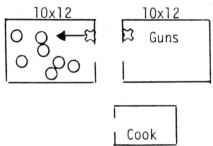

Store at Port Valdez, August 21, 1898.

out of the case since it was bought, nor will it be till I have use for it. This is a diagram of the tents and position of the men [see page 43]. The round dots represent the men as they were sitting at the time. The stars show where the bullet passed through the two tents. The arrow shows its course. Had the ball passed through the first man, it would have killed one sitting back of him also. It was a sad affair and is a warning to the boys to be careful of firearms in the future. We had two doctors, as there were one hundred tents right around us and all professions are represented. Everybody did all they could. Held an inquest this evening and appointed a coroner and notary public.

First law for this section was formed here tonight. One man was caught stealing the other day and he is now in irons on board ship to be taken back to the States. [According to Charles Margeson, another Copper River stampeder, a set of laws was established at a miners' meeting at Valdez which made stealing property worth $10 or more punishable by hanging. For lesser thefts, the penalty was having one's goods confiscated and being forced to leave Alaska. Although the punishment seemed severe, Margeson pointed out that a man's provisions were his life in that country.][15]

Lots of people arriving every few days. Wish I had my drugstore here. Could make my fortune in a little while. Would write to Len to come up and open [a drugstore] here, but I don't know how good the prospects will be after we cross the glacier and commence work. Should we strike rich diggings, there will be a booming town close by. There are two stores going up now. Of course they are crude affairs. [One enterprising party of gold seekers from Stamford, Connecticut, built a store in Valdez and stocked it with goods brought along for that purpose. Everything they sold brought them from two to four times its cost. Business was so good that they sent a man back to Seattle to purchase more stock.][16]

Do so hope I will be successful, for this is a terrible undertaking. It is not cold, but the atmosphere seems to penetrate one's marrow. I think it is on account of so much snow and ice. The coldest it has been since we came here [camp No. 2] is 26° above zero. I am wearing the same clothes I did when I left home.

We are now camped at the foot of the glacier. Most all of our provisions are on top of what is called 3rd bench of the glacier. It is about 10 [about 15] miles from there to the summit. I think it will take us 2 or 3 weeks to reach the top. [The distance from the top of the third bench to the foot of the fourth bench was approximately eight miles and the rise in elevation was 1,920 feet. The fourth bench was six miles long and had a rise of 1,050 feet. It began with a steep rise about a quarter-mile in length, and this was followed by a gradual climb in a northerly direction to the foot of the fifth bench, which was also called the "foot of the summit." The slope to the summit was almost a mile in length, and over this distance the rise in elevation was 1,000 feet, again necessitating the use of block and tackle.][17] It snowed 18 inches

On the Glacier Trail.

night before last and blew all the next day, which blockaded the trail. Don't think the snow can last much longer as it is drawing towards spring.

It is now 11:10 at night. I am sitting up with the corpse and writing letters to keep awake. It seems hard to bury a friend in this lonely country, but it can't be helped. One man was buried yesterday, age 52. He worked too hard and ruptured a blood vessel. There are now nearly two thousand people between here and the Copper River. Expect you will see an account of the shooting here but have no idea [if] it will be a correct one, as news which travels so far is liable to be changed a little. [On April 8, the *San Francisco Chronicle* carried the following account of Murfin's death.

L.R. Murfine was shot and killed on the morning of March 23rd. With his partner, he was engaged in pulling a heavily loaded sled across the ice from their camp, ten miles from the edge of the glacier, to the summit. A rope on the sled needed tightening, and both men were working on the knot. His partner's revolver in some way became loose in his belt and fell out. It struck the sled in such a way that it was discharged, the bullet striking Murfine and inflicting a wound from which he died shortly after. The unfortunate was a young man, but leaves a widow and family at Sleepy Eye, Minn.][18]

Guess I had better quit writing or it will cost me more than 2¢ to post this letter and I must be sparing with my stamps. How are the dear little ones, God bless them. I pray for you all every night and long to see you. Watch over them dear wife with tender care, for I will see you and them in a short time. Expect to get this letter out tomorrow. Have not heard from you since I struck Alaska. In fact there has not been any boat in carrying mail from Seattle since we landed here. Good night dearest. Keep up a strong heart and all will end well, I am sure. Don't forget to write once a month at least.

Lovingly,
your husband,
H.S. Conger

Friday, March 25, 1898
Weather: Cloudy; Thermometer: 26°
Roy was buried at 10:30 A.M. Sixty-two were gathered at the grave. Sang "Shall We Gather at the River." The minister's text was from Revelations, 7th chapter. Read the whole chapter. Snowing again.

Sunday, March 27, 1898
Weather: Clear and windy; Thermometer: 24°
All the boys have gone after wood. Saw men hauling goods on two sleds with one horse. Horses are just the animals in this country. Dogs are no good. A man broke his leg yesterday. Took a picture of Roy's grave today.

Monday, March 28, 1898
Weather: Snowing; Thermometer: 22°
The boys have gone on 3rd bench to move goods farther on. They
took dinner with them. Saw two goats drawing loads. They work
all right. Washed clothes today. M.J. Hessian cooked bread and
got dinner for the first time since we arrived here. He will cook in
my place and I will go on the trail tomorrow. Dreamed last night
that Lizzie would not recognize me. Also that I saw her at a
banquet flashing her diamonds and telling of her great wealth.

Tuesday, March 29, 1898
Weather: Snowing; Thermometer: 22°
Went out this morning with 9 of the boys and hauled 150 pounds
ten miles up the glacier. I never was so stiff and sore as tonight.
One man froze both hands while crossing the summit of the
glacier today. It is raining here now at 8:45 P.M.

Wednesday, March 30, 1898
Weather: Snowing; Thermometer: 30°
Started on the trail this morning but gave it up. Storm was too
bad. Could not see the trail. Went down to the bay this afternoon.
Horses there for sale. Stores and one restaurant. Sugar worth
$12.75 per C, flour, $8.00. Fifteen doctors here.

Thursday, March 31, 1898
Weather: Cloudy; Thermometer: 30°
Went out on trail this morning. Two of the boys have got swollen
jaws or a kind of neuralgic pain. Steamer *Excelsior* arrived today.
The trail was bad. Had to break one mile through 18 inches of
snow. Did not get into camp till 8 o'clock.

Friday, April 1, 1898
Weather: Cloudy; Thermometer: 26°
All went out on the trail except Reigel, who was sick with sore
throat. Gosh, I am lame. 130 passengers were unloaded here from
the *Excelsior.*

Saturday, April 2, 1898
Weather: Cloudy and snow; Thermometer: 28°
Went on trail this morning. [There] was a blizzard on 4th bench.
Was lame in left knee. Trail getting in bad condition. Bought a
pair of ice creepers for $2.50, pair shoes $4.00, 2 oz. arnica [a lini-
ment for sprains and bruises] 50¢.

Sunday, April 3, 1898
Thermometer: 28°
Did not go on the trail on account of wind and snow. Reportedly,
gold was found over the trail, 75¢ per pan, but it is doubtful.
Steamer *Alliance* arrived today.

Monday, April 4, 1898
Thermometer: 30°
Snowed during the forenoon. The afternoon was warm, still, and
bright. Saw a good many snowslides. The roar was like that produced from thunder. J.B. Buckley became snow-blind and had to
turn back from the trail. Corcoran was sick with big-jaw. [Snow
blindness and scurvy plagued a large number of the gold seekers
on this trail. Exposure to the sun's ultraviolet rays, reflected from
the ice and snow of the glacier, caused a painful eye inflammation
which usually resulted in temporary blindness. Topographer
Oscar Rohn suffered from snow blindness while crossing a nearby
glacier with a prospector in 1899. "By the time we got to the
crevasses," he wrote, "the pain in our eyes was such that neither
of us cared seriously how soon we fell into one."[19] The gold
seekers used a variety of devices to avoid this affliction. The best
protection was provided by close-fitting goggles, carved from the
soft poplar wood found at Valdez. The inside surface was
blackened to reduce the glare from the small amount of light
emitted through the tiny eye holes.[20] The symptoms of scurvy, a
disease caused by a severe vitamin C deficiency, develop slowly.
Fatigue and pain in the muscles and joints are among the early
characteristics of the disease. Since these vague symptoms
parallel the common complaints of hard physical labor, it is

Valdez Glacier near top of Third Bench, showing transverse crevasse and ridge topography in ice, 1898.

Up the trail from top of Third Bench.

Wooden eye protectors

understandable that the disease went unrecognized in Alaskan prospectors for several months. However, many physicians on the trail overlooked even the more obvious signs of the disease such as swelling and inflammation of the gums (big-jaw?), which bleed easily, and discoloration of the skin, especially of the legs, caused by subcutaneous bleeding. The general impression was that the condition was rheumatic. It was often called "black leg rheumatism."[21]]

Tuesday, April 5, 1898
Thermometer: 32°
This is a bright looking morning. Some wind. Afternoon is windy with a driving snow. Trail is filled up. "A horse, my kingdom for a horse." Am lame and tired after 20 mile jaunt.

Thursday, April 7, 1898
Weather: Windy; Thermometer: 32°
Could hear a child's voice this morning. Party of half-breeds. One

man sprained his ankle today. Coasted 2 miles coming down the glacier. We are taking goods on top of 3rd bench tonight.

Friday, April 8, 1898
Thermometer: 30°
We worked all night on the benches and today will haul 12 miles and return. This has been a lovely day. Sledding was good. Guyer was snow-blind and we had to sled him home. One man stole a sled and they gave him a hearing last night.

Saturday, April 9, 1898
Weather: Clear; Thermometer: 26°
Hauled goods to 4th bench. Sleighing was good. Coasted 6 miles coming back. Guyer is still blind. A good many parties are splitting up. They are dissatisfied. Expect to move camp tomorrow to foot of [the summit of the] glacier. This has been a warm day. Snow is melting rapidly. Snowing some tonight.

Sunday, April 10, 1898
Weather: Snow; Thermometer: 30°
Moved from Camp No. 2 to Camp No. 3, a distance of 16 [18] miles and all uphill. Pitched one tent at 10:30 P.M. We are now at the foot of the summit of the glacier. Ate supper with the Hudson boys. Bought 4 dozen fresh herrings at 25¢ per dozen. This is Easter Sunday, but no eggs did we see.

Monday, April 11, 1898
Weather: Snowing; Thermometer: 20°
Got up at 8:30. Pitched cook tent and made coffee. Went down to fourth bench and brought up 5 loads. The summit [slope] is 4,860 feet long [with a grade of about 20 percent] and we are going to block and tackle our goods up.

Tuesday, April 12, 1898
Weather: Windy; Thermometer: 20°
M.J. Hessian went on the trail and Neil took his place cooking. It

Middle of Fourth Bench Camp, looking south.

is colder here than at our last camp but the air is drier. Made one trip to the 4th bench. Had to . . . [leave][22] our loads on account of blinding snow.

Wednesday, April 13, 1898
Thermometer: 20°
It snowed and blowed all night. Blankets were covered with snow in the tent. This is tough. Fourteen miles from wood[23] and chances are we may be hemmed in here and perish. Face is peeling. [According to one prospector, the reflection of the sun's rays from the snow and ice on the glacier resulted in "boiled lobster-like and peeled up red onion-like faces."][24] Buckley was taken sick last night. The storm is terrific. Never saw the like. Unable to get out of our tents. Am afraid our tents will blow down and bury us beneath the snow.

A tent at the Fourth Bench.

Thursday, April 14, 1898
Thermometer: 24°
The storm still unabated. Some of the Fram party[25] stayed in our camp last night. They could not get through. Did not leave our tents all day. Have wood enough for only 2 days. At bedtime the stars are shining.

Friday, April 15, 1898
Thermometer: 22°
Got up at 5:45. Found it snowing but no wind. Can see some of the men breaking trail. Don't think we can make our cache today. Drifts of snow in front of tent 8 ft. high. Made one trip to the 4th bench for wood. Stayed in camp part of the afternoon. Put a plaster on my thigh.

Sunday, April 17, 1898
Weather: Cloudy with snow; Thermometer: 20°

I am cooking again. All the boys have gone after loads except Druey, who was sick this morning. Reigel played out on the way. He is now in camp laid up with contractions of the muscles.

Monday, April 18, 1898
Thermometer: 14°
The sun rose in view this morning for the first time in a week. Dick Baasen was taken with the big-jaw this noon and had to lay off.

Tuesday, April 19, 1898
Thermometer: 14°
This bids to be a fair day. I got up at 3:30 A.M. and it was daylight then. We have 17 hours of daylight now. The snow here is 100 feet deep. The boys did not get in till 10 o'clock last night. We commence tackling up the summit this afternoon.

Wednesday, April 20, 1898
Weather: Clear; Thermometer: 14°
We are working on the summit. Some of the boys are nearly blind. The reflection of the sun from the snow is terrifying. Steamer *Valencia* is in with 450 passengers. [Among the passengers were members of the Copper River Military Expedition. The federal government had responded to the public demand for information about Alaska by appropriating funds for several geographic and geologic investigations of the district. These explorations, begun in the spring of 1898, were conducted by two military parties and four U.S. Geological Survey (USGS) teams. Because a principal objective of these early investigations was locating practical routes of travel from tidewater to the Yukon gold fields, the reconnaissances were confined to the valleys of the larger rivers. Two U.S. Army detachments composed the Copper River Military Expedition of 1898. A USGS geologist was detailed to each detachment at the request of the War Department. Captain Edwin F. Glenn, Twenty-fifth Infantry, commanded one detachment which moved inland from

Cook Inlet along the Matanuska River. After crossing the Copper River plateau and the Alaska Range, some members of Glenn's party succeeded in descending the Delta River to the Tanana. The second detachment, headed by Captain W.R. Abercrombie, Second Infantry, moved inland by way of Valdez Glacier. Because of Abercrombie's decision to return to Seattle to procure pack animals for the expedition, the main part of this detachment did not get started over the glacier until August 5 and succeeded in advancing only as far as Copper Center.][26] Am nearly out of wood. Wood is 10¢ per pound here. Steamer *City* [of] *Seattle* lost on the rocks. 300 souls perished. [Conger was misinformed about the fate of the *City of Seattle,* as it remained in service on the West Coast until 1921. Several other ships ran aground in Alaskan waters in April of 1898 and two ships collided, but no human casualties were reported. The American bark *Mercury,* driven ashore in Skagway's harbor on April 11 and subsequently abandoned, was the only total loss reported for April. However, according to a *San Francisco Chronicle* news story on May 21, 1898, less than half of the ships suffering damage in Alaskan waters in the preceding six months had been reported because steamship companies were attempting to suppress such information. Allegedly, the *City of Seattle, Al-ki,* and *Oregon* were among the many ships which had been grounded, requiring extensive repairs.][27]

Thursday, April 21, 1898
Thermometer: 10°
This is the brightest morning I have seen since we came to this camp. Got up at 4 o'clock and got an early breakfast. Finished hauling from the 4th bench today. Took 2 Kodak pictures of the summit. This is a great hill to coast down. Most everybody who is on the trail is more or less blind.

Friday, April 22, 1898
Thermometer: 14°
This is a beautiful day. All the boys are working on the summit.

Slept on a sled last night. Expect mail today. Can hear someone playing a cornet. Neil Hessian went to the beach to see about buying a horse.

Letter dated April 22, 1898, Summit of Glacier, Alaska
[This letter was written on both the 22d and 23d at the Summit Camp, located at the foot of the summit.]
My Dear Lizzie,

Received tonight the first letters I have had since reaching this soil (or ice and snow). They were both from you, March 15 and 22, and you don't know how glad I was to get them. Had to stop at intervals during the reading to allow my eyes to dry sufficiently to proceed. The man who brought the mail is distributing it in one of our tents and there is a string of men going in and out. Expect they will keep it up nearly all night. He brings the mail once a month and goes as far on the trail as the advanced prospectors have reached. [According to Jackson, the mail carrier, four men had reached timber in the interior by March 2; however, a military explorer reported that the leading parties had not progressed beyond the summit by mid-April. It was difficult to pinpoint the progress of a party of gold seekers on the trail, as their supplies were scattered in piles or caches at various points along the trail. Because most gold seekers carried a one to two year supply of provisions, a number of tedious trips over the same ground was necessary to advance to the next desired camping place. The last of the series of load to be moved was always the tent and camping equipment. But sometimes this load was moved twice as far as the forward cache of supplies to avoid setting up the base camp so often. Thus, the location of the base camp did not indicate a party's general progress.][28]

There is a company of government soldiers and surveyors at Valdes who are going to survey a route through to Circle City.

We will move camp from here tomorrow over the summit of the glacier and down on the other side 12 miles to timber. This glacier is 30 miles long from timber to timber. Wood has to be hauled to last through [the trip]. We bought ¼ cord and paid $10 for it. A fearful storm raged here commencing Sunday [the 10th] and lasting 3 days. I thought for a while we would be blown away or snowed under. This is a bad place to be in during a storm, for the trail fills up in five minutes after a party of ten have gone over it. Thank God we are [almost] over the glacier.

Some say we are on the wrong trail. If so, there are others (some 2,500). [Confusion probably arose because the general direction the gold seekers were traveling was north. Soon after setting up camp at Valdez, Captain Abercrombie's expedition was visited by a group of prospectors seeking information about the route. In his report, geologist F.C. Schrader, who accompanied the expedition, wrote:

> As the route over Valdes Glacier had been supposed to lead within a short distance to a small lake, the supposed source of the Tasnuna River, which river was known to lie about due east of Valdes, the band of prospectors who for more than a month had been slowly forging their way a score or more miles up the glacier in the bleak mountainous waste of snow and ice, with no indications of the Tasnuna country in sight and no idea as to wither they might be going, held a meeting and sent a committee to the commander of our camp for such geographic information of the route and region as might be furnished. As such information was not extant, the region being practically unknown, Lieutenant Brookfield and the writer were detailed to make a hasty reconnaissance of the summit of the glacier and mountains and return to camp with the results of the observations.

Schrader and Brookfield did not reach the summit until May 3, and the following day Schrader made the first topographical observations of the glacier. He found that its true trend, from Valdez to the summit, was a little west of north, while the interior slope (Klutina Glacier) descended to the northeast. He concluded that the altitude of the summit was 4,800 feet.][29]

I cooked breakfast for 2 men from St. Cloud[30] this morning [the 23d]. They had been down to Valdes for supplies and were unable to reach camp yesterday, so stayed here all night. There are 12 men in one camp who are from there (St. Cloud). They are R.R. conductors and engineers.

Bought a pie the other day from a lady and paid 25¢ for it. It tasted home-like but I could make a better one myself if I had the facilities for doing so. Am baking corn bread this morning and writing between bakes. Darn the stuff, it sticks to the pan and falls to pieces if I touch it. Have been mixing a little whole wheat flour with it heretofore, but have run out of that, as all of our flour, with other provisions, are on top of the summit and I have got to use what we have in camp. Expected to move today but can't till tomorrow. Guess the boys will think I am trying to kill them or work myself out of a job by giving them such poor "chuck" food. I eat 3 times as much as I did at home and I imagine the others eat 6 times as much as I do. What a task it is to cook for so many in a 8x10 tent, and on a small sheet iron stove, particularly so when one has to melt snow for water, which I have had to do since we struck the glacier. But we will soon reach plenty of wood and water.

There are about 25 doctors on the trail and 10 or 12 women with their husbands. Saw one poor little lady yesterday whom I think will never reach home again, for she had a bad cough and looked so puny and frail. She was dressed in a mackinaw, same as a man, only her coat was a long sack. She looked cute and her suit was becoming. Others wear the ordinary home garments. Some of them are good looking and smart, while others are coarse and ugly. I admire them for their pluck just the same.

Have seen and heard several snowslides. They make a noise like distant thunder. I heard they had a slide near Dyea which buried 150 people. [The avalanche occurred near Chilkoot Pass on April 3, 1898. By April 9, 54 bodies had been recovered and the search for 7 still missing was called off so traffic along the trail could resume.][31]

Am glad you got the picture. Sent Len one but he did not say

he got it. Have taken 12 Kodak views of the glacier and surrounding country and will have them developed when . . . [page
four of this letter was lost] . . . and hearing talking and laughing, I
stopped and looked in. You were at the head of a sumptuously
spread table and were flashing diamonds and telling of your great
wealth. I stood there a few minutes and then walked away. [This
is an account of the dream Conger speaks of in his diary entry of
March 28.]

So you met Miss Hessian, did you? She wanted to come to
this country with her brothers but it is just as well she did not. If
we strike anything, it will be time enough then for our wives and
sisters to come.

Borguson has caught up and passed us. He and company had
a light outfit. I tell you, it takes lots of food to feed one in this
country. A good many are buying more whenever they can find
someone who is selling out and going back (and there are a good
many). Neil Hessian went down to the beach yesterday to try and
buy a horse. We heard there were some there for sale. If we can
get one, will make better time. They were selling a while ago for
$125 to $300. Sugar is 13¢, flour 10¢, wood 10¢, and other things
in proportion. If I only had a store at Valdes or anywhere on the
trail, could get rich in a short time. [This letter is resumed on
April 25.]

Sunday, April 24, 1898

Weather: Windy; Thermometer: 14°
Moved over summit of glacier and down to timber, a distance of
12 miles. Plenty of wood and water. Trout in the creek. Snow 4
feet deep. Spruce timber. The glacier is long and steep from this
side. Not so bad as the other, however. Rabbits and ptarmigans
abound. Quite home-like here. Believe there is gold here. Seventy
miles [actually about 56 miles][32] from here to Copper River. This
is camp No. 4. [This camp was called both Timber Camp and
Twelvemile Camp. The latter name was derived from the fact that
the gold seekers believed it was 12 miles from the summit of the
glacier. The distance measured by Schrader was 10 miles.]

A typical hand sled.

Monday, April 25, 1898
Weather: Cloudy; Thermometer: 16°
All of the boys have gone up to the summit for loads. The boys
did not get in till after 11 at night. Bad storm and sled tipped over
several times. [The only difficulty encountered in descending the
six-mile inland slope of the glacier was keeping control of the
heavily loaded sleds on the steeper parts of the grade. The hand
sleds had flat steel runners, were 6 to 7 feet long, about 18 inches
wide, and built 6 to 8 inches off the ground for stability. The
decks were composed of three inch-wide hardwood slats, braced
for strength. Attached to the right-front of each sled was a gee
pole used for steering and steadying the load, while the pulling
power was provided by a man with a rope strung over his
shoulders.][33]

Over Valdez Glacier — 61

Notes—

1. F.C. Schrader, "A Reconnaissance of a Part of Prince William Sound and the Copper River District, Alaska, in 1898," *Twentieth Annual Report of the USGS,* Part 7 (Washington: Gov. Printing Office, 1900), pp. 351, 373-76, 381-82; Oscar Rohn, "A Reconnaissance of the Chitina River and the Skolai Mountains, Alaska," *Twenty-First Annual Report of the USGS,* Part 2 (Washington: Gov. Printing Office, 1900), pp. 403, 405.

2. W.R. Abercrombie, "Supplementary Expedition Into the Copper River Valley, Alaska, 1884," *Compilation of Narratives of Explorations in Alaska* (Washington: Gov. Printing Office, 1900), p. 391.

3. Rohn, "A Reconnaissance of the Chitina River . . . Alaska," *Twenty-First Annual Report of the USGS,* p. 401; Map headed "Three All-American Routes to the Valley of the Yukon," *Seattle Post-Intelligencer,* March 18, 1898, p. 16, said to be compiled from data obtained by Abercrombie in 1884. The text with this map states that "The most favored route is from the head of Valdes Inlet across the glacial morraine to the lake in which the Tasnuna River heads, down the Tasnuna to the Copper. . . ."; U.S. Coast and Geodetic Survey Map No. 3091, published in April of 1898, Gov. Documents, Shields Library, Univ. of California, Davis; Maps published earlier and carried by prospectors also indicated that the route led eastward. See Conger's map, page 35, and Basil Austin, *The Diary of a Ninety-Eighter* (Mount Pleasant, Michigan: John Cumming, 1968), pp. 44-45. Also see "Gold in the Remote Creeks," *San Francisco Chronicle,* Dec. 5, 1898, p. 5; C.H. Remington, *A Golden Cross? On the Trails from Valdez Glacier* (Los Angeles: White-Thompson, 1939), p. 24.

4. Charles Margeson, *Experiences of Gold Hunters in Alaska* (Hornellsville, N.Y.: Charles Margeson, 1899), pp. 60-61, 95; The route taken by the Copper River Indians to Cook Inlet followed the Tazlina River and went over Tahneta Pass, following the route of what is now the Glenn Highway to Knik Arm. W.C. Mendenhall, "A Reconnaissance from Resurrection Bay to the Tanana River, Alaska, in 1898," in *Twentieth Annual Report of the USGS,* p. 303.

5. "Murder and Lynching on Copper River," *San Francisco Chronicle,* Feb. 3, 1898, p. 1; Margeson, *Experiences of Gold Hunters in Alaska,* p. 62; Remington, *A Golden Cross,* p. 8.

6. Alfred H. Brooks, *Blazing Alaska's Trails,* 2d ed. (1953; rpt. Fairbanks: Univ. of Alaska Press, 1973), pp. 29-36; E.F. Glenn and W.R. Abercrombie, "Report of Lt. R.M. Brookfield," *Reports of Explorations in the Territory of Alaska, 1898* (Washington: Gov. Printing Office, 1899), pp. 397-400; Schrader, "A Reconnaissance of a Part of Prince William Sound," *Twentieth Annual Report of the USGS,* pp. 352-53, 369.

7. Table of distances by glacier trail in Schrader, "A Reconnaissance . . . 1898," *Twentieth Annual Report of the USGS,* p. 366. Subsequent distances and elevations on the glacier route noted by the editors are from this table unless otherwise specified.

8. Neil D. Benedict, "The Valdes and Copper River Trail," (unpublished manuscript in Alaska Historical Library, Juneau), 1899, p. 1.

9. Benedict, "The Valdes and Copper River Trail," pp. 22-25.

10. Glenn and Abercrombie, "Report of W.R. Abercrombie," *Reports of Explorations . . . 1898,* p. 346; Benedict, "The Valdes and Copper River Trail," pp. 176-78.

11. "Terrible Trip to Alaska" *San Francisco Chronicle,* March 30, 1898, p. 4; W.R. Abercrombie, "Report of the Wilson Mining Co.," *Copper River Exploring Expedition, 1899* (Washington: Gov. Printing Office, 1900), p. 48.

12. Schrader, "A Reconnaissance . . . 1898," *Twentieth Annual Report of the USGS,* p. 349; Remington, *A Golden Cross,* p. 5; Eric Beerman, "Spanish Admiral Antonio Valdez," *The ALASKA JOURNAL®,* 9 (Spring 1979): 38-43.

13. A typical sleeping bag used by Alaskan gold seekers in 1898 weighed 15 to 20 pounds. It consisted of three separate bags, one inside the other. The outer bag was made of rubber, the middle, of goatskin with the hair turned inside, and the inner bag, of heavy mackinaw. Margeson, *Experiences of Gold Hunters,* p. 10.

14. "From the Copper River," *San Francisco Chronicle,* April 8, 1898, p. 5; Also see the *Seattle Post-Intelligencer,* April 8, 1898, p. 6.

15. Margeson, *Experiences of Gold Hunters,* pp. 63-64.

16. Margeson, *Experiences of Gold Hunters,* pp. 65-66.

17. Glenn and Abercrombie, "Report of Lt. Brookfield," *Reports of Explorations . . . 1898,* pp. 398-400; Schrader, "A Reconnaissance . . . 1898," *Twentieth Annual Report of the USGS,* pp. 351, 366.

18. "From the Copper River," p. 5; An identical account appeared in the *Seattle Post-Intelligencer,* April 8, 1898, p. 6.

19. Abercrombie, "Report of Oscar Rohn on Exploration in Wrangele Mountain District," *Copper River . . . 1899,* pp. 123-24.

20. Austin, *The Diary of a Ninety-Eighter,* p. 28; Benedict, "The Valdes and Copper River Trail," pp. 147-49; Margeson, *Experiences of Gold Hunters,* p. 84.

21. Abercrombie, "Report of Leroy J. Townsend, M.D., on Scorbutus or Scurvy," *Copper River . . . 1899,* pp. 44-47; *The Merck Manual of Diagnosis and Therapy,* ed. David N. Holvey, M.D., and John H. Talbott, M.D., 12th ed. (Rahway, N.J.: Merck, 1972), pp. 1056-59.

22. Word omitted is illegible in the original; it appears to be "leave."

23. From the foot of the summit, the distance to timber was 11 miles in the interior and 20 miles on the seaward side of the glacier. Benedict, "The Valdes and Copper River Trail," p. 27; Glenn and Abercrombie, "Report of Guy H. Preston," *Reports of Explorations . . . 1898,* p. 407; Schrader, "A Reconnaissance . . . 1898," *Twentieth Annual Report of the USGS,* p. 366.

24. Remington, *A Golden Cross,* p. 17.

25. The Fram party, composed of Finns, Norwegians, and Swedes, sledded several knock-down boats of the bateau style over the glacier. Remington, *A Golden Cross,* pp. 14, 98.

26. Schrader, "A Reconnaissance . . . 1898," *Twentieth Annual Report of the USGS*, pp. 347-48; Alfred H. Brooks, *The Geography and Geology of Alaska: A Summary of Existing Knowledge* (Washington: Gov. Printing Office, 1906), pp. 127-29; Glenn and Abercrombie, "Report of Capt. E.F. Glenn," and "Report of Capt. W.R. Abercrombie," *Reports of Explorations . . . 1898*, pp. 5-123, 295-351.

27. Gordon Newell, *Pacific Steamboats* (New York: Bonanza, 1958), p. 123; "Cottage City Runs Aground," *San Francisco Chronicle*, April 27, 1898, p. 12; "Steamers in Collision," *San Francisco Chronicle*, April 13, 1898, p. 4; "The Islander Crippled," *Seattle Post-Intelligencer*, April 13, 1898, p. 8; C.L. Andrews, "Marine Disasters of the Alaska Route," *Washington Historical Quarterly*, 7 (Jan. 1916): 25, 29, 35; "Alaskan Charts Bring Disaster," *San Francisco Chronicle*, May 21, 1898, p. 4; also see *San Francisco Chronicle*, April 12, 1898, p. 5.

28. "Over Valdes Glacier," *Seattle Post-Intelligencer*, March 30, 1898, p. 16; Glenn and Abercrombie, "Report of Lt. Brookfield," *Reports of Explorations . . . 1898*, pp. 394-95; Austin, *The Diary of a Ninety-Eighter*, p. 25.

29. Schrader, "A Reconnaissance . . . 1898," *Twentieth Annual Report of the USGS*, pp. 350-53.

30. Probably St. Cloud, Minnesota. Conger's wife received her education at St. Cloud Teachers College.

31. "Travel Over Buried Corpses," and "Victims of the Great Avalanche," *San Francisco Chronicle*, April 17, 1898, p. 20.

32. F.C. Schrader's table in "A Reconnaissance . . . 1898," *Twentieth Annual Report of the USGS*, p. 366, heretofore used to denote distances along the trail, is not consistent with the distances quoted in his text from the head of Lake Klutina to Copper Center — see pp. 388-89, 392; The distance quoted here has been ascertained from his text, p. 388, and approximates the distance as measured on a 1952 USGS quadrangle of this area.

33. Schrader, "A Reconnaissance . . . 1898," *Twentieth Annual Report of the USGS*, pp. 352-53; Austin, *The Diary of a Ninety-Eighter*, pp. 22, 25, 36; Remington, *A Golden Cross*, pp. 16, 19; Benedict, "The Valdes and Copper River Trail," p. 1.

Chapter 4—

Down the Klutina River to Copper Center

The gold seekers' spirits rose considerably upon reaching the narrow Klutina River valley. A few leading parties got through the upper part of the canyon on sleds, but by mid-May the melting snow forced an end to this mode of travel and boatbuilding was energetically begun to continue the journey to the Copper River. At this point, the prospectors (and the government explorers who followed them) were still unaware of their true geographical position and because of published accounts of the route, they believed the waters ahead were navigable.[1]

Several camps were established along the upper Klutina, a Copper River Indian name meaning "Glacier River." A few tents were located near the foot of Klutina Glacier but most of the gold seekers descended the mile-wide valley for four miles to the timber line before setting up camp. Here the valley doubles in width and they established Twelvemile or Timber Camp. It was the largest camp between the glacier and Klutina Lake, having approximately 100 tents throughout much of the summer. Downstream were other camps named for their distance from Timber Camp. At Threemile Camp a California party set up a portable saw mill it had sledded over the glacier, giving this locality the alternate name of Sawmill Camp. The California party did very well selling lumber for boatbuilding, and it continued to prosper throughout the summer by deriving income from a two-masted schooner it had constructed for ferry service on Klutina Lake.[2]

Where the upper Klutina River entered Klutina Lake, a point of land extended into the lake for a quarter of a mile. Here another camp was located which was aptly named Peninsula

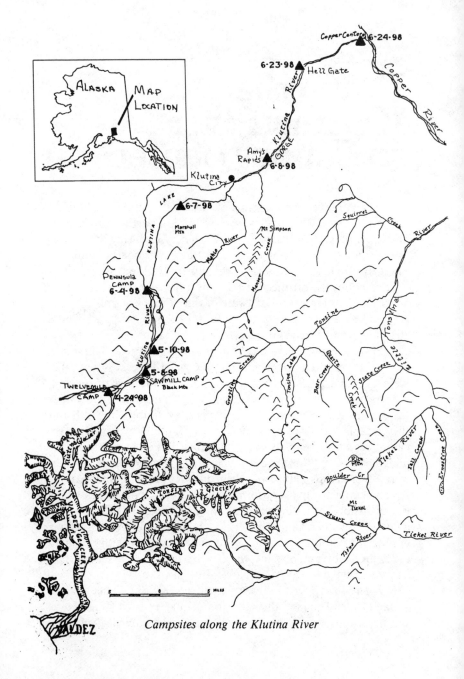

Campsites along the Klutina River

A tent at Twelvemile Camp.

Camp, but alternately called Twentyfourmile Camp for its supposed distance from the summit of Valdez Glacier. Because of its
windy location and the fact that the peninsula had been burned
over, Peninsula Camp offered relative freedom from mosquitoes.
From July to September of 1898, this camp had about 50 tents.
Another large camp, known as "Klutina City," was located at the
foot of the lake, along its northeastern shore.[3]

At the foot of Klutina Lake the mountainous terrain
diminishes, and the lower Klutina River, which drains the lake,
enters the plateau terrain of the Copper River basin. The surface
of the plateau is a nearly level moss and timber covered area,

A shoal at Twelvemile Camp.

dotted with small lakes and swamps. The Klutina entrenches itself increasingly deeper into the thick layer of glacial gravels and silts which compose the plateau terrain, falling about 620 feet in its 25-mile course to the Copper River. This gradient, together with the river's boulder-filled channel, created fierce rapids which halted boating for many gold hunters. A large camp known variously as Amy's Rapids or Amy's Landing was established at the head of these rapids, about four miles from the foot of the lake. This camp extended a mile or more along the Klutina and became a base camp or cache-site for many gold seekers who did not wish to risk their entire outfits by shooting the rapids or lining their boats downstream.[4]

Within a mile or so of the mouth of the Klutina, the precipitous bluffs along its banks almost disappear and at the junction of the Copper and Klutina rivers another large camp

Schooner Manhattan *on Klutina Lake.*

Sawmill, looking upriver toward elbow.

Tents on east side of Peninsula Camp.

called Copper Center was established on a low flat or terrace. It became the headquarters for all travel up or down the Copper River. The mouth of the Klutina was the first location reached on the Valdez Glacier trail which had been explored previously, having been noted on the maps drawn by Lieutenant Allen on his journey up the Copper River from its mouth in 1885.[5]

Letter dated April 25, 1898 [Continuation of April 22 letter]

Well, we have made another move since last writing. We are now 13 miles from last camp, just over summit of glacier and down into timber. Have plenty of water and good dry spruce wood too. Am chewing some [spruce] gum now. All I have to do is to just step outside of my tent and gather it. This is quite a nice

West end of Mosquito Avenue, Klutina City.

place to camp and I believe there is mineral here. I heard today that a man was in here a year ago and took out 60¢ per pan, gold. I don't believe it though.

The snow is 4 feet deep but will soon go and I am afraid it will leave us in the lurch, as it is 70 [56][6] miles from here to Copper River. Don't know as we will reach there very soon. Some of the parties are going no farther than the lake, which is 14 miles from here, and wait there until it breaks up, when they will go down it and follow the river which empties into the Copper. But that way is a very dangerous one on account of the swiftness of the stream. A party tried to go down that way and all lost their lives but one. No! We are going to take the second river but will have to cross another chain of mountains before reaching it. [Because of the indications on their maps, the gold seekers erroneously believed that the first river they encountered after crossing

Lower end of bluffs, looking down toward Copper Center.

the glacier was the Tasnuna, or one of its tributaries. They believed the "second river" was the Konsina, called "Tiekel" on today's maps. In reality, the first river was the Klutina (about 35 miles northwest of the Tasnuna) and the second, the Tazlina. Conger did not cross the mountains to the "second river" as he planned. A trail led northward from the northwest elbow of Klutina Lake, crossing a low divide to the Tazlina; but the low marshy country over which it passed made this route impracticable after the snow melted.][7]

I froze my right ear and my nose yesterday while crossing the summit of the glacier; did not have on my Klondyke cap. It was awful stormy on top but was mild and calm after reaching 3 miles this side.

You probably will notice that some of the words written here are blotted. It was not tears that did it but perspiration from my brow. Am baking bread and have to keep the flap of the tent closed in order to prevent the stove from cooling off too rapidly. Consequently, there is produced from this spruce wood great heat. When I get a loaf of bread into the oven, I sit down with my head bending over my table and write till I think it (the bread) is done. With my head inclined, the moisture which accumulates must necessarily fall on the paper (not in the dough), so please excuse the blots. Am cooking beans, bread, coffee, and apples, all at one time. I have to bake ahead so the boys will have lunch for tomorrow.

I got up at 3:30 this morning and it was daylight then. I do not require the same amount of sleep here as I did in Minnesota, seemingly so. The days are 19 hours long. That is, we have that amount of daylight. The temperature this morning was 16° above zero. Not cold, but would seem so in Minnesota at this time of the year. I think along in January and February it gets awful cold here.

Have not seen an Indian yet and don't expect to till we get far up the Copper River. Our journey has only commenced as regards destination, but I think the hard part is over. That is, the uphill part. It is nice and level, probably a little downhill, where we are hauling now, but don't know, soon it may end. Have had to use block and tackle 3 times since starting to get goods up and over the glacier. One place we used 4,080 feet of rope. Others joined in with us, and all worked together. I tell you, it is slow and tedious. All a man can haul up these places on a sled is 100 pounds and then he has got to have creepers on his boots to prevent him from slipping. We tried to buy a horse but could not get any, and I am glad of it now, for we are over the glacier and the snow is quite soft here and liable to go off with a rush.

It is now 11:15 and I have just finished baking 12 loaves of bread and will quit until this afternoon when I will bake 6 more which will last till tomorrow noon. As I have no one to get dinner for but myself, think I will take a half hour off and get some more spruce bows to carpet my tent floor. You don't know how nice they smell. It makes me think of being in the woods in old Minnesota. Would like to write to Len, but am afraid I won't have time, as the mail carrier may come any minute and I can send mail out only once a month. So if I miss him, good-by for another month. You can let Len read this letter, that is if you are in Mora. Address me same as before. Port Valdes, c/o Pacific Steam Whaling Co., Seattle.

4:15 — It is snowing here, or half snow and rain. It must be rough on the glacier today. The boys have not returned yet. Tomorrow is M. Clifford's birthday. [His son, Martin Clifford, was one year old.] Have been looking around to find something to send him, but I can't find even moss (of which there is an abundance), it being covered with snow.

I am confident that I shall come home rich, but when that will be I am not prepared to say. You don't know how gray my hair has turned in the past two months. You won't believe it but it's almost white. My mustache is yellow. Picture to yourself the combination, if you can. Don't think you will know me by and by. Am fat and my health never was better than it has been the past two weeks.

12:15 at night: Have just finished washing my supper dishes. The boys did not get in till nearly 11 o'clock. Had a bad storm and the trail was nearly obliterated. One in the party is so badly done up that he can't go on the trail for a while, so I am going to take his place and he, mine. This is the reason why I finish this letter tonight, for I will not have time to write anymore for I don't know how long. Now dear, write to me twice a month and I will answer whenever I can. Kiss the little ones for me and give kind regards to all who may inquire about me.

Lovingly,
Horace

Tuesday, April 26, 1898
Weather: Wind and snow; Thermometer: 20°
Neil Hessian is cook now. I went on the trail this morning. Made one trip to summit and coasted down with 500 lbs.

Wednesday, April 27, 1898
Thermometer: 26°
Commenced cooking again this morning. Hessian's eyes became

Hardsledding, Twelvemile Camp, May 25, 1898.

so bad he could not stand the heat of the stove. Four of the boys tried hauling at night but gave it up. Don't think we will work this forenoon. Saw a flock of geese going south. Snowed all day and blowed a hurricane. Seven of the boys took loads to 6 mile cache.

Thursday, April 28, 1898
Weather: Windy; Thermometer: 30°
Went on the trail this morning. Neil Hessian is cook. Tried to reach the summit but had to give it up on account of storm. Some [others] tried, too, but gave it up. I took 11 sacks 6 miles to lower camp. Trail was slick. Met Jackson, the mail carrier, today.

Friday, April 29, 1898

Thermometer: 30°

Started out to reach the summit of glacier but gave it up on account of snow and wind. Snow is getting soft. Two of the boys are making a sled. [Even after the snow melted, sleds were used to haul goods over the cobble-strewn riverbanks. See photo, page 75.][8] All stayed around camp all day.

Saturday, April 30, 1898

Weather: Snow; Thermometer: 30°

Storm still rages on the glacier. Can't reach the summit. Four boys went to the lake today. Jackson is here, snow-bound. Went to foot of summit and returned. 4:30 — commenced raining.

Sunday, May 1, 1898

Thermometer: 34°

Still raining. All in camp. Snow softening underfoot. Almost impossible to get about. Guyer came up from the lake. Goods partly under water.

Monday, May 2, 1898

Thermometer: 34°

Storm ceased and we started up glacier. Reached summit. Found goods buried under 9 feet of snow. Three snowslides at foot of summit and two killed. [The blizzard dumped from 8 to 12 feet of snow on the upper reaches of the glacier, burying caches and resulting in a series of avalanches which began on the night of April 30. Two men died under the snow at the foot of the summit and were carried over the summit and buried at Twelvemile Camp. Another was so seriously injured by the force of the cascading snow that he died aboard the *Morgan City* while homeward bound on May 6. Trying to locate buried caches was a tedious task, as the new trail, broken after the storm, was found to lie as far as a half-mile to the side of the old trail. The goods in some caches were never recovered, having been swept away in the avalanches. During the same storm, three men died in an

Camp below the summit and summit before the slide.

Summit from camp below, taken after the slide.

Looking toward Sawmill Camp.

avalanche on the second bench of the glacier but their fates were not discovered until the snow melted later in the season.][9] Did not reach camp till 3 in the morning, wet to the skin. Did not go to bed. Trail is rotten. Will build rafts and float down to the lake. Birds of all kinds have made their appearance.

Wednesday, May 4, 1898
Thermometer: 26°
Clearest and brightest morning for a month. Went to the summit and finished hauling, except for Guyer's bag and 8 sacks which were buried beneath the snow. The snow is melting fast. [On this day, geologist F.C. Schrader and Lieutenant Brookfield of Abercrombie's expedition made the first topographical observations of the glacier. They were the first members of the expedition to reach the summit and subsequently returned to Valdez.][10]

Thursday, May 5, 1898
Weather: Clear; Thermometer: 22°
Made one trip 3 miles down the canyon. Snow awful soft. Bassen and Guyer both blind. Some bare ground on the side hills. Neil shot a ptarmigan and a squirrel.

Friday, May 6, 1898
Weather: Cloudy; Thermometer: 28°
Corcoran came up from lower camp last night. Guyer went on the glacier to look for his clothing bag. Snow is going fast. Fell in the creek and got wet all over. Made a trip to 3 mile cache. Mike Beatty and Mike Hessian stayed in today.

Saturday, May 7, 1898
Weather: Clear; Thermometer: 20°
Could hear men working all last night building boats. Made a trip at 4 this morning. Went on the crust [of the snow]. It was good. Got back to camp at 10:30. Feet wet as usual. Can see tents and caches on every high bluff. Water is rising.

Sunday, May 8, 1898
Weather: Cloudy; Thermometer: 30°
Arose at 3:30 and took loads 2 miles down the canyon. Moved camp to Flin's Bluff [near Sawmill Bluff] and had to crawl on hands and knees to get there. Camp is on bare ground for first time. This is our 5th camp. John Amel and I broke 2 miles of trail this afternoon on snowshoes. This is a good place for a camp.

Monday, May 9, 1898
Weather: Clear; Thermometer: 26°
Arose at 2:30. Only for these freezing nights, we could do nothing. [The snow was too soft to haul loaded sleds in the daytime. The same conditions prevailed on the lower benches of the glacier at this time of year, limiting the labor of packing or sledding to the hours between nine at night and approximately nine in the morning.][11] Can hear red-breasted robbins chirruping.

Cache near the river.

Made one trip to 7 mile cache. Mike Hessian went down to the lake this morning. Five men broke a new trail this afternoon.

Tuesday, May 10, 1898
Weather: Clear and windy; Thermometer: 34°
Moved from camp No. 5 to No. 6 and will build our boats here. M.J. Hessian and Buckley came up from the lake today. This is a windy place to camp but plenty of wood, water, and spruce timber. Have to ford the creek to reach this point. Carry our stuff loaded on sleighs over stream.

Thursday, May 12, 1898
Weather: Snow and rain; Thermometer: 28°
Hauled all goods from last cache. Bad day. Trail nearly worn out.

Whipsawing

Party started to make new trail. Can haul 600 pounds 18 miles on ice at the lake. Have got one log on horses ready for sawing. Start mill tomorrow. Got some nice logs out. Saw a good many ducks and geese.

Friday, May 13, 1898
Weather: Stormy; Thermometer: 34°
Arose at 2:30. Started across the creek on Bassen's back and he fell and we both got wet, so had to return. Whirley and I cut down 3 trees and sawed them into [boards] for boats. Reigel went with the trailbreakers. Two whipsaws in operation. Sawdust flying. [A

Shipyard

Boatbuilding at Sawmill Camp.

Boatbuilding, showing caches on bank.

Boats, with river view.

whipsaw is a coarse-toothed saw, five to seven feet long, with a handle fastened to each end. It is normally operated by two men. Because of the length of the saw, logs were placed on supports erected about seven feet above the ground, or a similar distance above a saw pit. Using chalked lines as guides, one man stood on top of the stripped log and pulled up the saw, while a second man stood below the log and pulled down the saw. This operation reportedly ended many longtime friendships, for the man on the bottom, his eyes filled with sawdust, often complained that he had the worst of the deal.][12]

Saturday, May 14, 1898
Weather: Cloudy; Thermometer: 32°
Arose at 3:30. Buckley and I got up a woodpile in the forenoon. Pulled the whipsaw in the afternoon. Ripped off edging from 24-foot boards with a hand saw. Dick Bassen went to the lake. Some boats are on the creek already.

Sunday, May 15, 1898
Weather: Clear; Thermometer: 38°
Ran the ripsaw all day. Have more neighbors. One woman 10 feet from our tent. All are getting out lumber for boats. Three months today since I left Kasota. Mosquitoes are out in full blast. They are as large as sand flies.

Monday, May 16, 1898
Weather: Rain; Thermometer: 36°
Arose at 5. Went to work at 6:30. Saw 4 whipsaws at work on one log. Sawed boards are ¾ inch thick, 8 inches wide, 30 feet long. About 20 saws are at work now. Did not rain much. Cleared off in the afternoon.

Wednesday, May 18, 1898
Thermometer: 30°
This is a fine morning. Looks like spring. Worked all the forenoon with the whipsaw. Saw and heard some loons.

Skiff at Twelvemile Camp, May 25, 1898.

Thursday, May 19, 1898
Thermometer: 28°
Bright beautiful morning. Froze an inch of ice last night. Commenced dressing lumber for our boats. The canyon at this point is about 2 miles wide. The mountains are rocky and very abrupt. The river is 3 rods [49½ feet] wide, swift, and 3 feet deep opposite our tents. Whirley made yeast bread. It was very good.

Friday, May 20, 1898
Weather: Clear; Thermometer: 28°
Commenced to build our scow. Slow work, for none of us are boat builders. Wind blew hard and cold. One man shot a beaver and 3 ducks.

Sunday, May 22, 1898
Weather: Clear; Thermometer: 26°
The river which flows past us here is the Tesnuna [really the Klutina]. Went prospecting but the snow was too deep. One of the party shot a mink and two martens.

Monday, May 23, 1898
Weather: Clear; Thermometer: 32°
Worked on one of our boats. Had duck soup for supper. A fleet of 9 bateaux went downstream. [A bateau has a flat bottom, raked bow and stern, and flaring sides.] Played whist in the evening and got skunked.

Tuesday, May 24, 1898
Weather: Clear; Thermometer: 34°
Finished one boat today and hauled it out on the beach to caulk. [There] was an auction here today. Some [persons] going back. Flour sold for $18 and sugar $30 per C. Nails 40¢ per pound. Bacon 20¢.

Letter dated May 24, 1898, Headwaters of the Tesnuna River, Alaska
Dear Lizzie,
    Received today your letters of April 5th and 20th. I was down in the woods making a boat when I heard someone cry out, "Jackson." He is the mail carrier. Saw and hammer dropped to the ground, and one grand rush was made for mail. We all got a liberal supply. You don't know how anxious we all are to get mail, particularly so now that our country is at war. Saw a paper of May 2nd which gave an account of Admiral Dewey's battle and success. [The U.S. had declared war against Spain in April of 1898 and on May 1 the American fleet, under Commodore George Dewey, entered Manila Bay in the Philippine Islands and with the battle cry "Remember the *Maine*," destroyed the Spanish fleet without losing a single American vessel. The victory earned Dewey the rank of admiral.]

Scow at Twelvemile Camp, May 25, 1898.

We are now over the glacier and only 6 miles from where we were when last I wrote. Had a hard time getting this far on account of the softness of the snow and the amount of water to contend with. At times I would sink into the snow and slush up to my waist, and would go deeper only for my arms, which I threw out from each side to support myself. Imagine one hauling a sled with 300 lbs. on it under such conditions and you have Alaska, the land of the midnight sun. One can see the reflection of the sun at midnight on any clear night. Can see to read a paper at any hour of the night without a light. It is now 10 o'clock in the evening and I am writing without any light, only that of heaven. This is indeed a peculiar country. Snow is fast disappearing and in a few days will have bare ground, although it freezes a little every night.

We are building our boats out of red fir, which is quite plentiful. Have one boat done and lumber sawed for 4 more. I am head mechanic and I assure you that I find boatbuilding quite difficult. Will build 3 bateaux, 1 skiff, and 1 scow. We whipsawed 800 feet of lumber and I can tell you that it took lots of hard work. There are about 50 men doing the same kind of work all around us. Some have got their boats built and [have] gone down the river, which is easy to navigate. It is 45 miles from here to the Copper River. A good many have reached there and some have returned to buy supplies and report the trip as very pleasant. [This must have been a bit of propaganda, as the lower 20 miles of the Klutina River consisted of a succession of treacherous rapids.] We are all well and feel confident that we will strike it rich if health and provisions will hold out.

This must be a beautiful country in the summer. Moose and caribou roam here during the summer months, also bear. [The discovery of antlers, clawed-up earth, gnawed willow branches, and well-worn animal trails would lead to this premise.] Have seen cranberries and a kind of berry which looks like a blueberry. Fish have commenced to come up the river from the lake, 7 miles below, but you can't catch them with a hook, only with a seine.

Went prospecting with an old miner from California and found a piece of white quartz which carried free gold. Did not find the ledge though. The mosquitoes have started their songs and are making [prospecting] very disinteresting for us. They are about ½ inch long and when they fly by your face, quite a breeze is created by their wings.

There was a snowslide on the summit of the glacier May 2nd. Two were killed and about 30 were dug out from under 10 feet of snow. The place where we were camped just a week before was covered thirty feet deep with snow. It had been storming five days previous to the slide and to give you an idea of the amount of snow that fell on the summit, let the following illustrate: we had a cache (or a pile of provisions) standing on top of the snow, which was piled as high as a man could reach, and after the storm had ceased, we went on the glacier to look for our goods, but not a trace or any sign to indicate their whereabouts could be seen. We got some long poles and probed into the snow in the vicinity where we thought they ought to be. Finally, after two hours poking, we struck a box and dug down through 9 feet of snow and found it to be our lost grub. We had another pile which had been unloaded from a sled just before the storm, consisting of 8 sacks of flour and two clothing bags belonging to one of the boys, which cannot be located. Probably after the snow melts some (if it ever does), we will be able to find it. This is all we have lost since arriving here.

We will have to buy more food if we stay in this country two years. But at the prices things are selling for now, our money would buy very little. Tried to buy some nails today to finish building our boats with. Found one man who had ten pounds left but he only wanted *100 lbs.* of flour for them and flour is worth $18 per C. Just think of that! Will make pins for our boats before paying that price. [This letter is continued on May 26, 27, 29, 30, 31, and June 2.]

Thursday, May 26, 1898
Weather: Cloudy and rainy; Thermometer 38°
Guyer and Reigel left for Port Valdes this morning to buy nails for the completion of our boats. August Grund died last night with what is supposed to be scurvy. Thirty-eight years old and resided in San Francisco. A good many more are sick.

Letter dated May 26, 1898 [Continuation of May 24 letter]
Dear Lizzie,

It is 10 o'clock at night but as I have just finished writing to Len, could not quit until I had written you a few lines. We finished one of our boats today and started another. Sent some Kodak films East to be mounted and finished. So you write to L.C. Fredrickson, Sleepy Eye, Minnesota for one of each when finished. I think there were 9 different views. When you write to him, say that you are the wife of H.S. Conger, who is with Reigel and the Hessian party now in Alaska, and he will send them free by you paying the postage.

May 27th — The wind blew so hard on the point where we

have our tents pitched that it broke one of the ridge poles. A party going down this stream near where it flows into the Copper River lost a thousand dollars worth of their provisions by allowing their barge to get away from them.

Friday, May 27, 1898
Weather: Windy; Thermometer: 38°
Finished one more boat today. Bought a cardigan jacket, $3.00; suspenders, 75¢; plug of tobacco, $1.50 from a man who is going back. M.J. Hessian is sick.

Letter dated May 29, 1898 [Continuation of May 24 letter]
It rained all day yesterday and nobody worked. Last night or during the day, someone stole 140 feet of our lumber, which necessitates our sawing some more to complete our boats. It would go hard with the party who stole it, could we locate them. Probably there would be a hanging.

Saw a man yesterday with half a sack of mountain trout. He caught them with a net. A man camped just above us shot a beaver yesterday which weighed 30 lbs. They will have fresh meat for a few days, at least. We are in latitude 61°-32′,[13] so a surveyor told me the other day. [A five-member advance reconnaissance party from Captain Abercrombie's expedition, led by guide J.J. Rafferty, was in this vicinity at the time. Following Abercrombie's instructions to explore for practical routes to the Interior, Rafferty had started over the glacier on May 3 and reached Copper Center on June 9. Most of the other members of Abercrombie's expedition made short reconnaissances in the Prince William Sound area while waiting for Abercrombie's return from Seattle with the pack animals.][14] If you look on the map, you can determine where we are at. In my opinion, nobody knows the exact location. Some say when we reach the Copper River, we will be above Woods Canyon. I hope it is so, but doubt it. [Wood Canyon extends for several miles along the Copper River where it enters the Chugach Mountains, south of Taral. It contains a narrow gorge where portage was almost unavoidable.]

Klutina River, near the outlet of Lake Abercrombie (Klutina), 1899.

Monday, May 30, 1898
Weather: Cloudy; Thermometer: 38°
Worked on our last boat this afternoon. Guyer and Reigel returned today from Port Valdes. Quite a town is growing there, 300 people. Wholesale and retail drugstore there.

Letter dated May 30, 1898 [Continuation of May 24 letter]
This is Decoration Day and we have got our flag hoisted. We cast lots tonight to see who would name our boats and I came within one of first choice. Had I won, should have named my boat "Lila" [His daughter's name].

May 31st — Neil Hessian, Baasen, Guyer, and Druey Whirley went up to the summit of the glacier today to look for our lost cache, as this will probably be the last chance we will have, for we sail in a few days for greener fields. M.J. Hessian and Reigel went to the lake this morning to return a rope we had while on the glacier. Corcoran and I finished the last boat this afternoon. Beatty and Buckley pitched and caulked those we had already made. This has been a lovely day and I could fancy that the snow melted as fast as though warm water had been poured upon it. Am going prospecting tomorrow and expect to find something.

Thursday, June 2, 1898
Thermometer: 40°
Tried to melt some of the pitch found on the trees here, but it was no good for boats. Got too thick and would not stick. Some of the boys went hunting. I made a pair of oars.

Letter dated June 2, 1898 [Continuation of May 24 letter]
Well, I did not find much on my prospecting trip, only a hard country to get through. The boys returned from the glacier with our lost provisions. This is a very windy day and we are all in camp taking a rest, for we expect to set sail tomorrow. I will not have time to write more for some time to come. So I will say good by with love and fond hopes. Kiss the dear children for me and give kind regards to those who may ask about me.

Lovingly,
your husband,
H.S. Conger

Friday, June 3, 1898
Weather: Windy; Thermometer: 40°
Finished patching up the boats, for some of them leaked. Guyer, Beatty, and Reigel went out gunning.

Saturday, June 4, 1898
Weather: Cloudy; Thermometer: 32°
First day of boating. Broke camp at 6:30 and loaded our provisions into our boats and started for the lake. Did not go

Dangerous bend below Twelvemile Camp.

more than a mile before Baasen was swept off the stern end and passed out of sight. Two minutes later the boat struck a stump and swamped, leaving Reigel hanging to a dead tree. Parties below caught part of the sacks; ten we never more shall see. I came near smashing my boat a number of times. Was stranded 6 times. Had 3 ton on board. Corcoran was with me. Reached the lake at one o'clock in the morning wet to the skin. Some of the boys lost clothes and grips. [In addition to stumps and their large protruding roots, several other hazards to navigation existed along the upper Klutina in the 13 miles between Twelvemile Camp and Klutina Lake. Just below Twelvemile Camp, at a point where the stream bed suddenly narrowed, the force of the current channeled boats first toward one projecting point of land and then immediately toward another on the opposite bank. Many boats which were entrapped at these spots by the rushing waters were capsized and their cargoes lost. Just before reaching the lake, two spruce trees, standing a short distance apart in the strongest part of the current, also had to be avoided.][15]

Sunday, June 5, 1898
Weather: Cloudy
Made a trip up the river 6 miles. Four of us hauled a boat up. We were 8 hours going up and 1 hour and 15 minutes coming down. Young Whirley fell out of the boat. We are camped at the head of the lake.

Monday, June 6, 1898
Clear with prevailing winds. We are raising the sides of two boats. Some of the boys are sawing lumber for them now. Others are drying fruit that got wet during the wreck. Some have sailboats for crossing the lake but most all of them are bateau shape. Saw one screw propeller. [One Doctor Ottaway had a small steam launch, about 14 feet long, with which he did a thriving business of transporting men on Klutina Lake when the exodus from the valley began in mid-summer.][16]

Tuesday, June 7, 1898
Weather: Windy
Started from head of Lake Margurette with five boats and one scow. [Klutina Lake was originally called "Lake Margarete." This name was applied by Lieutenant Abercrombie in 1884 to designate the unnamed lake in the Creole's description of the glacier route. Subsequently, it was known as Lake Abercrombie and then Lake Klutina. The lake is merely a kidney-shaped enlargement in the channel of the Klutina River.][17] Bought one boat for $30. The scow was rigged with sail and Neil Hessian, M. Beatty, and Guyer went in it. Our boat took water and nearly swamped. Camped at 11:15 at night for it was too rough to go farther. Early in the morning, five men returned disgusted. This is a beautiful lake, 30 miles long, 3 miles wide, skirted with timber and smooth hills. [These dimensions generally agree with those reported by other gold seekers, as well as members of the military

Dr. Ottaway's launch

expedition. However, current USGS maps indicate that the present length of Klutina Lake is about 16 miles. In 1898 geologist F.C. Schrader found evidence that the lake was formerly much larger and deeper. He noted that lake filling was rapidly going on at the head of the lake by detritus being brought in by the Klutina and Hallet rivers. At the same time, the Klutina River was cutting its way deeper and deeper into the plateau terrain of the Copper River basin at the outlet of the lake, causing a "rapid diminution of the lake in size and volume."][18]

Wednesday, June 8, 1898
Weather: Clear
Left the borders of Lake Margurette at 6:30 in the morning. Had

Head of rapids

good sailing for 10 miles. Had to tow Buckley's boat. Went down the Klutena River four miles to head of the rapids. [This is the first time Conger refers to the river as the "Klutina," indicating the gold seekers had learned their correct geographical position.] One boat got stuck in the sand. This is camp No. 8 and it is a pretty place to camp. Most everyone is caching their goods here except 3 months' supply.

Thursday, June 9, 1898
Weather: Clear
Saw two men shoot the rapids early this morning. Others made the same attempt but most of them got swamped. Walked down the stream 5 miles and it looked mighty wicked that far. Went up on top of a high hill and could see Mt. Wrangele in the east, also Copper River and some of its tributaries.

Friday, June 10, 1898
Weather: Clear
This has been a warm day and the mosquitoes bite like sixty. M. Beatty, J. Reigel, Dick Baasen, and Frank Guyer are going to shoot the rapids in a few days, so we are dividing our stock now. We are no longer under contract. Every man for himself.

Saturday, June 11, 1898
Weather: Hot and clear; Thermometer: 102°
M.J. Hessian and I walked down the Klutena River to the Copper, a distance of 25 miles. The Klutena is very swift and rough its entire length. Saw a good many wrecks on the way. [Ninety-five per cent of the gold seekers who attempted to shoot the treacherous Klutina Rapids in the spring of 1898 wrecked their boats. Captain Abercrombie conservatively estimated the value of the lost supplies he saw strewn along the riverbanks in August of 1898 at $20,000.][19] The Copper is about 250 yards wide at the mouth of this stream, swift and deep. The country is densely covered with small spruce, quakinasp [quaking aspen], and birch trees. Little game and no fish so far.

Sunday, June 12, 1898
Weather: Clear and hot
Returned to the head of the [lower] Klutena. Not so hot as yesterday. Two men nearly got drowned. River raised a foot. Fires raging. [Forest fires were numerous in the Klutina and Copper River valleys in the summer of 1898, particularly in late summer. Most of these fires were started by embers from camp-fires left smoldering in the dry moss; however, explorers attributed the thousands of acres of previously burned-over areas they saw to the Native practice of burning the dense undergrowth for better visibility in hunting and to reduce the great numbers of mosquitoes.][20]

Monday, June 13, 1898
Weather: Clear; Thermometer: 72° at 1 P.M.

Hung around camp nearly all day. A good many have started to pack to the Copper River, taking 50 lbs. each. Hard proposition it is. [A trail followed the north side of the river, alternating between the mud of the riverbank and the top of the 500- to 600-foot clay and gravel bluffs encompassing the river.]²¹ Was an auction sale in front of our tent. Clothing, trinkets, guns, and ammunition sold for less than they cost in the States. This is quite a town. About 100 tents are pitched here. The water has risen 3 feet since yesterday. Most everybody is afraid of the rapids.

Tuesday, June 14, 1898
Weather: Clear; Thermometer: 72° at 1 P.M.
Lots of people coming in but very few going out. M. Beatty, Dick Baasen, Jack Reigel, and Frank Guyer shot the rapids. We have been packing up some provisions to take down to Copper River. Expect to be gone 3 months. Have built a cache high above ground and will leave most of our stuff here. This is called William's Landing, P.O. Headwaters of the Klutena River. [Captain Abercrombie later named this spot "Amy's Landing" for W. (William?) S. Amy, an early prospector who swamped his boat here and stopped to dry out his outfit. Those who followed him also stopped, and a large, temporary settlement was thus established. Contrary to Conger's statement, a post office never was established here and the Klutina River heads in the glacier of the same name; however, in 1898 the name "Klutina" often was applied only to the lower river, below the lake.]²²

Wednesday, June 15, 1898
Weather: Clear
Started for Copper River with three boats. Swamped one but did not lose anything. We are now camped on the banks of the Klutena, where the mosquitoes darken the sun. [June and July are considered the worst months of mosquito aggravation in Alaska. These insects are numerous not only along watercourses but above timber, where they breed in the wet moss. To repel the pests, the Natives anointed themselves with pitch and lampblack.

A cache at Copper Center.

Most of the gold seekers protected themselves with long heavy gloves and wire masks covered with mosquito-proof netting. Without this relief, life was made unbearable by the insects. Captain Abercrombie reported that he saw men without head nets "scream with pain and fright when passing through a swale of high grass. The insects, rising in clouds, would crawl into their eyes, mouth, and nose, almost smothering them."][23]

Thursday, June 16, 1898
Moved on down the river 3 miles. We are lining our boats down. [In this practice, several men on or near shore controlled the boat by holding onto a rope attached to the stern of the boat. One man stayed in the boat, using a pole to guide it around boulders or

Klutina River near head of rapids.

other obstructions and keeping it off the shore. On the lower Klutina, this procedure was extremely difficult because the swiftness of the current, which averaged about 14 miles per hour, compelled the men controlling the rope to move very rapidly over the rough terrain along the riverbank.][24] It rained hard for two hours but we got a tent up so did not get wet from the rain. But was wet up to my waist from wading in the river.

Friday, June 17, 1898
Weather: Clear
Made another move downstream. Saw 2 trunks, 3 boxes, 4 sacks (one of which we caught), sack of clothing, and several other bundles floating downstream. Some poor fellow has lost all. [Some parties had packed their provisions in paraffin outer sacks which were waterproof, while others used standard canvas outer

sacks. It was said that flour packed in the canvas sacks would wet through only a quarter of an inch, forming a paste which confined the air in the sack, thereby giving it buoyancy for long distances if not punctured or agitated too much.][25] Corcoran and Buckley went back after their robes. Got soaking wet and had to change clothes twice.

Saturday, June 18, 1898
Weather: Clear
Made another drive down the river. Got wet again as usual. Came near swamping two boats. This is a mighty dangerous stream to line or shoot a boat down. Beatty and party got their goods wet. The scow came near sinking with them.

Sunday, June 19, 1898
Weather: Clear
Did the same as yesterday only we discarded one boat and now are carrying all our goods in two boats. Met men returning from 30 miles up Copper River. They report there is nothing there (that is, no gold), but plenty of the dear little mosquitoes.

Monday, June 20, 1898
Weather: Clear
Still going down the river. M.J. Hessian swamped a boat today but nothing was lost. Beatty and party lost their boat. Have got a lame back. This is my 35th birthday. Time is creeping on.

Tuesday, June 21, 1898
Weather: Cloudy
Swamped another boat today. Got everything wet, even the clothes on my back. Came near losing my boat.

Wednesday, June 22, 1898
Weather: Clear
Am drying the stuff that got wet yesterday. Corcoran and M.J. Hessian have gone hunting. Two boatloads of provisions

Klutina Valley looking southwest; Devils Elbow in right center, 1899.

were lost belonging to two Jews. Picked a bouquet of 9 different flowers. Among them, lots of roses, but not an odor could I distinguish. [Wild flowers were abundant, with as many as 25 varieties in bloom at the same time in this area. The ripened hips of the wild roses found along the Copper River contributed to the Native food supply.][26]

Thursday, June 23, 1898
Weather: Cloudy
Made a good run today. Did not get anything wet. We are camped tonight at "Hell Gate," 7 miles from Copper River. [This was an area of extremely dangerous rapids, which, according to prospector Neil Benedict, received its name "both because of its own merit and because of its resemblance to the famous Hell Gate in the East River near New York City." Large signs had been posted, warning the argonauts of both Hell Gate and Devils Elbow, a mile downstream.][27]

Looking up the Klutina from Copper Center.

Friday, June 24, 1898
Weather: Cloudy
We are laying off a half day to pitch our boats, as they have sprung a leak. Started again this afternoon and reached Copper Center, the mouth of the Klutena River. A good many are stuck here, for it is almost impossible to go up Copper River, as the water is too high. [The river was near the high water mark at this time, with its current running about eight miles per hour.][28] Some have gone upriver 35 miles and returned and sold what they had left and said there was no gold to be found as far as they went.

Saturday, June 25, 1898
Weather: Cloudy
Rained some. Am resting for a few days. Don't know how I am going up Copper River. Bought some bacon for 11¢, coffee for 20¢. Lots [of men] selling out for what they can get. Nearly everyone discouraged. One man drowned.

Monday, June 27, 1898
Weather: Clear
Am loafing again. Shook hands with some Indians. Also gave dinner to 3 and bought one salmon. They ask one dollar for a fish no matter what the size. Showed one a looking glass and it tickled him very much. [The aboriginal inhabitants of the Copper River basin were Indians belonging to the Ahtna group, and like all of Alaska's interior Indians, they were of Athabascan linguistic stock. The name "Ahtna" comes from the Indian name for the Copper River. The name "Copper" River is a misnomer because it is the translation of the Indian name for the Chitina (Chittyna) River — "chitty" meaning copper and "na" meaning river. Lieutenant Allen, who established relations with the Copper River Indians in 1885, described them as "docile and mirthful," but in 1898 they were still popularly regarded by outsiders as hostile and aggressive. The gold seekers and government explorers quickly discovered that this belligerent reputation was undeserved. They consistently described the Natives as peaceful, hospitable, and honest. On several occasions Captain Abercrombie witnessed these Indians wading out into the rivers to rescue the property of some gold seeker whose boat had been wrecked upstream. After piling the retrieved goods on shore, the Indians would travel out of their way in an attempt to notify the owner of their location.][29]

Tuesday, June 28 1898
Weather: Clear
Wind blew hard all day. Andrew Whirley and I walked up the Copper River to the Tasslena [Tazlina], a distance of 10 miles, and returned same day. Passed 7 men towing their boat up. Am very tired tonight.

Letter dated June 30, 1898, Copper Center, on the Copper River at the mouth of the Klutena, Alaska
My Dear Wife,
    Jackson came last night and brought two letters from you, May 1st and 24th. I have been waiting here three days for the

Klutina River, near its mouth.

letter I knew would surely come before going any farther, for when I leave here God only knows when I will hear from you again. This is as far as the mail is carried, for people branch out in all directions from here, some going down the river to the Chittyna, or Chillyna, as it is spelled on the enclosed map [see page 35], others up the river in search of the yellow. I have [not] decided which way I shall go yet but think up the river, probably to the headwaters, and possibly on over to the Tanana and on to Dawson if nothing is found on the way. There is no gold here, although you can find colors most anywhere. A good many are turning back, completely disgusted and discouraged. Dick Baasen and Druey Whirley of our party left for home yesterday. Numbers [of men] are leaving daily.

I have bought some more flour and bacon. $10 for flour and 11¢ for bacon. [I] intend to stay this winter at least. I don't see how I can ever return without at least as much as I left with. It

Copper River, near the mouth of the Klutina.

would be humiliating in the extreme. I am going to send you $20 in this letter, taking my chances on it reaching you. I judge by your letter that your small allowance must be getting very low and I think I can spare you this much, for I have grub enough to last me till spring and can find enough work upon reaching Seattle to pay my way back should I get broke. But I think when you see me again I will have enough to pay for a night's lodging, at least.

I am sitting on a five gallon tin can, under some quakinasp trees, on the bank of the rushing Klutena while writing this letter. The wind is blowing quite hard and here the mosquitoes (the only living thing I have seen) are few. I wish I could blot out the sound of these mighty waters, for it is anything but pleasant. [This river] is no babbling brook, I can assure you. Thousands and thousands of dollars worth of goods have been swallowed up by it. We lost some but were more fortunate than most others.

Ever since embarking in our boats from the head of Lake Margurette to this point, it has been one continual strain upon the nervous system, besides fraught with danger on every side. There

Shooting the rapids.

have been only two drowned so far, something marvelous taking all into consideration.[30] I shot two boats down the Klutena Rapids, a distance of 25 miles, in 2 hours and 55 minutes. This is the time it takes to go through providing you do not hit any rocks. And if you do hit them you will probably never get through with all in the boat. You can judge the swiftness of the stream by the time it takes to go through. The White Horse Rapids, going to the Klondyke, are nothing to compare with it, so I have been told by a man who has seen both. [The White Horse Rapids, less than a mile in length on the Yukon River, were not as dangerous as they were often represented. According to Alfred H. Brooks of the USGS, no more than half a dozen lives were lost in running them in 1898.][31] The distance [of the Klutina Rapids] is so far and the strain on the nerves too great. Can get fifty dollars for each boat I shoot down, but would not do it for twice that amount, even if it only takes a few hours. There is no chance to stop and rest after once starting, for the banks on both sides are too high and current too swift. Had a picture taken while entering the rapids and I told Baasen to send you one. There are four of us in the boat.

There are hundreds of people at the head of the rapids waiting for the water to subside so they can safely go downriver. We left most all of our grub there, only bringing enough along to last each man 3 months, the time we consider it will take to reach the headwaters of the Copper and return. If we are successful in locating any claims, [we] will return and sled our stuff up the river this winter. If nothing is found, will go down [the Copper] in the spring or over on the Tanana. This is a large valley, covered over with small pine and quakinasp. [Of the pine family, the spruce is dominant in the Copper River valley, although hemlock, fir, and cedar are also present. Prominent among the deciduous trees are balm of Gilead, quaking aspen, willow, alder, and birch. Timber line is about 2,000 feet, above which a dense growth of moss and dwarf shrubbery occurs.][32]

Now dearest, take good care of yourself and the children. Kisses for you and the babies.

Lovingly,
your husband, Horace

Friday, July 1, 1898
Weather: Cloudy
Corcoran and I fixed up our boat. Four of us expect to start for upper Copper River tomorrow. One man sold flour for $4.00 per C, bacon 10¢, sugar 8¢. Most everything is cheap now, for so many are going back disgusted. The prospects so far are not very bright. Doubt if there will be much found here this season. There is no game so far. The Indians are catching a few salmon but they are not very plentiful. [The Copper River Indians cured large numbers of salmon for winter use, but according to a member of Abercrombie's party, these people were improvident and invariably went hungry before the next salmon run. Lieutenant Allen stated that the upper Copper River Indians were the most

destitute people he observed in Alaska. He described those he encountered between the Tazlina and Sanford rivers as the thinnest, hungriest people he had ever beheld. At the time of his visit on May 24, 1885, they were living solely on roots.][33]

Notes—

1. E.F. Glenn and W.R. Abercrombie, "Report of Capt. Abercrombie," and "Report of Guide J.J. Rafferty," *Reports of Explorations in the Territory of Alaska, 1898* (Washington: Gov. Printing Office, 1899), pp. 300, 439; Basil Austin, *The Diary of a Ninety-Eighter* (Mount Pleasant, Michigan: John Cumming, 1968), p. 44; "New Route to the Yukon Over American Soil," *Seattle Post-Intelligencer,* Nov. 18, 1897, p. 1.

2. F.C. Schrader, "A Reconnaissance of a Part of Prince William Sound and the Copper River District, Alaska, in 1898," *Twentieth Annual Report of the USGS,* Part 7 (Washington: Gov. Printing Office, 1900), p. 357; C.H. Remington, *A Golden Cross ? On the Trails from the Valdez Glacier* (Los Angeles: White-Thompson, 1939), p. 36; Neil D. Benedict, "The Valdes and Copper River Trail," (unpublished manuscript in Alaska Historical Library, Juneau), 1899, pp. 47-51, 56, 178.

3. Schrader, "A Reconnaissance . . . 1898," *Twentieth Annual Report of the USGS,* pp. 357-58; Benedict, "The Valdes and Copper River Trail," pp. 69, 78, 178.

4. Schrader, "A Reconnaissance . . . 1898," *Twentieth Annual Report of the USGS,* pp. 384-85, 391-92; Benedict, "The Valdes and Copper River Trail," pp. 80-82.

5. Benedict, "The Valdes and Copper River Trail," pp. 80, 89; Schrader, "A Reconnaissance . . . 1898," *Twentieth Annual Report of the USGS,* p. 358.

6. Schrader, "A Reconnaissance . . . 1898," *Twentieth Annual Report of the USGS,* p. 388.

7. Austin, *The Diary of a Ninety-Eighter,* pp. 44-45, 51; Luther W. Guiteau, "Alaska Gold Rush Diary," Serialized 1928 in the Freeport, Illinois, *Journal-Standard* (manuscript in Alaska Historical Library, Juneau), diary entries of April 17 and 22, May 2 and 3, 1898; Schrader, "A Reconnaissance . . . 1898," *Twentieth Annual Report of the USGS,* pp. 350, 366-67.

8. Benedict, "The Valdes and Copper River Trail," p. 44.

9. Glenn and Abercrombie, "Report of Lt. R.M. Brookfield," *Reports of Explorations . . . 1898,* p. 400; Schrader, "A Reconnaissance . . . 1898," *Twentieth Annual Report of the USGS,* pp. 352-53; Benedict, "The Valdes and Copper River Trail," pp. 30-33; "Crushed by Tons of Snow," *San Francisco Chronicle,* May 20, 1898, p. 4; Charles Margeson, *Experiences of Gold Hunters in Alaska* (Hornellsville, N.Y.: Charles Margeson, 1899), pp. 92-94.

10. Schrader, "A Reconnaissance . . . 1898," *Twentieth Annual Report of the USGS*, p. 353.

11. Glenn and Abercrombie, "Report of Lt. Guy H. Preston," *Reports of Explorations . . . 1898*, p. 405; Schrader, "A Reconnaissance . . . 1898," *Twentieth Annual Report of the USGS*, p. 353.

12. Murray Morgan, *One Man's Gold Rush: A Klondike Album* (Seattle: Univ. of Washington Press, 1967), pp. 111, 120; Austin, *The Diary of a Ninety-Eighter*, p. 48.

13. Conger recorded 61°-32″ in the oiginal; however, the "seconds" notation was probably an "error in his wiring," as 32 minutes is a more accurate coordinate for his location.

14. Glenn and Abercrombie, "Report of Guide J.J. Rafferty," *Reports of Explorations . . . 1898*, pp. 433-50.

15. Benedict, "The Valdes and Copper River Trail," pp. 60-63.

16. Margeson, *Experiences of Gold Hunters*, p. 142; Benedict, "The Valdes and Copper River Trail," p. 48; Schrader, "A Reconnaissance . . . 1898," *Twentieth Annual Report of the USGS*, p. 358.

17. W.R. Abercrombie, "Report of a Supplementary Expedition into the Copper River Valley, Alaska, 1884," *Compilation of Narratives of Explorations in Alaska* (Washington: Gov. Printing Office, 1900), p. 391; Also see "Bitter Against the Copper River," *San Francisco Chronicle*, July 12, 1898, p. 2.

18. Schrader, "A Reconnaissance . . . 1898," *Twentieth Annual Report of the USGS*, p. 390. With the exception of the length of Klutina Lake, the distances along the Klutina River reported by both the military explorers and prospectors closely approximate measurements taken from a 1952 USGS quadrangle.

19. Glenn and Abercrombie, "Report of Guide J.J. Rafferty," and "Report of W.R. Abercrombie," *Reports of Explorations . . . 1898*, pp. 443, 311.

20. Glenn and Abercrombie, "Report of W.R. Abercrombie," and "Report of E.F. Glenn," *Reports of Explorations . . . 1898*, pp. 62, 310, 333; Schrader, "A Reconnaissance . . . 1898," *Twentieth Annual Report of the USGS*, pp. 357, 390; Alfred H. Brooks, *Blazing Alaska's Trails*, 2d ed. (1953; rpt. Fairbanks: Univ. of Alaska Press, 1973), p. 92.

21. Schrader, "A Reconnaissance . . . 1898," *Twentieth Annual Report of the USGS*, p. 358.

22. Glenn and Abercrombie, "Report of Lt. P.G. Lowe," *Reports of Explorations . . . 1898*, p. 358; W.S. Amy, with a party of eight men representing the "Copper River Mill and Mining Company," sailed to Alaska aboard the *Wolcott* on Nov. 10, 1897. "News of the Ocean and Waterfront," *San Francisco Chronicle*, Nov. 11, 1897, p. 10.

23. Brooks, *Blazing Alaska's Trails*, pp. 91-92; A.C. Harris, *Alaska and the Klondike Gold Fields* (n.p. 1897), p. 218; Glenn and Abercrombie, "Report of W.R. Abercrombie," *Reports of Explorations . . . 1898*, p. 333.

24. Glenn and Abercrombie, "Report of Guide J.J. Rafferty," *Reports of*

Explorations . . . 1898, p. 441; Benedict, "The Valdes and Copper River Trail," pp. 62-63; Schrader, "A Reconnaissance . . . 1898," *Twentieth Annual Report of the USGS,* p. 392.

25. Remington, *A Golden Cross,* p. 39.

26. Glenn and Abercrombie, "Report of W.R. Abercrombie," *Reports of Explorations . . . 1898,* p. 331; Schrader, "A Reconnaissance . . . 1898," *Twentieth Annual Report of the USGS,* p. 370.

27. Benedict, "The Valdes and Copper River Trail," p. 88; Glenn and Abercrombie, "Report of W.R. Abercrombie," *Reports of Explorations . . . 1898,* p. 311; Guiteau, "Alaska Gold Rush Diary," June 8, 1898, entry.

28. Glenn and Abercrombie, "Report of Guide J.J. Rafferty," *Reports of Explorations . . . 1898,* p. 444.

29. Henry T. Allen, "Report of a Military Reconnaissance in Alaska, Made in 1885," *Compilation of Narratives,* pp. 471, 474; Robert A. McKennan, *The Upper Tanana Indians,* in Yale Univ. Publications in Anthropology, No. 55, ed. Irving Rouse (New Haven: Dept. of Anthropology, 1959), p. 22; Glenn and Abercrombie, "'Report of W.R. Abercrombie," *Reports of Explorations . . . 1898,* pp. 323, 329; "Eager to Do Battle With Alaska Braves," *San Francisco Chronicle,* Aug. 10, 1897, p. 2; "To Look for a Route," *Seattle Post-Intelligencer,* Feb. 4, 1898, p. 2; Margeson, *Experiences of Gold Hunters,* p. 18; Harris, *Alaska and the Klondike Gold Fields,* p. 531; Also see John R. Swanton, *Indian Tribes of North America,* Smithsonian Institution, Bureau of American Ethnology, Bulletin 145 (Washington: Gov. Printing Office, 1953), p. 529; Cornelius Osgood, *The Distribution of the Northern Athapaskan Indians,* Yale University Publications in Anthropology, No. 7 (New Haven: Yale Univ. Press, 1936), p. 7.

30. Charles Kelly of Providence, R.I., and one L.J. Mytinger were two prospectors drowned in the Klutina about this time. The date of July 11 given by Benedict for Mytinger's death may be an error, as this date coincides with James Buckley's drowning on the Copper. See Conger's diary entry for July 11, 1898. Benedict, "The Valdes and Copper River Trail," pp. 43, 64-65; Margeson, *Experiences of Gold Hunters,* pp. 126-28.

31. Brooks, *Blazing Alaska's Trails,* p. 358; Alfred H. Brooks, "A Reconnaissance in the Tanana and White River Basins, Alaska, in 1898," *Twentieth Annual Report of the USGS,* p. 433; Morgan, *One Man's Gold Rush,* p. 112.

32. Schrader, "A Reconnaissance . . . 1898," *Twentieth Annual Report of the USGS,* p. 370; Glenn and Abercrombie, "Report of W.R. Abercrombie," *Reports of Explorations . . . 1898,* pp. 332-33.

33. Glenn and Abercrombie, "Report of Lt. P.G. Lowe," *Reports of Explorations . . . 1898,* p. 368; Allen, *Compilation of Narratives,* pp. 437-38.

Chapter 5—

A Prospecting Trip in the Chistochina River District

Lacking navigable waterways, the Copper River gold seekers journeyed across swamps, hacked through thickets, climbed rugged hills, and followed boulder-strewn canyons in their search for the yellow metal. Overcoming these obstacles to travel consumed most of their time and energy, but in the limited extent of ground they were able to prospect, they usually found a few colors per pan. The origin of this gold was not generally understood in 1898. Though many prospectors knew that fine particles of gold are carried long distances by swift-flowing rivers, few realized that the fine gold located in the low-lying areas of the Copper River region had been carried into the region by glaciers, which pulverized and thoroughly distributed the heavy metal in the glacial gravels and silts which cover bedrock to a great thickness. Paying quantities of gold were discovered at higher elevations in the Copper River region, however, where the gravel sheet is thin. Here streams reworked the auriferous gravel beds, concentrating the precious metal at, or near, bedrock.[1]

Gold mining began in the Copper River region in 1900 but the total production up to 1959 was only one per cent of Alaska's total output. The bulk of the gold came from placers in the Chistochina and Nizina districts, where bedrock is accessible. The initial locations were made in 1898 along the Chisna — a main tributary of the Chistochina River, which heads in the ice covered slopes of the Alaska Range. Slate Creek and Miller Gulch later became the largest producers in the Chistochina district. The productive placers along the upper Nizina, a tributary of the Chitina, were not discovered until 1902. The extensive copper deposits in

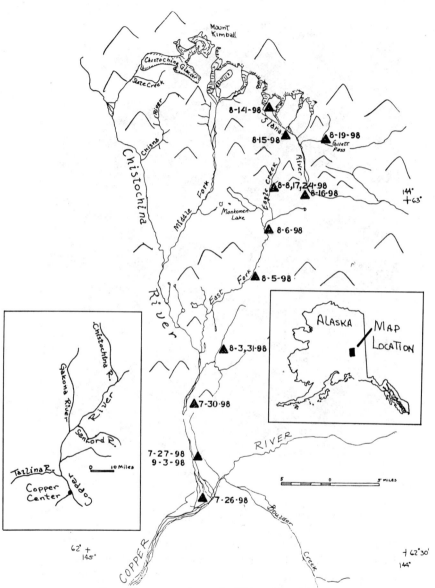

Campsites on a trip to the Chistochina District

Panning

the Chitina district, worked by the Kennecott Company from 1900 to 1938, yielded little gold; however, the initial "discoveries" were made by gold seekers who entered the Copper River region in 1898. According to Oscar Rohn, the location of the copper vein was disclosed to the prospectors by the Natives for a "consideration of flour and provision."[2]

Saturday, July 2, 1898

Corcoran, Buckley, and I packed 709½ lbs. over to the Copper and started up the river at 2:30 P.M. [See appendix for itemized list of supplies.] Made seven miles before camping. Met a good many returning.

Sunday, July 3, 1898

Weather: Cloudy

Made only a 3 mile pull. Passed under a clay bank one thousand feet high. Rocks and dirt constantly falling. Two men nearly lost their lives by the caving off of tons of dirt. Am lamer tonight than I have ever been. Am afraid this daily wetting will do me up. Bad looking country here. Nothing to sustain life, only what you bring in.

Monday, July 4, 1898

Weather: Cloudy

Am traveling upriver with a party of 11 men. Made 7 miles today. The river is very swift in places. Fired my first shot since coming to Alaska. This being the 4th, thought I would celebrate. We had the Stars and Stripes up all day.

Tuesday, July 5, 1898

Broke camp at 9 A.M. but made only 4 miles owing to rain. Bought 2 salmon from some Indians. Paid $1.00 for them. Panned out some dirt and got several colors. Copper River is very wide at this point (21 miles up from the Klutena) owing to a vast number of bars and shoals. Navigation is slow and tedious.

Wednesday, July 6, 1898

Weather: Clear

Made only 4 miles today. Stopped four hours on the way to prospect a dry creek. Found colors only. Saw a fresh moose track but did not see his mooseship. Gosh, the mosquitoes are awful thick tonight. Think it is going to rain. Crossed over to the other side of the river. High clay bank. Could not get around.

Thursday, July 7, 1898
Weather: Windy
Traveled only four miles. Found one place where the bank projected over the river so far that we had to throw a line over to another party. Very dangerous. Saw several parties returning. It is getting more discouraging every day. The farther up we go, the worse it gets.

Friday, July 8, 1898
Made only three miles today, for we swamped one boat belonging to another party. They lost most all of their stuff that was in it. This has been the hottest day for two weeks.

Saturday, July 9, 1898
Weather: Clear
Started upriver this morning at 7 sharp. Made seven miles before camping. Passed by some very dangerous clay banks. [At] one place there had been a slide a few days . . . [ago][3] of about one hundred thousand tons of dirt.

Sunday, July 10, 1898
Rained some last night. We are resting today. Did some washing. The Gacona [Gakona] River is just opposite. Expect to go on till the Christischina [Chistochina] is reached.

Monday, July 11, 1898
Weather: Cloudy
Started out this morning in good spirits, but before we had gone one mile, Jim Buckley fell into the river and was drowned. Have not recovered the body as yet. Will remain here a few days in hopes that we may find the body. He fell off the bank while pushing the boat away from shore and was carried out into the swift current. [Several days before this incident, a one-armed man called Dickey (possibly the same man Conger saw aboard the *Excelsior*) reportedly drowned in the Sanford River.][4]

Sanford River and Mount Drum

Tuesday, July 12, 1898
Spent all day looking for Buckley's body but could not find it. It rained quite hard and thundered a number of times during the day. The river is rapidly rising.

Wednesday, July 13, 1898
Weather: Clear
We started on our journey again this morning. I went back 2 miles to look for poor Jim. We camp on the sand bars now, for the mosquitoes are not so bad. The Copper River is certainly the muddiest stream on earth. One can almost walk on the water it is so thick. The country looks just the same as it did 50 miles back.

Thursday, July 14, 1898
Weather: Clear
Crossed the Sanford River today. It was not deep but very swift. The water has a brick color. Eight men camped with us from

upriver. They say there is nothing up there. The color of the Copper at this point is that of white clay mixed with black dirt and water.

Friday, July 15, 1898
Weather: Clear
The wind blew very hard down the Copper in the afternoon. We moved along quite smoothly today. The water seems to be getting smoother the farther up we go. My boots are almost gone. Will soon be barefooted. Five months today since I left Kasota. Oh, what a change.

Saturday, July 16, 1898
Weather: Cloudy
We traveled seven miles today. Saw an Indian who was one hundred years old. Bought a salmon. It rained in the afternoon and we all got wet. The river is a mile wide here with bars in between. Color of the water is like that of muddy coffee. We are getting nearer to the mountains. Am abreast of Mt. Sanford [elevation 16,237 feet] which is all covered over with snow.

Sunday, July 17, 1898
Weather: Clear and hot
Rested all day. Did some washing and then went up on a hill to look over the country, but the mosquitoes were so thick had to give it up.

Monday, July 18, 1898
Weather: Cloudy
Made four miles today. The riverbanks were very bad and the water is in many shallow channels. There are 20 men besides ourselves camping here tonight, bound for the same place.

Tuesday, July 19, 1898
Weather: Cloudy
Traveled only 3 miles today. Came to a bluff where we have to

pack around. The dirt and moss hangs over the edge 20 feet in places and is liable to drop any minute. Some fell yesterday which shook the ground like an earthquake. Will make my bed on moss tonight. Picked some berries which look like blackberries, only these are red and grow low to the ground like a strawberry. [Among the wild berries found in the Copper River region are several varieties of currants, blueberries, raspberries, dewberries, crowberries, bearberries, huckleberries, and cranberries.][5]

Wednesday, July 20, 1898
Weather: Cloudy
Made only two miles this day. The river is so badly broken up into channels that it is almost impossible to go up. This is the point where Lieutenant Allen abandoned his boats and packed up. [Allen abandoned his boat on the Copper about 17 miles above the mouth of the Chistochina on May 30, 1885. Continuing north, he crossed Suslota Pass in the Mentasta Mountains and reached the Tanana, which he descended to its mouth on the Yukon. He concluded his investigations for 1885 by exploring the Koyukuk River.][6]

Thursday, July 21, 1898
It rained all night and we are compelled to remain where we are for today. We are camped on a bar or island of gravel and driftwood. Was afraid the water might rise during the night and drive us off. Picked some currants and made sauce.

Friday, July 22, 1898
Arose at 6 o'clock and started upriver. Made four miles even if it did rain. The river at this point is 5 miles wide, cut up into a hundred channels. Picked some red raspberries but they are somewhat different than those at home.

Saturday, July 23, 1898
We started in the afternoon and traveled 3 miles. It rained all day. Saw 34 returning from the Christuchina today.

Sunday, July 24, 1898
Weather: Rain
Two Indians came to our camp this morning. They had been
packing for some white men. One of them could talk quite good
English. He said the gold was too small to be of any good. He was
well posted in the geography of this country and could locate
every mountain and rivulet. [Some of the Copper River Indians
spoke both broken English and Chinook Jargon. The latter was a
common tongue understood by all Northwestern Indians. It was
intermixed with the simplest words of the Native American,
English, and French languages. Initially employed by the
Hudson's Bay Company traders in their intercourse with the
Natives, its use was later encouraged by missionaries, who
brought it into general use. Though missionary influences were
absent among the Copper River Indians, some of these Natives
had come into contact with whites on their trading voyages to the
coast and during infrequent visits to the Yukon long before white
men penetrated the Copper River basin.][7]

Monday, July 25, 1898
Weather: Cloudy
Reached one branch of the Christochina River today. Met several
[men] who were just returning from the Tanana. They say there is
nothing there. The Christochina has several outlets and is a swift,
muddy stream. [Schrader provided the following description of
the 48-mile-long Chistochina River, which heads at the glacier of
the same name.

> *On its way to the Copper, the river has intrenched
> itself in a narrow bluff-walled canyon several hundred
> feet deep into the Copper River Plateau. Here it flows
> at a rate of about 10 miles an hour. The stream bed is
> very rough and bowldery. . . . In its lower reaches the
> river widens considerably and is beset by a great
> number of islands and sand bars. It finally flows over
> a large delta and empties into the Copper through a*

*great many channels, of which the most southerly is
about 3 miles south of the main channel.*][8]

Tuesday, July 26, 1898
Weather: Cloudy
Made a short pull to another branch of the Christochina, which
we will go up for a ways although several have come down saying
there was nothing there. A good many have gone over to the
Tanana and on to 40 Mile [Fortymile]. [Many of the gold seekers
who had intentions of pushing on to the Tanana became
discouraged and turned back after meeting a party of prospectors
who had spent a fruitless winter on that river. The Tanana party
had crossed the divide hoping for better luck on the Copper.][9]

Wednesday, July 27, 1898
Weather: Cloudy
Pulled our boats four miles up the Christochina River. It is very
swift where deep, but it spreads out into many channels which are
shallow and full of shoals. The water is not clear. Traded two
bandana handkerchiefs for 2 salmon.

Thursday, July 28, 1898
Started out this morning with Mr. Rope to investigate the river
and trail in view of either packing or towing one boat upriver 30
miles and then pack from there. It rained so that we had to turn
back. Met 7 men who had been up 40 miles and found nothing.
They saw a few men sluicing, but they were getting nothing.

Letter dated July 29, 1898, Christochina River, Alaska
Dear Lizzie,
As this is the first time I have had a chance to send any mail
down since leaving the Klutena, will write you a very few lines so
that you will know I am alive and well. I am 90 [about 70] miles
from the Klutena. Towed a boat all the way and will go 15 miles
more with it up this stream, then pack on my back God knows
where.

There has not been any gold found so far, nor do I think there will be this year. Some have gone to the head of the Copper and Slona [Slana] and returned without finding anything. Others have gone on over to the Tanana with the same results. A good many have started to pack on to 40 Mile Creek near Dawson. I don't think I will try it till winter and maybe not then. I am at a standstill and don't know what to do. I hate to go back broke, for what will become of us then, just think of it. I have almost given up in despair of making anything here. Half of those who came in here have gone back.

Poor Jim Buckley was drowned on July the 11th near the mouth of the Gacona River. He was pushing the boat out from shore with a pole when his feet slipped and he fell in over his head. He, being unable to swim, was soon swept out into the current, which is very swift. We were unable to find his body.

I left the Hessian party, or part of it, at Copper Center and came up here with Buckley, Whirley, and John Corcoran. I wrote to Mrs. Buckley today but it may be months before she gets the letter.

It has been raining nearly every day since we left the Center. I am glad that my health has been so good. My gum boots are all worn out and so too are most all my socks. Will use sacks in the future. I put some white patches on my pants today. You would laugh to see me, I know.

Oh, how I would like to get a peep of you and the dear little ones. I do hope they are well. Keep up hopes dear and don't worry about me, for so long as God gives me good health, I will pull through all right. Give my love to Len and Myrtle [his brother and sister-in-law]. Would write [them] but my paper got wet and I lost most all I had with me.

The Indians are few and quite civilized. They live mostly on salmon. They are well pleased to have the white man with them because the white man's muck-muck (food) is better than theirs. [In 1898 the Copper River Indians numbered abut 300. They were divided into two main groups: the *Midnoosky* (a Russian word adopted by the lower river Indians), who lived from the mouth of the Tazlina and its branches southward, and the *Tatlatans,* or upper river Indians. The people of these groups differed very little but Lieutenant Allen noticed a variation in their language. Each group was subdivided further, with each clan strictly adhering to a particular district in hunting and fishing. Captain Abercrombie noticed that it was not unusual for a tribe on one side of the river to go hungry because the salmon were running on the opposite bank, in the territory of a neighboring tribe.][10]

Remember me to all. Love to you dear.

From your hubby,
Horace

Saturday, July 30, 1898
Weather: Cloudy
Thirteen of us started this morning up the Christochina River. We made 6 miles. Have grub enough for one month's prospecting.

Sunday, July 31, 1898
Weather: Rain
Someone got up quite early and killed 2 ducks and picked a pan full of currants. The water here is like ice water. Picked some fine red currants. They were the largest I ever saw.

Monday, August 1, 1898
Weather: Rain
Had a tough time of it today. We came to places in the river where no boat could pass through and live. Had to cross and recross [the river], cut trees and brush. Camped in a swamp.

Tuesday, August 2, 1898
Weather: Cloudy
Had to go back ¼ of a mile with our boats and crossed the river 3 times. At noon we were opposite where we camped the night before. Went huckleberrying in the afternoon. Got a nice lot, but gee whillican, they are sour. [Government explorers made special mention of the immense quantity of blue huckleberries growing in

this vicinity in August of 1898. The berries were unusually large and grew on dwarf bushes not over a foot in height.][11]

Wednesday, August 3, 1898
Weather: Quite clear
We finished towing boats today. Start packing tomorrow. We are 4 miles up the first clear water stream that leads into the Christochina on the right. Can go no farther with boats owing to shoals and shallow water.

Thursday, August 4, 1898
It rained in the forenoon and we did not work. Started in the afternoon with 50 lbs. each and packed 5 miles through swamps and over creeks and returned in the evening.

Friday, August 5, 1898
Weather: Cloudy
Organized a company consisting of 14 members, seven of whom go back to Copper Center while the balance prospect till the grub is gone. We traveled 10 miles and camped on a clear water stream which we named Decker Creek. Found several nice colors in this stream. It is the first clear water stream running parallel with the Christochina on the east. [This stream was probably the East Fork Chistochina.]

Saturday, August 6, 1898
Weather: Cloudy
Made one trip back 5 miles in the forenoon and then went on up Decker Creek 4 miles. Saw one side of a pair of moose horns which measured 4 feet. Saw plenty signs of bear but bruin himself did not appear.

Sunday, August 7, 1898
Weather: Cloudy
This morning seven of our party go back to Copper Center, leaving seven here to prospect. I am elected to remain. Sunk a

prospect hole 3 feet deep. Could go no deeper on account of water. Got several good colors.

Monday, August 8, 1898
Weather: Clear
Started packing on up Decker Creek and went about 7 miles where we will stay for a week. [Since Conger made no mention of a large lake (Mankomen), he probably went up Eagle Creek, an eastern tributary of the East Fork Chistochina.] The hills look smooth at a distance but upon a nearer approach they are found to be covered with brush 4 feet high. Whirley got hurt. Fell down with a pack on his back and struck a stub just over the heart.

Tuesday, August 9, 1898
Rope and I went out prospecting in the morning but did not find a color. The balance of the boys packed up from our last camp. In the afternoon all went after huckleberries. It rained quite hard during the day.

Wednesday, August 10, 1898
This has been the finest day since I left Copper Center. Had a frost last night. Seven of us started out prospecting this morning but did not find a color. The rock is mostly all granite and badly broken up and lies very loosely.

Thursday, August 11, 1898
Weather: Cloudy
I went prospecting all day. The rest of the party rested in the forenoon but went down the creek 3 miles and packed up some flour in the afternoon. Had gopher stew for dinner. I did not eat much of it.

Friday, August 12, 1898
This has been a nice day and we packed up a week's rations and started in a northerly direction across the hills. Killed some pheasants with stones. [Pheasants were not introduced into

Alaska until the 1930s, and then they were failures. The willow ptarmigan and spruce grouse, both found in this area, were tame, unsuspecting, and easily killed. But since Conger has previously mentioned ptarmigan (April 24 and May 5), the birds referred to here were probably grouse. Because the spruce grouse was easily approached and slaughtered, it became known by the common name "fool hen." Conger was not alone in referring to these birds as pheasants. Two members of Abercrombie's expedition made the same mistake.][12] Speared a trout with a shovel. Picked a nice mess of berries. I found the largest speck of gold yet discovered.

Saturday, August 13, 1898
Weather: Clear
Broke camp at 7:30 A.M. and traveled north to the headwaters of the Slona, which we reached a little after 1 P.M. Will camp here for a few days and prospect. Saw the Hudson boys. They were returning from the Robinson Creek where they left 3 men to prospect.

Sunday, August 14, 1898
Weather: Cloudy
Started north this morning and went 8 miles to the extreme head of the Slona River. It flows out from beneath a glacier in two different channels. Saw where someone had made a cache up in a tree. Prospected a clear water stream on the left going up and found colors. This is an awful rocky country and the hills are very steep. Lots of iron, granite, lime, slate, and some quartz, but no ledge of quartz. [Quartz is the commonest rock in which gold is found. On a mountain side, prospectors look for an outcropping of a gold-bearing quartz vein, sometimes called a ledge.] Ate bread straight for dinner, flapjacks for supper.

Monday, August 15, 1898
Raining hard this a.m. I am sitting under a large spruce tree where no water can reach me, for the limbs all grow downward, caused

by the heavy snows. Broke camp at 3:30 P.M. and went down the river 4 miles. Crossed a clear creek and camped in the timber on the mountainside.

Tuesday, August 16, 1898
Weather: Rain
Started in a N.E. direction and traveled till noon, then bore S.E. for 2 hours, when we discovered that we were not on our course. Kept on going in a S. of S.E. direction till we came to a canyon where there was timber, where we camped for the night midst a heavy fog and rain. Had only a little bread for each man. The storm ceased about 9 in the evening.

Wednesday, August 17, 1898
Ate the balance of our bread for breakfast, which was 4 bites per man. Still foggy and off our course. However, we started in a S.W. direction and kept bearing a little west till the end of the mountains was skirted. The fog cleared up enough so that a high mountain was reached and camp located. We had nearly circled it. Reached that long looked for haven at 1:30 P.M., and maybe we did not fill up on flapjacks.[13]

Thursday, August 18, 1898
Three of us went out prospecting in the morning but it rained so hard, had to turn back. Whirley remained in camp and the other 3 went after flour. In the afternoon we all stayed in camp.

Friday, August 19, 1898
This has been a fine day. We packed up 6 days' grub and started in a N.E. direction and traveled 10 miles. Camped on a clear water stream that flows into the Slona. Found where the Eagle Mining Company had located a claim on July 6. Don't think it is worth a cent. Picked 2 gold pans full of huckleberries, but gee whiz they are sour, for we have no sweetening. Six flapjacks, seven men, seven knives. Frost last night.

Saturday, August 20, 1898
Weather: Clear
Five of us went prospecting in a canyon running east but found
nothing, only pyrites of iron, the same as the Eagle Company
found. These are the worst chopped up hills I ever saw and all
covered with granite. One of the boys caught 60 nice trout. Have
seen no game so far, only a few . . . [grouse].[14] Froze ice.

Sunday, August 21, 1898
Rained all day and we did not prospect. Some of the boys caught
a nice string of trout for dinner. This has been the most lonesome
day I have experienced since arriving in Alaska. The mosquitoes
are about all gone. My thoughts all day have been of those at
home, especially so of my family.

Monday, August 22, 1898
It rained a little. Wind blew a gale last night. Went fishing today.
Caught 102 trout. Have quit prospecting (for there is nothing
around here) and gone to sporting.

Tuesday, August 23, 1898
Went fishing again and caught 82. Ate them all in two meals. It
rained very hard in the p.m. and I got wet through.

Wednesday, August 24, 1898
Weather: Cloudy
Broke camp this morning and went back to where our grub is.
Was out of salt and had to eat fish without it. Killed one duck but
it won't go very far among seven hungry men, for we all eat like
bears.

Thursday, August 25, 1898
Weather: Clear
It was very cold last night. Froze ice one inch thick. Stayed in
camp all the forenoon. In the p.m. went over the hill and finished
sinking a shaft we commenced some time ago which had run into

a clay. We were anxious to see what lie beneath. Found plenty of water but no gold.

Saturday, August 27, 1898
Weather: Clear
Some of us took flour back to our last camp. We are preparing to leave here for our boat Monday. I went over the hill 4 miles and prospected a small creek. Got 7 colors out of 5 pans of dirt. No good. Anderson caught 70 trout, so we will have a feast for supper. It hailed quite hard during the afternoon.

Sunday, August 28, 1898
Weather: Clear
It being Sunday, we are at rest. Shot 4 . . . [grouse][15] and gathered some spruce gum. Saw the auroras or northern lights last night, also the moon, which seemed to keep in a straight line to the horizon and did not rise. The North Star is nearly straight overhead.

Monday, August 29, 1898
Weather: Rain
Started on our back trail and went as far on Decker Creek as where we left the other boys on August 7. I went out prospecting and found 7 colors to the pan, about one cent's worth of gold. Too small. It won't pay. We are on our way back to Copper Center but it may be 10 days before we get there, for we shall do a little hunting on our journey.

Tuesday, August 30, 1898
Weather: Cloudy
Went . . . [down][16] Decker Creek to first camp and packed down and over the hills to within 4 miles of our boat, where we will pack tomorrow. Went back to Decker Creek and camped for the night.

Wednesday, August 31, 1898
Rained nearly all night. Blankets got wet and so did we. Started at

Washing

10 A.M. for the stream where our boat is. Reached there at 3 P.M. Found things musty in the tent and my robe was getting moldy. The mosquitoes are all gone but the gnats have taken their place.

Thursday, September 1, 1898
Weather: Cloudy
Arose at five and went back on our trail for the balance of our grub and got back to the boat at 12 . . . [noon].[17] In the p.m. I did my monthly washing but before it was finished some of the Hudson party came along and I had a chat with them. They have

just returned from the Robinson River [probably Robertson River] and report it favorable. It rained hard.

Friday, September 2, 1898
Had to go back on my trail 3 miles to find my knife which I lost yesterday. It rained hard all day. The water is rising rapidly in the rivers. We start down the Christochina tomorrow and go as far as our other boat.

Saturday, September 3, 1898
Weather: Clear
Started at 9 in the morning down the Christochina and reached our other boat at 1 P.M. This is where we were camped at the time I wrote to Lizzie last July 29. Guess we are the last ones left on this river. Picked a nice lot of cranberries but they will be quite tart, I reckon, without sugar.

Sunday, September 4, 1898
It rained all night and is still raining. The water ran through the tent, around us, and out. Three of the boys are getting our morning repast of flapjacks, coffee, and bacon. Lit a candle tonight for the first time since May 1.

Monday, September 5, 1898
Weather: Clear
Started down Copper River this morning with 7 men and 2 boats. Went about 25 miles and had to stop on account of high wind. The river channels are filled with debris. There are 4 tents here besides our own, but who owns them remains to be found out. Found one boat, wrecked, containing a shovel and some rope. The boat was upside down. Name on boat is J.W. Masner. Goodal and party are the ones who are camped here. They are going over to the Tanana.

Tuesday, September 6, 1898
Started this morning from 8 miles above the Sanford and camped

at the mouth of the Taslena. The wind bothered us. Struck one rock but did no damage. Met more parties bound for 40 Mile.

Wednesday, September 7, 1898
Left the Tasslena at 8:20. Arrived at Copper Center (10 miles) 9:20. Over half the people have gone out. Provisions and clothing are being given away, there being no sale. Shovels sell for 10¢, picks 5¢, coats and pants 75¢, flour $1.50 per hundred, etc. Buckley's body was found on the 5th instrument [September 5] at Copper Center. It drifted 45 miles. Nothing has been found on my 2 months' trip.

Notes—

1. Walter C. Mendenhall, "A Reconnaissance from Resurrection Bay to the Tanana River, Alaska, in 1898," *Twentieth Annual Report of the USGS,* Part 7 (Washington: Gov. Printing Office, 1900), pp. 319, 322-23; A.H. Koschmann and M.H. Bergendahl, *Principal Gold-Producing Districts of the United States* (Washington: Gov. Printing Office, 1968), pp. 13-14.

2. The output of the Chistochina district through 1959 was 141,000 ounces, all from placers; the Nizina district produced 143,500 ounces, and all but 60 ounces was from placers. Koschmann and Bergendahl, *Principal Gold-Producing Districts,* pp. 13-14, 9; Clarence L. Andrews, *The Story of Alaska* (Caldwell, Idaho: Caxton Printers Ltd., 1938), pp. 212, 292; Dempsey, Hazlett, and Meals were the initial locators on the Chisna. W.R. Abercrombie, "Report of Addison Powell, Guide," *Copper River Exploring Expedition, 1899* (Washington: Gov. Printing Office, 1900), p. 133; Oscar Rohn, "A Reconnaissance of the Chitina River and the Skolai Mountains, Alaska," *Twenty-First Annual Report of the USGS,* Part 2 (Washington: Gov. Printing Office, 1900), p. 437.

3. Omitted word is "since."

4. Luther W. Guiteau, "Alaska Gold Rush Diary," serialized 1928 in Freeport, Illinois, *Journal-Standard* (manuscript in Alaska Historical Library, Juneau), diary entry for July 11, 1898.

5. Capt. Edwin F. Glenn and Capt. W.R. Abercrombie, "Report of W.R. Abercrombie," *Reports of Explorations in the Territory of Alaska, 1898* (Washington: Gov. Printing Office, 1899), pp. 330-31; F.C. Schrader, "A Reconnaissance of a Part of Prince William Sound and the Copper River District, Alaska, in 1898," *Twentieth Annual Report of the USGS,* p. 371.

6. Lt. Henry T. Allen, "Report of a Military Reconnaissance in Alaska, Made in 1885," *Compilation of Narratives of Explorations in Alaska* (Washington: Gov. Printing Office, 1900), pp. 439, 468.

7. Glenn and Abercrombie, "Report of Guide J.J. Rafferty," *Reports of Explorations . . . 1898,* p. 444; Allen, *Compilation of Narratives,* pp. 440, 442; Robert A. McKennan, *The Upper Tanana Indians,* in Yale Univ. Publications in Anthropology, No. 55, ed. Irving Rouse (New Haven: Dept. of Anthropology, 1959), p. 28; Frederic R. Marvin, "The Chinook Language," in *The Yukon Overland: The Gold Digger's Handbook* (Cincinnati: Editor Publishing Co., 1898), pp. 144-45.

8. Schrader, "A Reconnaissance . . . 1898," *Twentieth Annual Report of the USGS,* p. 394.

9. "Victims of Copper River," *San Francisco Chronicle,* Sept. 19, 1898, p. 3; "Hundreds Trying to Work Their Way Out," *San Francisco Chronicle,* Aug. 21, 1898, p. 15; "Little Gold on Copper River," *San Francisco Chronicle,* July 18, 1898, p. 3; also see Neil D. Benedict, "The Valdes and Copper River Trail," (unpublished manuscript in Alaska Historical Library, Juneau), 1899, pp. 113-17.

10. Allen, *Compilation of Narratives,* pp. 419, 441, 471; Schrader, "A Reconnaissance . . . 1898," *Twentieth Annual Report of the USGS,* p. 368; Glenn and Abercrombie, "Report of Capt. Abercrombie," *Reports of Explorations . . . 1898,* p. 327; also see Cornelius Osgood, *The Distribution of the Northern Athapaskan Indians,* Yale Univ. Publications in Anthropology, No. 7 (New Haven: Yale Univ. Press, 1936), p. 7; and John R. Swanton, *Indian Tribes of North America,* Smithsonian Institution, Bureau of American Ethnology, Bulletin 145 (Washington: Gov. Printing Office, 1953), p. 529.

11. Mendenhall, "A Reconnaissance . . . 1898," *Twentieth Annual Report of the USGS,* p. 284; Glenn and Abercrombie, "Report of Capt. Abercrombie," *Reports of Explorations . . . 1898,* pp. 65, 69.

12. Ira N. Gabrielson and Frederick C. Lincoln, *The Birds of Alaska* (Harrisburg: Stackpole, 1959), pp. 50, 292-95, 298-301. Addison M. Powell and H. Brian Pearson referred to pheasants in W.R. Abercrombie, *Copper River Exploring Expedition, 1899* (Washington: Gov. Printing Office, 1900), pp. 135, 151.

13. This was a vernacularism having the opposite meaning of the words. Another illustration of this usage is in the following passage, spoken by men who had just arrived at Sheep Camp after crossing the Chilkoot Pass: "They at camp congratulated us on getting over, and showed us where we could get something to eat, and maybe we didn't get over there quickly." Chicago Record, *Klondike: The Chicago Record's Book for Gold Seekers* (Chicago: Monarch Book Co., 1897), p. 335.

14. Omitted word is "pheasants." See editors' comment for Aug. 12, 1898.

15. Omitted word is "pheasants." See editors' comment for Aug. 12, 1898.

16. Omitted word is "up."

17. The letter "M" has been deleted. This abbreviation signifies "meridian," an obsolete usage meaning "noon."

Chapter 6—

Settling in for the Winter

In August, while Conger was in the Chistochina district, the main part of Captain Abercrombie's military expedition reached Copper Center over the trail established by the gold seekers. Because of the lateness of the season, they abandoned their original plan of continuing the survey to the head of the Copper River district. Instead, Captain Abercrombie and two packers made a hasty reconnaissance to Mentasta Pass in the Alaska Range, while geologist F.C. Schrader, in charge of 13 men and 17 horses, proceeded southward down the west bank of the Copper River. Abercrombie returned to Copper Center from Mentasta Pass on September 27 (while Conger was visiting Amy's Rapids). The army commander intended to proceed to Klutina Lake, but upon learning of the hardships suffered by the members of his Copper River party, he obtained a boat and headed downriver to join them.[1]

The Copper River party had encountered many obstacles to travel on their downstream journey. The high bluffs along the river were discontinuous, being cut at frequent intervals by long, steep-sided canyons. Therefore, travel was easier along the river flats, though it was hindered by mire and quicksand which often entrapped the animals. At places where the river was actively engaged in undercutting the adjacent bluff, the men and horses were forced to climb 500 or 600 feet to the overhanging bluff, where considerable trail cutting was necessary to advance through the thick underbrush. While crossing the Tonsina, a western tributary of the Copper, Private Archer was drowned and most of the party's provisions were lost when a raft got caught in the river's swift current. At Taral the horses were abandoned due to the rugged mountainous terrain ahead, and the journey was

*Dewey Creek and mountains on east side of Copper River, opposite
the Tiekel River, 1899.*

continued alternately on foot and in a boat procured from prospectors. Abercrombie rejoined his men at a camp made on Dewey
Creek, just opposite the mouth of the Tiekel. The expedition then
continued down the Copper, reaching the Tasnuna River on
October 1. At this point, Emil Mahlo, a topographical assistant,
suffered a heart attack and several men subsequently escorted him
down the Copper by boat while the remainder of the party
attempted a return to Valdez across the unexplored Tasnuna
River valley.[2]

    Though the expedition was expected back in Valdez by
October 23 to catch the last steamer out to the States, completing
the journey on schedule was somewhat in doubt. Nighttime
temperatures were near freezing; the fresh snow level was grad-
ually decreasing on the surrounding mountain sides; and the men
lacked heavy clothing and footgear, which had been lost along
with their provisions in crossing the Tonsina. In addition, travel
across the rugged Tasnuna country proved tedious. To avoid the
mire of the river valley, the party hacked a trail through a dense

growth of alder and devil's club at the foot of the steep mountains, but in some places it was necessary to wade through long stretches of waist-deep water, where the footing consisted of anchor ice and slippery boulders. A long, impassable gorge was encountered which necessitated cutting trail while climbing 400 feet up the steep canyon walls. However, with the exception of Lieutenant Lowe, who had proceeded to the Yukon via Mentasta Pass, the explorers arrived back in Valdez in mid-October. They left to winter in the States on October 26 aboard the steamer *Excelsior*.[3]

Remaining behind was the quartermaster's agent of the expedition, Charles Brown. He was the government's representative in Valdez charged with carrying out relief operations, an action authorized for all mining regions of Alaska by a federal law passed in December of 1897. During the months of August, September, and October, Brown had issued rations to over 300 men who had returned from the Copper River valley without resources. Some had lost their outfits in the Klutina Rapids, while others had simply abandoned their supplies in their haste to get out of the country before winter. Since most of these men lacked the severe symptoms of scurvy evident in those arriving later, the destitute among them were able to work at jobs provided by Brown to earn their keep until steamers arrived to take them south. Through the labor of these men, many improvements were made in the government facilities at Valdez: a cabin, smoke house, and stable were constructed; hay was cut for the pack animals; gravel was hauled for roads and footpaths; and assistance was rendered in the establishment of a relief station on the glacier. More than one-third of these gold seekers were carried south free of charge by steamers of the Pacific Steam Whaling Company, while the others saved enough of their earnings to pay for second-class passage.[4]

Meanwhile, in the Copper River valley, an estimated 300 gold seekers who refused to give up the hunt were settling in for the winter by building cabins, cutting firewood, and replenishing their outfits through the auctions of those selling out.[5]

A typical restaurant

Thursday, September 8, 1898
Started up the Klutena [from Copper Center] to look after my cache. Found a few things missing. M.J. Hessian and Neil are going out. [See appendix for a list of items in the cache at the head of the rapids.]

Friday, September 9, 1898
This has been a fine day. People building cabins right and left, and good ones, too. There are twice as many people here [at Amy's Rapids] as at the Center. Two restaurants. Meals 25 and 50 cents. One saloon. A few are selling out at a big sacrifice, for grub and tools are very cheap. Bought some baking powder. Paid 50¢ per pound. The water is much higher than I ever saw it.

Saturday, September 10, 1898
Quite a number of us walked up to the head of the [lower Klutina] river where they were having a rifle shoot. A good many are camped there. One of our party took second prize. Five ladies took a hand in the shooting. Mrs. Dowling won first money. [A

member of Abercrombie's party reported the kind treatment Mrs. Dowling rendered to an army private who was suffering from typhoid fever on the summit of the glacier, and C.H. Remington, a prospector, wrote, "When men were about to give up, a woman by the name of Mrs. Dowling shamed them into a final effort and it saved them, because . . . she had the nerve, though undoubtedly was the weakest physically."][6] Saw the man who was hurt with bear. [A gold seeker named Hoffman, who was camped at the foot of Klutina Lake, had been severely mauled by a brown bear. Although accounts of the attack vary somewhat in their details, it seems that the unfortunate man had sailed across the lake alone to retrieve a knife lost on a prior hunting trip. During the search along Salmon Creek, with his attention directed toward the ground, he virtually walked into the bear, which had surrounded itself with a catch of salmon from the stream. With a slap from one of its huge paws, the surprised bear knocked Hoffman to the ground, simultaneously tearing loose half of his scalp. The animal then sank his large teeth into the man's lower jaw, fracturing it in five places and turning his face into an unrecognizable mass of flesh. When the bear retreated, the victim crawled to his boat. Though his scalp was flopping over his eyes, he succeeded in reaching the opposite shore. He was aided by several doctors camped nearby, but reports of his fate are conflicting. Margeson wrote that he lingered six days and died, while Remington stated that he was helped out to Valdez and then to the States.][7]

Sunday, September 11, 1898
This has been a lovely day. We walked down to Copper Center from the head of the rapids. Wore a pair of moccasins and the soles were so thin that [the skin on] my feet nearly peeled off. Some [men] came back today from Franklin Gulch, near 40 Mile Creek, and they report the prospects good. [Franklin Gulch was a mining camp located at the junction of Franklin Creek and South Fork Fortymile River, about 48 miles southwest of Eagle. Howard Franklin discovered gold in this vicinity in 1886.][8]

Brown bearskin at Copper Center.

Letter dated September 12, 1898, Copper Center, Alaska
Dear Lizzie,

I have just returned from the headwaters of the Slona [Slana] River. Upon my arrival here I found 4 letters from you. I will answer them now and send them out with the Hessian boys, who will leave here day after tomorrow.

There are only three of us now left of the original party — A. Whirley, John Corcoran, and myself. I think they will remain with me. I found nothing during my 2 months' trip north. Went 125 miles up the Copper and its tributaries. Passed around the head of the Slona River. It comes out from under a glacier in 3 different channels. I walked around all three of them on the glacier. It is a hard looking country and much harder to travel

Valdez Summit and mountains at head of glacier; prospectors returning from Copper River, 1898.

over. I found one small particle of gold, about the size of a half a grain of wheat. It is the largest piece found to date. I do not think there is any gold in paying quantities this side of 40 Mile Creek. Some have gone down to Spirit Mountain but met with the same results. [Spirit Mountain, 7,287 feet in elevation, is located three and four-tenths miles southeast of the junction of the Uranatina and Copper rivers. Lieutenant Allen reported that the coast Natives were superstitious about the mountain and smeared their faces with charcoal and ashes when approaching it. In 1885 an old Native told Allen that "formerly much fire and smoke were emitted from the mountain, and that now terrific rumblings were at times heard, all the workings of a Mighty Spirit." According to Allen, these sounds were the result of snowslides.][9]

Over half the people who came in here have gone out. Provisions are cheaper here than in the States. I am going to buy some more to be sure and have enough to last one year from now. I had nine sacks of flour stolen from the cache while I was up the river, but I have money enough to buy more. If I could sell what I have for anything, would try to come home, but could not reach Mora earlier than October 20th with good luck. [Horace and Lizzie were expecting their third child in October.]

View of crevasses on northern slope of the glacier.

They say it is almost impossible to cross the glacier at this time of year. Several parties have been lost while crossing. [By early fall, the exodus from the Copper River valley had developed into a mad race to escape from the country before winter. Those who chose the glacier route found that the everlasting northern sun had melted the snow cover from the surface of the lower reaches of the glacier, exposing rocks, ice, and numerous crevasses. While diligence was required in crossing this dangerous terrain, a greater risk was encountered at higher elevations on the glacier, where snow bridges of unknown depth and durability still covered the deep chasms. An unwary returning gold seeker narrowly escaped death at one of these spots on the day Conger wrote this letter. John R. Herman was at the rear of his party when he was suddenly missed by his companions. An immediate search located Herman wedged in a 40-foot crevasse from which he was rescued after a five-hour confinement. A snow bridge had been safely crossed by the other members of the party but had chosen the moment of Herman's passing to disintegrate.][10]

Some [persons] have gone out via Orca, down Copper River, but that, too, is dangerous, as you pass through a canyon where the ice drops off every half hour. Should the ice drop while a boat is within 40 yards, it will be drawn in and swallowed up. Seven men and one Indian were drowned while trying to pass this point. [Guide J.J. Rafferty, of Abercrombie's party, wrote the following description of this part of the lower Copper River, known as Abercrombie Rapids: "The head of Abercrombie Canyon was reached at 3 P.M. July 1. One side of this canyon was formed by a wall of immense bowlders, the terminal moraine of the Miles Glacier. The bed of the river is filled with these bowlders, over which the waters of the Copper, confined to a narrow channel between the glacier walls and the bluffs of solid rock, go tearing through at a high rate of speed." Rafferty bypassed this obstacle by portaging over a trail that ran along the face of the bluff on the right bank. At one place he encountered a snowslide which pitched dangerously toward the river. "A misstep," wrote Rafferty, "meant almost certain death." In the process of lining his empty boat down the canyon, "it received such rough usage as to spring the timbers and cause it to leak badly." The next danger reported by Rafferty was "from the swell caused by the ice breaking off from the Childs Glacier, which sometimes created such waves as to land a loaded boat 150 feet high and dry on the shore. The current swings directly toward the glacier on making the turn and it required all the strength at hand to keep from being carried with it. The river was filled with floating ice, some pieces being almost the size of a freight car."][11]

No dear, I have decided to remain here a part, or whole, of the winter. If possible, will boat or sled my stuff up Copper River and on over to 40 Mile Creek, 310 miles. If I am successful in getting there by June, will work till fall and then come home by way of the Chilcoot Pass. Gold has been found on 40 Mile in paying quantities.

My trip this summer has been one long to be remembered and, God grant, never to be repeated. After poor Buckley was drowned, 3 of us towed our boat on up the Copper till the Christochina was reached, thence up that roaring torrent (which is swifter than any of the others) till we came to a small stream on the right bank. We took our boats up this stream 4 miles, which was as far as we could go with them. Then [we] commenced packing on our backs and packed 50 miles through swamps, over rocky cliffs, and across small streams. We were lost two days in a fog and storm. Had nothing but dry bread to eat. Some of the party who had never been in the mountains before became very excited and would have thrown their blankets away only for me. They all seemed to look upon me as a guide, as I had some experience in the mountains before, but I confess [that] I was a little bewildered myself, for I had never seen a country like this before. It all seems to look alike. There is not enough difference in the lakes, streams, and hills to enable one to recognize them the second time. The mountains are a jumbled up mass of loose granite and one can feel them move while walking over them. After about five weeks of wading through water, and in moss up to my knees, I started back to Copper Center.

Buckley's body was found the day before we reached the Center, floating by the place where, nearly 2 months before, he started out alive. The remains were interred here under the auspices of the Masons. There was only $153.87 found on his body. His interest in the provisions did not bring much, nor did his clothing. [See "Buckley Account," in the appendix.] I think Neil Hessian will take the money to Mrs. Buckley. Poor Jim was no man for Alaska.

A good many are stiffened up with the rheumatism. One of

our party has it in his knees. This is a very healthy country. Most everyone has increased in weight. I weigh 167 lbs. notwithstanding the hardships I have gone through.

It is 30 miles to the head of the rapids. Tents and log cabins are scattered along the whole distance. There are some very nice buildings here. Everything is cheap except tobacco and whiskey. Whiskey is $20 per gallon and tobacco is $1.25 per pound.

Two men got badly hurt while hunting bear. One had his jaw broken and scalp torn off. They must have got into a den of them, for I have seen nothing, only tracks, since I have been here. I know of only one caribou and two moose having been killed so far. Game is very scarce. Caught some nice trout on a branch of the Slona.

This has been a transportation boom from the first and will probably extend throughout another year. Don't you believe a word you read or hear about gold being found on Copper River, for it is not so. Not an ounce has been dug out this side of the Tanana, although colors can be found most anywhere. Don't you worry about me, for I will look out for No. 1. I feel that I will strike something if health and grub will last long enough. If I should come home now, we would be but little better than beggars, and I think you can do without me for a while.

You don't know how I long to see you and the dear children. Have just finished reading, for the second time, your letter of June 20th [his birthday]. I, too, thought of you all that day and would have happily joined you in the picnic on the farm were I near enough, but a great gulf divided us. I went down the bounding Klutena River on that day and came near losing a boat load of goods. Received the pin (Remember the *Maine*) and I am glad her destruction has been avenged.

Have good cheer, mon ami, about your sickness [pregnancy], for I am satisfied you will be well cared for. It would be impossible for me to reach you in time for the event, should I start tomorrow. I shall not worry, for I know you are in good hands. But this does bother me: viz., that after Oct. 31, we shall not be able to get anymore mail until spring, as the steamers stop running and the glacier will be impassable. But I can't believe that 7 or 8 hundred people will be cut off from the world for so long a time. I think there will be some way provided whereby we can get our mail. I will write to you again before that time, but you will not get the letter till November. Get Len or someone to write me a few lines immediately after the arrival, for I shall be anxious.

A man was just in my tent with a petition to Congress for a money order P.O. at this point. I signed it, you may be sure, but I don't think it will materialize, for in the spring there will not be anyone here unless something is struck. And I don't think this is the best way to reach Circle City, Dawson, or 40 Mile.

Tuesday, September 13, 1898
Dear Wife,

Will finish my letter, started yesterday, now, for in the afternoon I will be too busy to write. Did not sleep much last night. My thoughts kept flying back to the ones left on the other side of the briny deep. Guess it must have been caused from drinking some coffee (which was strong) just before going to bed. This is a lovely morning, so bright and still.

Bought 1 pair rubber boots, coat and vest (sheep lined), heavy sweater, pair of lined pants, large hood, and a pair of German socks this morning for $4. These things are all new. The balance of Buckley's clothing will be auctioned off this afternoon and I am going to bid on his 12 lb. blanket. Think it will go for two dollars. It cost $10. The Hessian boys leave here tomorrow. M.J. is going to 40 Mile in the spring. He will go no farther than Seattle this winter.

The leaves are all falling off the trees and soon the howling blasts of old winter will be upon us. Take good care of yourself dear and don't run any chances. If you are in need of any money, don't hesitate to tell Len, for I know he will not let you suffer, for well he knows [that] if I am successful in this country (which I will be) all his encumbrances and liabilities will be swept away and the road to prosperity and happiness made clear. Have courage my dear. Never falter and all will end well. Did you get my letter of

Looking northeast across the Copper; Mount Drum in center, 1899.

June 30th? Sent you a $20 bill. When my diary is full, will send it to you. Have recorded every day's transactions.

Kiss the dear little tots for me two or three times. Kind regards to all my dear friends, for I often think of them all. Love to you my dear wife, and may God preserve your health and life for my homecoming.

Lovingly,
Horace

Tuesday, September 13, 1898
This has been a very fine day. Attended auction sale. Bought 200 lbs. flour at $6.50, 90 lbs. bacon at $15, one fur cap 60¢. Most of the stuff went very cheap.

Wednesday, September 14, 1898
Weather: Cloudy
The Hessian brothers left for the States this afternoon accompanied by quite a number from St. Cloud. Twelve men left last

night for the Tonsena [Tonsina River]. Another gold excitement to increase the price of grub.

Thursday, September 15, 1898
This has been a fine day. I moved part of my grub to where the cabin will be built. Some of us are going to build two cabins connected together. Four moose were shot today. There is quite an excitement on the Tonsena.

Friday, September 16, 1898
Rained a little in the forenoon. Clear and windy in the afternoon. Bought some moose meat, 25¢ per lb. Made a table.

Saturday, September 17, 1898
Fine day. Too nice to stay in camp, so went hunting. Got 2 squirrels and one . . . [grouse].[12] Everybody is all excited over the Tonsena gold diggings. Some have gone down the Copper, but most of the people go overland from the foot of Lake Margurete [Klutina].

Monday, September 19, 1898
Thermometer: 20°
Commenced my cabin. We cut 78 logs. Will build two cabins. Three men in each. Nice and warm all day but very clear and quite cold at night. Water in Copper River is falling rapidly. Everything is quiet today. Most of the men have gone to the Tonsena excitement.

Tuesday, September 20, 1898
Weather: Clear; Thermometer: 16°
Still working on my house. Expect to get the roof on this week. Will chink the cracks with moss. Smith came down from the head of the rapids. Said there was nothing in the gold excitement.

Wednesday, September 21, 1898
Thermometer: 16°

Covered both cabins with poles and mossed the top of one. It has been a nice, still day. Some are making ready to move upriver with their boats. Have got a bad cold and it has settled on my lungs. Cough badly at night.

Thursday, September 22, 1898
Thermometer: 32°
Rained nearly all night and all the afternoon today. Worked on our cabins in the forenoon. Covered both roofs with moss and one with dirt. Burt Carvey and party returned from Mt. Drum [a 12,010-foot peak in the Wrangell Mountains]. Located some claims. Don't know whether it is gold or not. Met Clark Moore, who was arrested with the Sontag party at the time they robbed the train in California. Had a big dinner today — ham and eggs, peaches and cream, sweet corn, etc.

Friday, September 23, 1898
Weather: Cloudy; Thermometer: 32°
Finished the outside of both cabins. Ripped up one boat to make a door and window frame. Visited with Mr. and Mrs. Flynn. They are well acquainted with Machelhargey [the hardware merchant] of Mora.[13]

Saturday, September 24, 1898
Weather: Clear; Thermometer: 28°
Finished the exterior of our cabin and put up the stove to dry the moss and logs inside before moving in. Got a large sheet of celluloid for a window and the color of it is green. The mail arrived today bringing me 4 letters.

Sunday, September 25, 1898
Thermometer: 32°
Lonesome, dismal day. Wrote letters most all day. Four boats left for Orca. Others to follow soon.

Letter dated September 25, 1898, Copper Center, Alaska
My Dear Wife,

Yesterday the mail arrived and brought me 3 letters from you, so I will answer all of them today and send them out by a man who goes down the river tomorrow to Orca. Well, nothing has transpired since last writing, only more excitement on the Tonsena, which I think is a fake; however, I start for there tomorrow (Monday) to satisfy myself. It means three weeks of good hard work packing to and from.

Have got my cabin built. It is a rough looking structure, but it will keep out the cold, at least. I may not live in it very much but have got it ready in case I need it. Have got an airtight heater to warm it up, and it is the only one in here. Could sell it for four times its cost.

Strange you never got my letter written while on the Christochina. In it I told you all about Mr. Buckley's death. You [surely] have got it by this time. If not, you have no doubt heard of Buckley's drowning and burial. The Hessian boys took the necessary papers to secure his insurance, together with $110.75 in cash, out with them. They will, or Neil will, deliver same to her.

I know the parties mentioned in the enclosed clipping, as they built their boats where we did and went down the rapids at the same time. They did not go any farther than to the mouth of the Klutena, and when I returned from the north, I found they had gone back home, except W.L. Dudley, who is still here. Their description of the trip and country is too true, except the swiftness of the rapids, which should read 12 miles instead of 50.

The picture you sent me is a bad one. You look as though you were standing up to be shot. Probably the sun was shining in your eyes at the time. Would not know Lila [age 33 months] at all, and of course, not the boy [M. Clifford, age 17 months].

Am glad that you are giving music lessons, for every little [bit] helps. But it seems you put it off to a late date, for you will soon be unable to attend to them for some time. Hope to be able to present you with a fine piano upon my return. I think you have done remarkably well in making your money last so long. I don't see how you managed it. I certainly thought, when I left home, that by this time I would be earning some money so that I could remit you some, but not a cent have I earned, nor am I likely to till spring. It was very wise of you to engage [Dr.] Cowan for the occasion. It will be over ere this letter reaches you and it may be spring before I learn the result. Imagine my suspense. We will have one more mail the last of October, and it may be the last till March. Can't find out for sure.

You did just right in selling those carpets, for, as you say, if we continue to live in that house we don't need them, and if in a better place, can buy new ones. You have my permission to sell any or all the things you have, for they are yours. I relinquish all claim.

I will close now for this month, but will write again the last of October. Many kisses for you and the children and may God preserve your lives.

Lovingly,
Horace

Monday, September 26, 1898
Weather: Rain
Went to the rapids and was awful tired when I reached there. Auction sales going on daily. This is Amy's Landing,[14] 30 miles from Copper Center.

Tuesday, September 27, 1898
Weather: Cloudy
Attending sales at Amy's Landing. Bought snowshoes and two pair socks. One qt. whiskey brought $4. Sugar 25¢ per lb. Flour $6.50 per C. Coffee 7 and 8¢, tea 5¢, beans 2¢, and clothing simply nothing.

Wednesday, September 28, 1898
This is a lovely morning after a cold, frosty night. A good many are returning from the Tonsena and report it a fake. Lots of auction sales today. Bought 37 lbs. oatmeal at 8¢. Whipsaw 15¢.

Thursday, September 29, 1898
Weather: Clear
Cold last night. Bought sugar today. Paid 23¢ per lb. Several boats started down rapids. Water very low. Coffee sold today for 4¢, flour 5½.

Friday, September 30, 1898
Weather: Clear
Left Amy's Rapids for Copper Center with 60 lb. pack. Was taken with contractions of the muscles of my legs. Had to leave half of pack by the wayside. It is a long tedious walk. Saw several boats swamped while trying to line down.

Saturday, October 1, 1898
Thermometer: 16°
Beautiful day. Just like fall weather in Minnesota. Made a door for my cabin and cased up the window. Oh ye of little faith, why linger in this desolate land. Rope found an old Russian war ax. [Russian explorers ascended the Copper River at least as far as the Tazlina River prior to 1850. See the prologue.]

Monday, October 3, 1898
Another fine day. Went after the balance of my pack in the forenoon, and in the afternoon we moved into our cabin. It seems nice to be in a house once more, even if it is a log cabin.

Letter dated October 3, 1898, Copper Center, Alaska
My Dear Wife,

As I have a chance to send a letter out tomorrow, will avail myself of the opportunity of sending you one of my latest photographs, taken in the wilds of Alaska. I hope when you get this letter you will be well and smart as ever.

Started last week for the Tonsena, but on my way, met some reliable friends and they advised me to stay away, as the strike was a fake, which later proved true. Another strike was reported today. This is a beautiful day, and I have been getting up a

*Copper Center, Alaskan home of H.S. Conger, October 3, 1898.
(Note Horace S. Conger in center.)*

woodpile, ready for any emergency. It was 6° above zero this morning and it did not seem at all cold.

[October 4, 1898]

Last night was the first time I slept in my new house, having moved in that day, and according to the old custom (of some people), I named each corner of the room. Commencing with the one I slept in, I named Lizzie; the one at the foot of the bed, Lila; the one behind the door, Clifford; and the one back of the stove, where it was warm, the Unknown. Old Father Morpheus [the Greek god of dreams] had a tight hold on me, but I did a [great] deal of thinking before he came around.

Another moose was killed day before yesterday about 10 miles from here. They are coming in awful slow for such a "game" country. No one crosses the glacier now, for it is considered too dangerous, but they go down the Copper to Orca. Don't know how we are going to get mail in here from this [time] on, unless some new route can be found to avoid the glacier. I talked with the mail carrier, and he said if it was possible to get in he would make another trip.

Now, my dear, look on the bright side of everything and keep up a strong heart. When anyone leaves here now for home, they say he is troubled with cold feet — the reason for going. Love to all and kisses for you and the babies.

Lovingly,
Horace

Wednesday, October 5, 1898
Weather: Clear; Thermometer: 8°
Did nothing this day, only smoke and eat. Five boats went down the Copper this morning.

Friday, October 7, 1898
Weather: Cloudy; Thermometer: 32°
The first and only steamer on Copper River left here today for Orca. Some have gone to the Chitnany [Chitina] to prospect.

Saturday, October 8, 1898
Weather: Clear; Thermometer: 32°
Have been reading *A Little Game with Destiny,* by Marie St. Felix. It shows the power of money and the evil thereof.

Sunday, October 9, 1898
Some Indians were in the cabin today and one of them had some very nice quartz. We had one of them sing "Marching Through Georgia" and "A Hot Time in the Old Town Tonight." Could understand him quite well.[15]

Monday, October 10, 1898
Weather: Clear; Thermometer: 14°
Did some patching and mending. Can buy a squaw for $10 to

cook and sew and get my pick of them all. Guess I will do it. Fred Scott and R. Walker came down from Amy's.

Tuesday, October 11, 1898
Weather: Clear; Thermometer: 10°
Same as yesterday. Am doing nothing now except sleep, eat, and read. Jack got a puppy and we call him "Atna."

Wednesday, October 12, 1898
Heavy hoarfrost last night. The trees look as though they were covered with light snow, and the particles simulate diamonds in the morning sun. Rope returned from the Taslena.

Thursday, October 13, 1898
Nice bright day. 6° above zero but does not seem at all cold. Scott and Walker went back to the rapids. Two girls were here selling tickets for a concert to be given at Amy's.

Friday, October 14, 1898
Weather: Clear; Thermometer: 2°
Went to the opera last night. Heard some fine violin playing. Two lady actors. One of them resembled Mary Brown very much and her name was Brown, too.

Saturday, October 15, 1898
Weather: Clear; Thermometer: 4° below
The coldest morning since my arrival in Alaska. Andrew Whirley, Rope, and Leo started for a week's hunt.

Sunday, October 16, 1898
Thermometer: 20°
We had our first snow last night. Fell about 1 inch and snowing a little now, 9:30 A.M. Have a terrible pain under right shoulder blade. Can scarcely sleep at night. Have felt it for a week. Made a gold cake (or a 5 egg cake) today.

Monday, October 17, 1898
Thermometer: 18°
Stayed alone all day. Jack went to help Mike build his cabin.
Snowed a little all day.

Tuesday, October 18, 1898
Weather: A little sun; Thermometer: 20°
Made some yeast bread, the first I ever tried to make, and it is lovely. 6:15 P.M. — Taken suddenly sick in the stomach. Feel a nauseous and sinking sensation.

Wednesday, October 19, 1898
Weather: Cloudy; Thermometer: 20°
Some of the Great Northern party came down the river with a scow. [The Great Northern party was composed of former employees of the Great Northern Railroad (see Conger's letter of March 4, 1899). During the summer of 1898 this party, headed by H.T. Smith of St. Paul, Minnesota, assisted a party of prospectors from Wisconsin, led by B.F. Millard, in establishing the "Millard trail." While some of the men cut the trail, others backpacked the provisions. In this fashion, they succeeded in building a 70-mile trail which began on the east bank of the Copper, near Copper Center, and skirted the base of Mounts Drum and Sanford while crossing the high country inside the big bend of the Copper River. The Millard trail merged with the Copper River Trail near the mouth of the Slana River.][16] Auction sale today. My eyes are getting sore. Guess it is caused from reading nights.

Thursday, October 20, 1898
Thermometer: 16°
Bright, cheerful morning. Some Indian dogs are tied up nearby and they howl like a pack of coyotes.

Friday, October 21, 1898
Thermometer: 16°

Millard Trail

Whirley, Rope, and party returned from Mt. Drum. They brought home 10 . . . [grouse].[17] Four Indians called on me. Saw a nice marten hide.

Saturday, October 22, 1898
Weather: Clear; Thermometer: 22°
Received a letter from M.J. Hessian at Valdes. He and party left on the 10th inst. aboard the *Excelsior* for Seattle. He has heard of parties who are located on Copper River and doing well.

Monday, October 24, 1898
Weather: Clear; Thermometer: 6°
Report of rich strike down on the Teikhell [Tiekel]. Uncle John

started for there this afternoon. I have ⅓ interest in a claim at Mt. Drum.

Tuesday, October 25, 1898
Thermometer: 10°
This has been a lovely day. Dr. Barrett has just returned from the Teikhell and says the outlook is good. Am reading *Emmett Bonlore,* by Opie Read.

Wednesday, October 26, 1898
Weather: Clear; Thermometer: 6° below
Corcoran went to the rapids. Whirley and I went out on a hunt. Walked 15 miles and got one grouse. Saw some awful big bear tracks in the snow.

Thursday, October 27, 1898
Weather: Snowing; Thermometer: 6°
Looks as though we are going to have sleighing soon. 7:10 P.M. — Did not snow much. Getting colder. Read *The Jucklins,* by Opie Read. It is good.

Friday, October 28, 1898
Weather: Clear; Thermometer: 0°
Did a washing and baked another one of those famous cakes of mine. Time is beginning to hang heavy upon my shoulders.

Saturday, October 29, 1898
Thermometer: 8°
This has been a beautiful day. Don't see how the weather can be so fine in this far northern country. The nights are grand. The moon seems to throw such a mellow light. Big ball tonight at Amy's Rapids.

Sunday, October 30, 1898
Weather: Clear; Thermometer: 2° below
This is the longest day of the whole seven. Am always glad when

the shades of night appear. Have just read *The Wives of the Prophet,* by Read. Oh, you destroyer of innocent souls, the day of judgement is near at hand.

Monday, October 31, 1898
Weather: Snowing; Thermometer: 4° below
Did not snow any to speak of. Corcoran returned from Amy's. Twenty men leave the lake for Valdes tomorrow. [By November of 1898, changing weather conditions began creating additional sources of peril for those attempting the crossing of Valdez Glacier. Quartermaster's agent Brown reported that on November 7, gale-force winds lifted John Bell, a guide, off the ice and carried him several yards. A week later, Mike Smith, a prospector, collapsed within a mile of the summit during a storm and subsequently froze to death. Mike Krohn, who began the ascent a day after Smith, met a similar fate after being stalled for four days at the summit in the same storm; the members of his party had sought shelter by digging a hole in the snow with their snowshoes, but the cave did not offer enough protection for Krohn, who died from the effects of exposure a week after reaching Valdez.][18]

Tuesday, November 1, 1898
Weather: Cloudy; Thermometer: 8°
Went up the Klutena 8 miles and packed down 50 lbs. flour. Ate my lunch at the "Gates of Hell," or Hell Gate. Will make another trip tomorrow if it does not snow.

Letter dated November 2, 1898, Copper Center, Alaska
My Dear Wife,
  I have been packing flour from seven miles up the Klutena to this place the past few days and at night my bones ache so that I sleep but little. Aside from that, my health is good. I have been waiting for the Klutena to freeze so that I could sled my stuff down, but it runs so swift that I do not think it will close up before January. The coldest it has been is 6° below zero. The days are

beautiful. No wind. Still and mild. There is about 3 inches of snow on the ground.

Today the mail came and brought me two letters from you, Sept. 7 and 18. Will answer them tonight. I wrote you the full particulars of Buckley's death 10 days after it occurred. I also wrote Mrs. Buckley. The Hessian boys are back by this time and she will learn all.

Lots of men are leaving here and going out, or at least as far as Valdes. A good many are waiting at Valdes for the government to send a boat to take them out, as they have no money. I hope I won't come home a pauper. Don't know who could have started the report that I was on my way back. Don't look for me till you see me. You know the time I am due to remain away. I would like to look in and see you and the children. Do so hope they will not have any more sickness.

I have got ⅓ interest in a claim near Mt. Drum but don't think it will amount to very much. I also have a claim on the Teikhell River, 100 [about 75] miles from here. Some good gold has been found there. I may move down there as soon as the Copper freezes up. Will be able to say definitely in my next letter. I hope it will prove rich enough, for it is only 30 miles from Valdes and will save that long tedious trip over the divide. [A new route to the Copper River valley via Thompson Pass was discovered about this time by the mail carrier (see chapter 7); however, the distance to the Tiekel by this route was about 50 miles.]

I suppose by the time you get this letter I will be "papa" again. Do so hope you will have no difficulty. Shall look anxiously for the November mail, and if I am on my way upriver when it is due here, will come back for it. I wrote you 3 times last month and sent the letters by parties going out. Sent one letter by Neil Hessian, but he did not leave Valdes till Oct. 10, as there was no boat in.

Now dearest, good night. Kiss the children for me and give my kind regards to all my friends.

Lovingly,

P.S. The sun rises at 8 and sets at 4.   Horace

Thursday, November 3, 1898
Thermometer: 0°
Been cold and raw all day. Party of 25 left this morning for the Teikhell.

Saturday, November 5, 1898
Weather: Clear; Thermometer: 8° below
Two of our fair damsels skipped out to the States with other men. Such is life, even in Alaska.

Monday, November 7, 1898
Weather: Cloudy; Thermometer: 8° below
The Copper is freezing over slowly and roughly. Some have commenced sledding up along the edges as far as the Taslena.

Tuesday, November 8, 1898
Weather: Hazy; Thermometer: 4° below
J.W. Anderson came down from Amy's. He says they have found some good diggings on Quartz Creek [a northwesterly flowing stream which empties into the foot of Tonsina Lake].

Wednesday, November 9, 1898
Weather: Clear; Thermometer: 6°
Uncle John returned from the Teikhell. He was lost 6 days. One auction sale and two dog fights today.

Thursday, November 10, 1898
Weather: Cloudy; Thermometer: 8°
Threatening snow all day. Tomorrow I start for the Teikhell. Have just finished reading *Quo Vadis,* a narrative of the days of Nero, by Henry K. Sienkiewicz. Nero was surely mad or he couldn't have spilled so much innocent blood.

Notes—

1. Edwin F. Glenn and W.R. Abercrombie, "Report of Capt. Abercrombie," *Reports of Explorations in the Territory of Alaska, 1898* (Washington: Gov. Printing Office, 1899), pp. 311-14; F.C. Schrader, "A Reconnaissance of a Part of Prince William Sound and the Copper River District, Alaska in 1898," *Twentieth Annual Report of the USGS 1898-99,* Part 7 (Washington: Gov. Printing Office, 1900), pp. 356, 358-59.

2. Schrader, "A Reconnaissance . . . 1898," *Twentieth Annual Report of the USGS,* pp. 359-63.

3. Schrader, "A Reconnaissance . . . 1898," *Twentieth Annual Report of the USGS,* pp. 363-65.

4. Glenn and Abercrombie, "Report of Quartermaster Agent Charles Brown," *Reports of Explorations . . . 1898,* pp. 451-53; P.H. Ray, "Alaska— 1897, Relief of the Destitute in Gold Fields," *Compilation of Narratives of Explorations in Alaska* (Washington: Gov. Printing Office, 1900), p. 499; W.R. Abercrombie, "Report of Capt. Abercrombie," *Copper River Exploring Expedition 1899* (Washington: Gov. Printing Office, 1900), p. 17.

5. Schrader, "A Reconnaissance . . . 1898," *Twentieth Annual Report of the USGS,* p. 368.

6. Glenn and Abercrombie, "Report of Lt. Guy H. Preston," *Reports of Explorations . . . 1898,* p. 407; C.H. Remington, *A Golden Cross ? on the Trails from Valdez Glacier* (Los Angeles: White-Thompson, 1939), p. 22.

7. Charles A. Margeson, *Experiences of Gold Hunters in Alaska* (Hornellsville, N.Y.: Charles Margeson, 1899), p. 172; Neil D. Benedict, "The Valdes and Copper River Trail" (unpublished manuscript in Alaska Historical Library, Juneau), 1899, pp. 159-60; Basil Austin, *The Diary of a Ninety-Eighter* (Mount Pleasant, Michigan: John Cumming, 1968), p. 66; Remington, *A Golden Cross,* pp. 52-53; "Hundreds Trying to Work Their Way Out," *San Francisco Chronicle,* Aug. 21, 1898, p. 15.

8. Donald Orth, *Dictionary of Alaska Place Names,* U.S. Geological Survey Professional Paper No. 567 (Washington: Gov. Printing Office, 1967), p. 353.

9. Orth, *Dictionary,* p. 907; Henry T. Allen, "Report of a Military Reconnaissance in Alaska, Made in 1885," *Compilation of Narratives,* p. 427.

10. Glenn and Abercrombie, "Report of Quartermaster Agent Charles Brown," *Reports of Explorations . . . 1898,* p. 452; A description of conditions on the glacier during the last week of August 1898 is provided by Benedict, "The Valdes and Copper River Trail," pp. 125-33.

11. Glenn and Abercrombie, "Report of Guide J.J. Rafferty," *Reports of Explorations . . . 1898,* pp. 449-50; The name Abercrombie Canyon, used by Allen, has been changed to Abercrombie Rapids, as there presently is no canyon there. Orth, *Dictionary,* p. 45.

12. "pheasant" in the original. See editors' comment for August 12, 1898, in preceding chapter.

13. "the hardware merchant" is from a repetitious sentence deleted from Conger's letter of September 25, 1898.

14. Conger previously referred to this location as "Williams Landing." See diary entry of June 14, 1898.

15. Charles Margeson, who left his Klutina Lake camp on October 8, 1898, to go Outside via the Copper River, mentioned an Indian boy with an accordian singing the same songs. Margeson, *Experiences of Gold Hunters,* p. 238; A year later, guide Edward Cashman found the Copper River Indians "very pleasant and sociable," and noted that they sang these songs. W.R. Abercrombie, "Report of Edward Cashman," *Copper River . . . 1899,* p. 168.

16. Benedict, "The Valdes and Copper River Trail," p. 95; Glenn and Abercrombie, "Report of Lt. P.G. Lowe," *Reports of Explorations . . . 1898,* p. 360; Oscar Rohn, "A Reconnaissance of the Chitina River and the Skolai Mountains, Alaska," *Twenty-First Annual Report of the USGS* (Washington: Gov. Printing Office, 1900), pp. 401-02.

17. "pheasants" in the original. See editors' comment for August 12, 1898, in preceding chapter.

18. Glenn and Abercrombie, "Report of Quartermaster Agent Charles Brown," *Reports of Explorations . . . 1898,* pp. 453-55.

Chapter 7—

Gold on the Tiekel?

Reports of placer prospects on Quartz Creek and the Tiekel River in the fall of 1898 led to the development of a trail from the Klutina River, near the head of the rapids, to a location on the Tiekel River about four miles above the mouth of Boulder Creek. The gold seekers followed Manker and Greyling creeks to the foot of Tonsina Lake, ascended the Quartz Creek valley to its head, and reached the Tiekel by way of a steep descent of about 2,000 feet known to prospectors as "The Drop." Upon reaching the Tiekel, some of the gold seekers descended the stream to its confluence with the Tsina and then prospected up this stream. The region over which this trail passed remained unmapped until the spring of 1899, when Captain Abercrombie returned to Valdez and started building a pack trail inland across Thompson Pass. This new entry route had been discovered by Jackson, the mail carrier, during the fall of 1898. Charged with delivering the mail to the most advanced prospecting camps, Jackson found his route from the Tsina back to Valdez by way of Valdez Glacier very circuitous, so he made several attempts to find a more direct route. A companion froze to death on one of these attempts, but Jackson persevered and succeeded in locating a return route across the divide into the Lowe River valley.[1]

Jackson's route proved practical for several groups of prospectors who ascended Keystone Canyon on the ice during the winter of 1898-99; thus Captain Abercrombie adopted it as the first leg of the military trail he was ordered to establish between Valdez and Eagle in the spring of 1899. The construction of this trail provided employment for many of the able-bodied gold seekers who had wintered in Valdez and the Copper River valley. Though trail construction advanced only as far as the summit of Thompson Pass in 1899, the surveying work was completed as far north as the Tonsina valley. Abercrombie's topographic officer, 1st. Lt. Walter C. Babcock, preceded the work crews, mapping

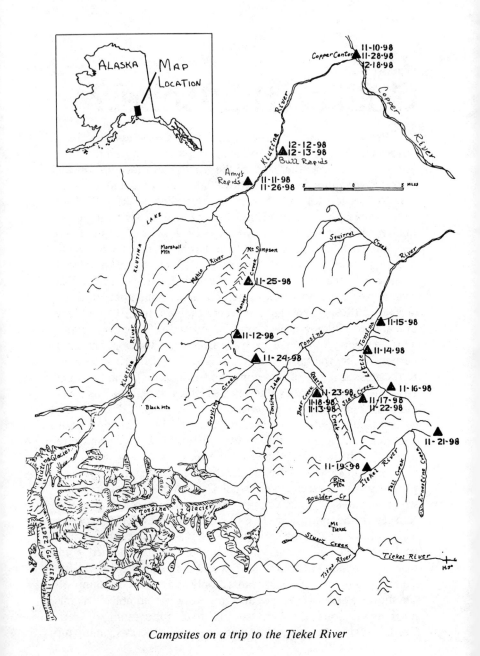

Campsites on a trip to the Tiekel River

the Tiekel, Tonsina, Little Tonsina, and Quartz Creek valleys. During the next few years, the pack trail, along with a telegraph line, was extended to Eagle, on the Yukon. After the gold strikes in the Tanana valley in 1902, a wagon road also was opened between Valdez and Fairbanks. Today's modern Richardson Highway, an outgrowth of these early road-building efforts, follows the Tiekel and Little Tonsina rivers, where Conger searched for gold in November of 1898.[2]

Friday, November 11, 1898
Left Copper Center at 6:30 A.M. Arrived at Amy's Rapids at 4 P.M. [The ice is] all broken up but must start tomorrow morning at daylight. [Go] over the mountains . . . [about 38 miles][3] to the Teikhell [Tiekel] where I expect to hit it rich. This has been a warm day, almost like spring.

Saturday, November 12, 1898
Thermometer: 34°
Left the Klutena this morning at 6:30 with 50 lb. pack. Traveled all day in a . . . [southeasterly][4] direction and camped under some pine trees. It was not very cold. Snow 6 inches deep.

Sunday, November 13, 1898
Thermometer: 30°
Left Greyling [Manker] Creek at 7 A.M. and bore east in our course. [The names of Manker and Greyling creeks, as they appear on present-day maps, were often, interchanged in 1898-99.][5] Ate dinner at Tonsena Lake. Saw about 200 king salmon which had been caught out of the lake. Saw a fine looking squaw. After dinner we crossed the lake and went up Quartz Creek 5 miles, then turned south up Bear Creek [and went] ½ mile where we camped in a log cabin. There are a good many claims here. [The following summer First Lieutenant Babcock reported finding a mining camp of 8 or 10 log cabins at the mouth of Bear Creek. He saw prospectors actively engaged in placer mining along lower Quartz Creek but judged the results of their

Southern half of Tonsina Lake, August 1899.

labor inadequate to pay for the expense of hand work. According to C.H. Remington, a prospector, the Quartz Creek mining district, formed on September 17, 1898, was not "a poor man's pick and shovel and sluicebox proposition." He reported that hydraulic mining on that stream produced only $800 of the precious yellow metal in 1900.][6]

Monday, November 14, 1898
Thermometer: 10°
Left Bear Creek at 7:30 A.M. Continued up Quartz Creek 3 miles, then went up Rainbow Gulch[7] and down Slate Creek to another stream which has no name [Little Tonsina] where we took dinner. Snow is about 8 inches deep and looks like more will fall soon. Went on down the canyon and across the valley. Camped on the side hill and found that we were lost.

Tuesday, November 15, 1898
Thermometer: 10°
Got up at 5 and found it snowing hard. We started in a N.E.
direction down the most crooked river I ever saw. Traveled all day
in a blinding snowstorm. Did not go more than 5 miles all day.
Still lost and guess we will retrace our steps before it is too late, as
our grub is limited. This is an awful rough country to pack over
and I wish I were out of it. [Making progress in the Little Tonsina
River valley was even more difficult in the summer. First Lieutenant Babcock reported that the entire valley was an immense
swamp, covered with a dense growth of six- to eight-foot willows
and patches of timber. He concluded that it would be impossible
to get a horse safely across this terrain. "I was wet from head to
foot," he stated, "and the legs of my trousers were torn off at the
knees."][8]

Wednesday, November 16, 1898
Thermometer: 6°
Retraced our steps made yesterday but have not found the canyon
we came down, so are still lost. Traveling in a S.E. direction. It
cleared up today. Snow now 1 foot deep. Sky clear tonight. Cold.
Sleep with all clothes on except boots. Wet every night from
perspiration and snow.

Thursday, November 17, 1898
Weather: Clear; Thermometer: 4°
Got up at one o'clock in the morning. Too cold. Could not sleep.
Started out at 7:30 in a S.E. direction but after going two miles,
found that we were not on our course, so returned to where we
camped last night and took dinner. After dinner we went . . .
[N.W.][9] and came into our lost canyon [Slate Creek] at 2 P.M.

Friday, November 18, 1898
Weather: Clear; Thermometer: 3°
Very cold last night but slept warm. Went back to Bear Creek
where we started from 5 days ago. We all feel quite happy to get

into a cabin once more. I am going back to look for the Teikhell tomorrow. The balance of the party are going on to Amy's Rapids.

Saturday, November 19, 1898
Weather: Clear; Thermometer: 18° below
Left Bear Creek this morning at 7 A.M. with Wm. Gardner and went south by east over a high divide [at the head of Quartz Creek]. Snow up to my waist and crusted just enough to let you break through. Traveled all day and reached the Teikhell at 4:30 P.M. nearly froze to death. This is a fine valley and looks favorable for gold.

Sunday, November 20, 1898
Weather: Clear; Thermometer: 28° below
Went down the Teikhell 7 miles and staked claim No. 9 below Boulder Creek. The claim is on the east side of the bank. Saw seven men who were locating claims. Did not get back to camp till late at night. Had a bright moon though. Located claim No. 8 for Jack Corcoran. Claim 600 feet in N.E. direction, thence 1,500 feet in S.E. direction, thence 600 [feet in] S.W. direction to bank of the river, thence northerly 1,500 feet to place of beginning. [First Lieutenant Babcock found the stakes of numerous placer claims along the north fork of the Tiekel and some of its branches the following summer. Most of the claims appeared to be abandoned; however, he noted that claims were still being worked on two of the Tiekel's largest branches, Fall and Ernestine creeks, where gold had been reported in paying quantities.][10]

Monday, November 21, 1898
Weather: Clear; Thermometer: 30° below
Located placer claim "Clifford," No. 37, and followed the [Tiekel] river to its head. Had to stop twice and thaw out my feet. Traveled 20 [probably about 10] miles and camped in a spruce swamp where there was plenty of dry wood. Burned about 3 cords during the night. It was so cold, had to sit around the fire with

blankets over shoulders, Indian fashion. [A low ridge separates the headwaters of the Tiekel from the Little Tonsina. Both streams rise in swampy terrain near the old mining locality of Ernestine. Babcock reported that this region was "thickly overgrown with dwarf willow and sparsely timbered with small but tall spruce trees."][11]

Tuesday, November 22, 1898
Weather: Clear; Thermometer: 31° below
Bitter cold all day. Got into a 5 mile patch of brush that was so thick that we had to cut our way. Tore my pants nearly off, also big holes in my boots. Struck an old Indian trail which led us into a canyon [Slate Creek] where we camped 5 days previous.

Wednesday, November 23, 1898
Weather: Cloudy; Thermometer: 32° below
Left our cold and dreary camp at 8 A.M. Arrived at Bear Creek at . . . [noon][12] where we found 3 fish, one of which we boiled and transferred to our stomachs, which were getting quite empty. Saw 6 men with sleds who had just arrived from Amy's Rapids. What a gloomy and desolate country this is. So still and cold. Not a breath of air. Tonight we are in caribou cabin.

Thursday, November 24, 1898
Thermometer: 2° below
Did not get up very early this morning on account of sleeping in a cabin. However, we started down the [Quartz Creek] canyon to Tonsena Lake in a blinding snowstorm. Found an Indian house there and bought two salmon. Got one of the squaws to mend my mittens. She used sinew for thread. One little girl was sick abed from eating fish. [A small band of Copper River Indians, headed by Chief Stickwan (or Stephan), inhabited this region. Their district encompassed the territory between the Klutina and Copper rivers south of Copper Center and adjoined Chief Nicolai's district near the mouth of the Chitina. These Natives occupied "stick" houses along the rivers, where they spent the

Family and house of "Stick" Natives above Taral on the Copper River, 1898.

summers catching and drying salmon. In the fall they departed to hunt and trap but returned to their houses when the snow became too deep for travel.[13] White men described these people as extremely honest and hospitable. "They would come out 3 or 4 miles to meet us and invite us into their houses, where they would share their food with us," wrote Edward Cashman, a guide with Abercrombie's 1899 expedition. "If our mittens or moccasins were torn they would take them from us and repair them." One night Cashman pointed out a rip in the pants of one member of his party to a "Klutch woman," or squaw. "She wanted him to take them off so that she could fix them," said Cashman, "but he was bashful and would not do so. Before he realized it, two Klutchers caught him by the arms and held him, while one pulled off his pants. He yelled at me to help him, but it was such a funny sight I could do nothing but laugh. The Klutcher fixed his pants in good shape," reported Cashman, "and was well pleased when I presented her with three old, red handkerchiefs."[14] Sinew from the legs and back of caribou was a main source of sewing thread among the northern Athabascan Indians. The universal sewing implement was the awl, made of bone from a variety of animals and sometimes from copper. The eyed sewing needle was practically unknown among these Natives prior to their contact with whites, though it was widely distributed among the Eskimo.[15]] Continued our journey up Manker [present-day Greyling] Creek but the snow was so deep we could travel but a little ways. Finally camped overnight under some spruce trees. Gardner froze his feet. A happy birthday, dear wife.

Friday, November 25, 1898
Weather: Snowing; Thermometer: 6°
Started for the Klutena in the morning but the trail was obliterated and we could find our way [only] with difficulty. Gardner broke through the ice and got wet to the waist. Was afraid that he would freeze to death before timber was reached, but we finally reached Moose Camp[16] where A.S. McDowell was camped, who fed us and gave us the best of care under the circumstances. Only for this gentleman, we would have suffered untold misery. How hard it is to suffer with cold and hunger.

Saturday, November 26, 1898
Weather: Clear; Thermometer: 6° below
Got a sled from McDowell and loaded our packs on and I pulled it down to the Klutena where we took dinner with our friend. After dinner, continued down the Klutena to Amy's Rapids where I stayed with Anderson and Co.

Sunday, November 27, 1898
Weather: Clear; Thermometer: 16° below
Went back up Greyling [present-day Manker] Creek to Moose Camp to get my claim on the Teikhell recorded. It was bitter cold all day. A good many are sledding over to Quartz Creek and Teikhell.

Monday, November 28, 1898
Weather: Cloudy; Thermometer: 26° below

Left Amy's Rapids at 8:30 A.M. and walked down to Copper Center. Did not get there till after dark. The day is only 6 hours long now, and one has to get started by daylight if he intends to go any distance.

Tuesday, November 29, 1898
Weather: Cloudy; Thermometer: 0°
Have been making a sleeping bag and putting some "gee" poles in my sleds [for steering purposes] preparatory to going up to the rapids and hauling the balance of my stuff down here, when I will go on up the Copper. The ice in the Copper is jammed here for ten miles. When the floe started, it made a noise like a snowslide. It threw boats clear up on the beach and some were crushed. Ice is piled up ten feet high.

Wednesday, November 30, 1898
Weather: Cloudy; Thermometer: 4°
Frosty all day but not cold. An auction today. The man has the scurvy and is going out. Miners going in all directions — some over to the Teikhell, some to 40 Mile, some to head of the Copper, and others down to the Chitana [Chitina]. No one has a sure thing. My legs ache terribly tonight. Think I have got rheumatism. [Joint and muscle pain are early symptoms of scurvy. See editors' comment in diary entry of April 4, 1898.]

Thursday, December 1, 1898
Weather: Cloudy; Thermometer: 4°
Did a washing today. The air looks full of snow. Bought an ounce of salicylic acid for which I paid 50¢. Have commenced doping myself for rheumatism. Learned today that it is almost impossible to sled up the Copper now owing to the ice gorge.

Friday, December 2, 1898
Weather: Cloudy; Thermometer: 4° below
The air still seems full of snow, yet none of it falls to earth. Charley Cy Wash, an Indian, was in the cabin. Had lots of fun

with him. He could talk English fairly well. ["Si-wash" was the Chinook Jargon term for "Indian." Traders sometimes bestowed white men's names upon Indians who visited their trading posts. As Native contact with whites increased, the abundance of "Johns," "Sams," Billies," etc., necessitated further geographic appellation such as "Tazlina John," or "Gakona Charlie."][17]

Saturday, December 3, 1898
Weather: Clear; Thermometer: 14° below
Cold, raw day. Walker and Bell left at noon for head of rapids. They are going over to the Teikhell. Just finished reading *Won By Waiting,* by (Lyall).[18] Too many tears in it to suit my taste.

Sunday, December 4, 1898
Weather: Clear; Thermometer: 8° below
Some parties returned from the Teikhell today. I was up to Flynn's visiting and returned books which I had borrowed. This day has not seemed like Sunday. The poker joint ran all last night. They caught some suckers down from the rapids. [Prospector Luther Guiteau identified the site of the poker joint as "Ed Melby's log cabin, which is nothing but a saloon, and a place to play poker."][19] A good many mules and horses are freezing to death. Don't think they have the proper food.

Monday, December 5, 1898
Weather: Clear; Thermometer: 20°
Intended to go to the rapids today, but hearing that the mail would be here today or tomorrow, concluded to wait. How awful short the days are now. Here it is 3 P.M. and dark.

Tuesday, December 6, 1898
Thermometer: 30°
Got up this morning at 5. Read till 6 and then got breakfast, and here it is 7:30 and dark as the shades of night. Snowed hard all day. About 10 inches fell. About 5 P.M. it started to rain and rained hard for 3 hours. Anderson came down the Klutena and said lots

of goods were scattered along the bank. They will all get wet, for no one expected this kind of weather.

Wednesday, December 7, 1898
Thermometer: 38°
It rained during the night and the water found its way through the roof of our cabin. A warm wind is blowing from the S.E. this morning. Two men froze to death while crossing the glacier last week. Five more tried to cross but had to give it up.

Thursday, December 8, 1898
Weather: Cloudy; Thermometer: 14°
Walked up the Klutena a mile to see how the trail was. Met some men coming down and they said the water was a foot deep over the ice, so that ends my sledding till it freezes over. Called on Mrs. Flynn and borrowed some more books. Can't move up Copper on account of water flooding the ice.

Friday, December 9, 1898
Weather: Clear; Thermometer: 4°
As the sun rises it shines with a mellow light like the spring of the year. Two Indians were here from Big Stone. They say "Hi low muc-muc" there, meaning that they have no food and are in a starving condition.

Saturday, December 10, 1898
Thermometer: 20°
Bert Carvey got bit by a dog in the fleshy part of the leg. It is quite a bad wound. Snowing hard.

Sunday, December 11, 1898
Thermometer: 14°
Has been snowing all day. Been reading *Titus: A Comrade of the Cross* [by Florence Kingsley]. It is a beautiful story. Am about out of grub here, so intend to start for head of rapids tomorrow.

Bull Rapids

Monday, December 12, 1898

Left the Center this morning at 7 o'clock with two sleds loaded with blankets, tent, stove, and some grub. Camped at Bull Rapids, where I will sled my plunder to from Amy's as the first relay. Cloudy all day but not very cold.

Tuesday, December 13, 1898

Left camp at 6:30 A.M., but it was so dark we had to go slowly for fear of falling into some air hole. Reached the cache at 10:30 and took everything out of boxes and put them into sacks to save extra weight. We loaded our sleds with 350 lbs. each and started [out] after eating our frugal dinner. Did not travel more than 2 miles before we unloaded part [of our goods], then went on till dark and 4 miles from camp, [where] we left two sleds and the three of us doubled onto one sled and reached camp at 6 nearly dead.

Wednesday, December 14, 1898
Weather: Cloudy
Went back for loads left yesterday. Got into camp before noon. Hauled up some wood in the afternoon. Been very warm all day. Almost a rain. Foggy most of the time. Dear me, how a man sweats in this country. Nearly everything I have on is wet when night comes if I have been working.

Friday, December 16, 1898
Weather: Cloudy
Corcoran and Whirley went to Amy's for our last two loads while I took a load down the river 8 miles. The sleighing is much better from here down. Can't understand why so much warm weather.

Saturday, December 17, 1898
Weather: Clear
This has been a nice day. We took 400 lbs. each down the river to where I went yesterday. Saw two ravens flying by. Guess they were going to a warmer climate.

Sunday, December 18, 1898
Weather: Clear
In the cabin at Copper Center tonight. Hauled 350 lbs. 16 miles and will have two more loads to haul, when I will have all of my stuff down here. Quite cold last night, though warm today. Sold two sleds for $1 each.

Monday, December 19, 1898
Weather: Cloudy
Made a trip upriver for more goods. Got back here at 12 . . . [noon].[20] Remarked all of my sacks and got some poles to make a portable bunk in the afternoon. Also repaired my snowshoes and put an ice plate on the heels of my boots.

Tuesday, December 20, 1898
Weather: Cloudy; Thermometer: 8° below

Started up the Klutena this morning to bring down the remainder of my grub but did not go far before I met the water coming over the ice with a rush. Had to turn back. It may be a week before I can get up but will try it by the land trail tomorrow, for I am afraid my goods will be under water if I wait too long.

Wednesday, December 21, 1898
Weather: Clear; Thermometer: 18° below
Went after the remainder of our plunder and such a time as we had. Found the river broke over the ice in two places. Had to pack our stuff a quarter of a mile through the timber and snow two feet deep. Did not have any dinner and got very weak about 3 o'clock, when we left our loads a mile from the Center. Will go back for them in the morning. It is 16° below zero [at] 8:30 P.M. and a cold, bright moon in view.

Thursday, December 22, 1898
Thermometer: 8°
Snowed most all day but tonight the moon seems to shine brighter than ever. Have finally got all of my stuff here and expect to move on up the Copper Monday if the weather will permit. Have been packing the clothing I am going to take with me. Will leave a good deal of it here, as I expect to come back this way next fall.

Friday, December 23, 1898
Weather: Cloudy; Thermometer: 2°
Did not get up this morning till 7, as I had nothing pressing and was in no rush. Traded 25 lbs. of tea for 25 lbs. coffee and sold 25 lbs. tea for $2.50. Did a whole lot of mending and packed up some boxes with provisions to take up country. Traded off two 10 x 12 tents for one 12 x 14, as I will have more room for my heater. Suppose most people in the States are busying themselves selecting their Xmas presents. It won't trouble me very much.

Saturday, December 24, 1898
Weather: Cloudy; Thermometer: 2°

Fixed up my sled and did some washing. Bought a loaf of honey bread for Christmas. [By August of 1898, Copper Center was boasting several "businesses," including a bakery operated by a husband and wife, a hotel, and a couple of restaurants.][21] Saw some parties who had come from Valdes and they report no mail there since October and probably won't be any in until March 1st. Seven Tanana Indians[22] came down from Mantaska [Mentasta] Lake with furs.

Sunday, December 25, 1898
Thermometer: 14°
This is the finest Christmas morning I ever beheld. Soft, beautiful day. So still and quiet. Had pancakes and maple syrup for breakfast. For dinner I have made a cake and some pies.

Monday, December 26, 1898
Thermometer: 2°
Still, mild day. Cut one end off a large trunk and converted it into a grub box. It was no small job either. Expect to start up Copper tomorrow. There are quite a good many sick about here. Some are almost helpless with rheumatism. [Leroy J. Townsend, a physician in the Copper River valley in 1898-99, reported that the "most astonishing errors" were made in identifying the scorbutic symptoms prevailing at that time. "Nor were these errors made by the layman alone, but by presumably reputable physicians," he said. "For instance, one case that came to my notice had been diagnosed and treated as gangrene of the feet and legs, thought to have been produced by too tightly constricting the parts with cords used in tying gunny sacks over the feet and limbs. The marked extravasations were responsible for this mistake. The patient died. Again, another individual who had been unfortunate enough to have his toes frozen had the same cause placed on these offending members in explanation of scorbutic symptoms, which subsequently developed. Another individual, in which the disease was just beginning to manifest itself, was told that the pain and stiffness in his leg were due to a sprain, and the slightest swelling

Hotel and post office, Copper Center.

and discoloration of the gums were the result of 'frosting' them.''
The general opinion, as expressed by several physicians in the
Copper River region, was that the condition affecting the
prospectors was rheumatic.][23]

Tuesday, December 27, 1898
Weather: Cloudy; Thermometer: 22° below
Arose this morning at 5:30 and left with 250 lbs. on my sleigh for
up Copper River. Went 5 miles and repeated the trip in the afternoon. Saw two Indians from Cooks Inlet. They report it dead
there.

Wednesday, December 28, 1898
Weather: Clear; Thermometer: 24° below
Worked all day but it was very cold (still cold). Nearly froze my
hands coming home tonight. Dreamed that Lila fell through a
hole in the floor of a building. It did not kill her but broke both

legs. I hollered out in my sleep and woke myself up. Auction sale today. Coffee 4¢, flour $12.50. Someone selling out nearly every day. Saw an Indian with a diamond ring on his finger. [Lieutenant Allen reported that bracelets and finger rings were almost unknown among the Copper River Indians in 1885.][24]

Thursday, December 29, 1898
Weather: Clear; Thermometer: 42° below
This has been the coldest day of the season. I started upriver this morning with a small load. Froze the end of my nose before I got back. We are all ready to pull up stakes and move camp. Intended to move tomorrow, but if it continues to be below [minus] 40 degrees, will remain where we are. It is too cold to tent out.

Friday, December 30, 1898
Weather: Clear; Thermometer: 46° below
This has been one of those days you read about. Too cold for comfort. Some tea was sold today for 1¢ per pound. Coffee 4¢, flour $11. Have got a bad cold on my lungs. Mercury has been congealed all day. [Temperatures below the freezing point of mercury, -38.8° F, could be determined from a large "spirit" or alcohol thermometer at the mail relay station at Copper Center.][25]

Saturday, December 31, 1898
Weather: Clear; Thermometer: 47° below
This is the last page of '98. I hope the coming year will be more prosperous to me than the past has been. Can't say as I have accomplished a thing since Feb. 15th. Have hauled what food I have eaten since then over 2,000 miles with sled and boat. Fought mosquitoes and battled against the coldest kind of weather. Have named this book one of "Great Expectations," but the last page will be filled and the book closed without one of my fond hopes being realized. Been quiet all day. Lungs very sore.

[On the first page of his diary for 1899, Conger has written the title, "Book of Short Comings and Long Goings."]

Sunday, January 1, 1899
Thermometer: 40° below
Bright sunshine all day. Shooting of guns and blowing of horns
last night. Heard "Home Sweet Home" played on the cornet. It
sounded lonely as the sounds stole out on the midnight air. Had
oatmeal pancakes and maple syrup for breakfast. Moose meat for
dinner.

Letter dated January 1, 1899, Copper Center, Alaska
My Dear Lizzie,

I presume you have not had a letter from me for nearly five
months. Some of the letters I sent out in September and October
were lost, as the parties [taking them out] lost everything they
had, and some, their lives. October mail is still in Valdes waiting
for a boat to come, which will not be earlier than Feb. 15th. We
are completely cut off from communications with the outside
world. Have plenty to eat, but it is very cold. Mercury has been
congealed for a week. Last night it was 58° below.

I have been hauling my goods up Copper River and have got
everything up five miles except tent and cooking outfit. Have been
waiting a few days, thinking the weather would moderate, but
guess it will continue [cold] throughout this month. Will break
camp Monday, Jan. 2nd, at all hazards. You will probably
wonder where I am going, as I went up the Copper over a hundred
miles last summer. Well, I am going still farther up, to the headwaters if I can get there. If not, [will go] to 40 Mile of Golofin
[Golovnin] Bay, 60 miles north of St. Michaels.

There has been some excitement over on the Teikhell River, a
western tributary of the Copper. About 100 men are sledding their
provisions over there now. I was in there 18 days during the
month of November and located the "Clifford," which is claim
No. 9 below Bowlder Creek. Had the claim recorded, which holds
good until Jan. 1, 1900. In the meantime, I will go on up the
Copper, and if anything is found there, I will have two chances. If
not, will come back this way in the fall, and if nothing has been
developed on the Teikhell, will go to the States. If I should strike

it in the north, I may not come back this way at all, for I am not stuck on boating on the Copper.

While I was on the Teikhell, the mercury showed 38° below and I had to camp out without any tent. Two nights I sat around the fire (and no small one either) with two pairs of blankets around my shoulders. Too cold to sleep. Thank God there was plenty of wood. Was lost three days in a snowstorm. The last two days I lived on dried salmon which I bought from the Indians. Don't know as there is much gold on the Teikhell or not. I saw a few nice colors, and a good many men are confident it is there in large quantities. If they should find good diggings there, it will be quite handy, as it is only 30 [50] miles from Valdes. Men are going in all directions from here —down to the Chittana, up to 40 Mile, over to Mt. Drum, and to Cooks Inlet. It certainly has been a dead letter so far. Nothing but the hardest kind of hard work and exposure.

Wish I could send you my diary for '98, but am afraid it might get lost. This letter will not leave here before the middle of February and you will not get it until the last of March. I write now, for I will not have a chance to send any mail out till sometime in the summer, if then. I think my mail will follow me up country as soon as it comes. The last letters I got [arrived on] Nov. 2nd. They were those written in September.

A good many have died here and on the glacier this winter. Those on the glacier were frozen to death. It was reported that 3 men had perished (froze) on the Teikhell but I doubt that, unless they got out of grub.

Where we built our boats last summer, the snow is now 12 feet deep. It has been very nice weather up to the present time. Christmas day was lovely, warm and still. Would not have believed that it could be so mild and pleasant had I not been here to see for myself. The changes come very suddenly. I call this a dead country, for you can stop still while walking in the woods and listen and not hear a sound, only the beating of your heart. That, I have heard a number of times. Everything seems so quiet. Not a leaf moves, not a bird chirrups, nor any sound to break the monotony. They say the wind blows hard here. Well, if it does, it must commence soon, for I will soon have one year passed here and there has not been wind enough to furl a flag half the time.

My health has been quite good so far, and my appetite better. A loaf of your brown bread with the beans and other dishes would just make me one square meal now. Ain't you glad you don't have to cook for such a gormandizer? I hope, dear, this letter will find you and the children well and not in want. I am awfully anxious to get my mail.

I have got an awful cute little puppy dog. He is as black as the shades of night, but a rascal, for he carries off my shoes and socks during the night. Would like to bring him home with me, but guess the expense would be more than I can stand unless, unless------.

Kind regards to all who may inquire about me. Kiss the dear ones for their papa and tell them to mind mama. Love and health to you, my dear wife, and may the blessings of God be with you.

Lovingly,
Horace

Notes—

1. W.R. Abercrombie, "Report of 1st Lt. W. Babcock," and "Report of Oscar Rohn," *Copper River Exploring Expedition 1899* (Washington: Gov. Printing Office, 1900), pp. 68-75, 89; Oscar Rohn, "A Reconnaissance of the Chitina River and the Skolai Mountains, Alaska," *Twenty-First Annual Report of the USGS,* Part 2 (Washington: Gov. Printing Office, 1900), pp. 402-03, 405. Rohn refers to the mail carrier here as "Johnson," but many other sources indicate his name was "Jackson."

2. Abercrombie, "Report of Capt. W.R. Abercrombie," and "Report of 1st. Lt. Babcock," *Copper River . . . 1899,* pp. 21, 26, 65, 68-75; Alfred H. Brooks, *Blazing Alaska's Trails,* 2d ed. (1953; rpt. Fairbanks: Univ. of Alaska Press, 1973), pp. 425-26.

3. "75 miles" in the original. Because this area had not been mapped, distances were estimated by those previously traveling the route.

4. "northeasterly" in the original. For reasons unknown to the editors, Conger's compass directions are sometimes erroneous. The magnetic declination for this location was approximately 30° E. in 1895; thus, an uncorrected compass would not account for the variance.

5. See Abercrombie, "Reports of Abercrombie, Babcock, and Quartermaster's Clerk John F. Rice," *Copper River . . . 1899*, pp. 19, 71-72, 96; E.F. Glenn and W.R. Abercrombie, "Report of Quartermaster Agent Charles Brown," *Reports of Explorations in the Territory of Alaska, 1898* (Washington: Gov. Printing Office, 1899), p. 453; C.H. Remington, *A Golden Cross ? On Trails From the Valdez Glacier* (Los Angeles: White-Thompson, 1939), pp. 41, 75; An exception was F.C. Schrader, who used the present-day name of "Manker" for the stream emptying into the Klutina. 'See "A Reconnaissance of a Part of Prince William Sound and the Copper River District, Alaska, in 1898," *Twentieth Annual Report of the USGS,* Part 7 (Washington: Gov. Printing Office, 1900), p. 392 and map No. 20.

6. Abercrombie, "Report of 1st. Lt. Babcock," *Copper River . . . 1899,* p. 71; Remington, *A Golden Cross,* pp. 59, 152.

7. A confluence of Quartz and Rainbow creeks is not indicated on present-day USGS maps; however, 1st. Lt. Babcock reported that Rainbow Creek was a main branch of Quartz Creek, emptying into the latter stream from the N.E. about five miles above its mouth. Abercrombie, "Report of 1st Lt. Babcock," *Copper River . . . 1899*, pp. 70, 73.

8. Abercrombie, "Report of 1st. Lt. Babcock," *Copper River . . . 1899,* p. 75.

9. "N.E." has been deleted. Since they had been traveling in a S.E. direction up the Little Tonsina River and had bypassed the mouth of Slate Creek, backtracking to Slate Creek would have necessitated traveling in a N.W. direction.

10. Abercrombie, "Report of 1st. Lt. Babcock," *Copper River . . . 1899,* pp. 70, 74.

11. Abercrombie, "Report of 1st. Lt. Babcock," *Copper River . . . 1899,* p. 75.

12. The letter "M" has been deleted. This abbreviation signifies "meridian," an obsolete usage meaning "noon."

13. Glenn and Abercrombie, "Report of Capt. W.R. Abercrombie," *Reports of Explorations . . . 1898,* p. 328; Remington, *A Golden Cross,* p. 76; Rohn, "A Reconnaissance of the Chitina River . . . Alaska," *Twenty-First Annual Report of the USGS,* p. 415.

14. Abercrombie, "Report of Edward Cashman," *Copper River . . . 1899,* p. 168; also see Glenn and Abercrombie, "Report of Guide J.J. Rafferty," *Reports of Explorations . . . 1898,* p. 444.

15. Basil Austin, *The Diary of a Ninety-Eighter* (Mount Pleasant, Michigan: John Cumming, 1968), p. 98; Cornelius Osgood, *The Ethnography of the Tanaina,* Yale Publications in Anthropology, No. 16 (1937; rpt. New Haven: Human Relations Area Files Press, 1966), pp. 78, 103; Robert A. McKennan, *The Upper Tanana Indians,* in Yale Univ. Publications in Anthropology, No. 55, ed. Irving Rouse (New Haven: Dept. of Anthropology, 1959), pp. 47, 67.

16. Moose Camp was located 10 miles above the mouth of the Greyling

(present-day Manker). It consisted of a lean-to of poles covered with spruce and fir boughs. Remington, *A Golden Cross,* p. 75; Another "Moose Camp" was located on the Klutina River, 10 miles above its mouth. See Marcus Baker, *Geographic Dictionary of Alaska,* 2d ed. (Washington: Gov. Printing Office, 1906); and Remington, *A Golden Cross,* pp. 84-85.

17. Frederic R. Marvin, *The Yukon Overland: The Gold-Digger's Handbook* (Cincinnati: Editor Publishing, 1898), p. 157; McKennan, *The Upper Tanana Indians,* pp. 26, 28, 142.

18. Edna Lyall was the pen name of Ada Ellen Bayly.

19. "Alaska Gold Rush Diary," serialized 1928 in Freeport, Illinois *Journal-Standard* (manuscript available in Alaska Historical Library, Juneau), diary entry of Sept. 2, 1898.

20. See footnote number 12.

21. Austin, *The Diary of A Ninety-Eighter,* p. 65; Guiteau, "Alaska Gold Rush Diary," diary entries of July 31 and Aug. 22, 1898; Shad Reid (unpublished manuscript in Alaska Historical Library, Juneau), diary entry of July 30, 1898.

22. The Natives living in the vicinity of Mentasta Lake were Copper River Indians. See McKennan, *The Upper Tanana Indians,* pp. 16, 21-22; Glenn and Abercrombie, "Report of Capt. Abercrombie," *Reports of Explorations . . . 1898,* p. 328.

23. Abercrombie, "Report of Leroy J. Townsend, M.D., on Scorbutus, or Scurvy," *Copper River . . . 1899,* p. 45.

24. Henry T. Allen, "Report of a Military Reconnaissance in Alaska, Made in 1885," *Compilation of Narratives of Explorations in Alaska* (Washington: Gov. Printing Office, 1900), p. 473.

25. Remington, *A Golden Cross,* p. 97.

Chapter 8—

Mushing up the Copper River

Though a few cases of scurvy were recognized in the Copper River valley in 1898, an epidemic was not apparent until early 1899, when symptoms of the disease became well developed. By that time, many of the afflicted prospectors had taken to the trail, unaware of the true cause of their increasing disabilities. As their condition worsened, many turned back toward Copper Center, the interior starting point. A few, unable to assist themselves, had to be hauled back, causing much suffering and inconvenience.[1]

On February 3, 1899, Dr. Leroy J. Townsend, who was performing the duties of attending physician at an improvised hospital at Copper Center, sent the following appeal to the quartermaster's agent at Valdez:

Dear Sir:

I beg to report to you herewith the serious condition which prevails in this camp. Scurvy has developed to an alarming extent. Two deaths have occurred and the hospital, which it was necessary to establish, is now full, and still throughout the camp are many who should be admitted. Up the Copper River the condition, I understand, is equally serious. Many are wholly without means and dependent upon others for nursing, medical attention, etc. We are in need, too, of some medicines, and of any fresh fruit or vegetables which may be had at Valdez. Two have volunteered their services to bring in these supplies and are now on their way to Valdez. Several men are suffering with frozen feet, and amputations in a number of cases will, no doubt, be necessary. If it be within your power to give any assistance, I would respectfully ask your immediate consideration.[2]

At Valdez, the quartermaster's agent, Charles Brown, was unable to comply with Dr. Townsend's request for medicines, having none on hand, even for his own use. The most he could furnish was some green potatoes and sauerkraut, and these meager supplies were taken into the interior by volunteers who succeeded in their endeavor only after being foiled in three attempts to cross the storm-ridden glacier. By early April, over 300 cases of scurvy had been reported and further assistance was not available until Captain Abercrombie returned to Valdez in late April aboard the steamer *Excelsior* with antiscorbutics and fresh food.[3]

The army commander began relief operations immediately after his arrival, sending parties with dog teams and supplies over the glaring ice of the glacier to bring out the helpless and establishing a log cabin hospital in Valdez. "That [the prospectors] had passed a terrible winter," said Abercrombie, "was beyond all question of doubt; that many of them had died from scurvy and being frozen to death was in evidence at the little graveyard that had sprung up since my departure the year before." Because of their long hair and beards, Abercrombie had difficulty recognizing many of the men he had come to know the previous year. They were a "motley looking crowd," he said, dressed in "mackinaw suits of all varieties and colors, faded and worn by exposure to the elements and their long journey over Valdez Glacier."[4]

Abercrombie ordered his quartermaster's clerk to set up relief stations at Amy's Rapids and at Copper Center, where he detailed enlisted men "to extend relief and encouragement to the demoralized and destitute prospectors." He reported that the army provided aid to 480 persons in Valdez and the Copper River Valley. Yet, Charles Remington, a prospector, depicted the army men as less than generous. He wrote that those in charge of the relief stations refused rations to starving prospectors, claiming they had orders to hang onto the provisions. He also reported a trailside encounter with an army party which was carrying fresh provisions: the army men boldly requested some sheep meat from the scorbutic prospectors in Remington's party without offering any fresh food to them in return.[5]

Conger did not witness the tragic developments in the heart of the Copper River valley in early 1899, for he started mushing up the Copper on January 2. On this leg of his journey he traveled beyond the range of Lieutenant Allen's explorations, reaching the head of the Copper River, on the north side of the Wrangell Mountains, by the end of March.

Monday, January 2, 1899
Thermometer: 34° below
Left Copper Center at 10 A.M. with camp outfit. Went one mile above the Taslena [Tazlina] and pitched our tent. Had a cold, hard job cutting hole in tent for heater, but she is humming now and warms the interior nicely. A few are camped here on their way upriver. An Indian was just in the tent who did not know what "Hello" meant. He is the first one.

Tuesday, January 3, 1899
Hauled the sled, loaded, all day. Did not reach camp till after dark. Then had to rustle wood. Oh, this is a picnic, this gold hunting on the Copper.

Wednesday, January 4, 1899
I got up at 4 this morning, made the fire, and prepared breakfast. Started for our loads at 6:15. Got back for dinner at 11. Hauled another load in the afternoon. Froze my nose badly. Saw icebergs coming down the river. They took everything before them. They were large cakes, 4 rods [66 feet] square.

Thursday, January 5, 1899
I hauled three hundred lbs. upriver in the forenoon. Corcoran and Whirley went downriver to first cache for the two last loads. We did not work in the afternoon. Cut wood. The Copper is open for about one mile above here and it roars, same as usual. The trail is good.

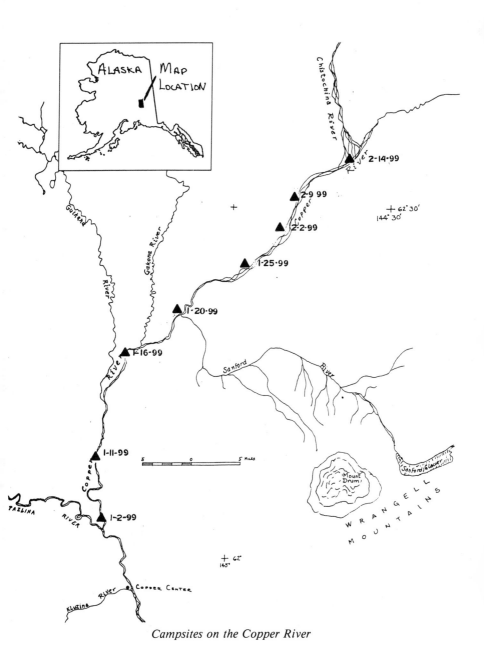

Campsites on the Copper River

Friday, January 6, 1899
Thermometer: 4° below
Made one trip upriver today. Snowed three inches during the night and made the trail very bad. My neck aches (that is, the back part of it does) like rheumatism, caused from pulling so hard in a stooped position.

Saturday, January 7, 1899
Weather: Much warmer and more snow; Thermometer: 6°
Made a full trip in the forenoon and half one in the afternoon. The sledding was bad through the fresh snow. Saw a man with four dogs hitched up two abreast. He had on a thousand lbs. Dogs (good ones) are the animals for this country. Saw a man with a quarter of moose meat on his sled. Wish I had a piece.

Sunday, January 8, 1899
Thermometer: 10° below
Did not get up very early as this is the Sabbath. Had oatmeal pancakes for breakfast and eggs for dinner. Read Christ's Sermon on the Mount. The other boys darned their socks and mended their shoes.

Monday, January 9, 1899
Thermometer: 4° below
This has been some such a day as one sees in Minnesota. Wind blew the snow into the trail as soon as a sled passed over. It was so rough in the afternoon, we did but little. We are all ready to move camp tomorrow if the wind does not blow.

Tuesday, January 10, 1899
Thermometer: 4° below
Did not go out today. Too windy and the trail filled full. Some Indians came down from the Chistochina. Among them was one I saw last summer while on that stream, who came near being drowned, only for me. He knew me at once.

Wednesday, January 11, 1899
Thermometer: 35°
This is camp Jan. 11th, about 8 miles above where we camped last. The first 3 miles was badly drifted, but from there on it was a sheet of glare ice. One can pull 5 or 6 hundred lbs. Two men froze their feet and they have gone back to the Center.

Thursday, January 12, 1899
Weather: Clear and very cold
Went downriver 3 miles and hauled up loads to camp. In the afternoon Whirley and I took 2 loads upriver 5 miles, opposite the Cocona [Gulkana] River. Corcoran stayed in camp and cut wood. Met two men hauling their loads back to Copper Center. One had a frozen toe and the feet of the other one were growing cold. [In the parlance of the trail, a man who turned back was said to be suffering from "cold feet." See Conger's letter of Oct. 4, 1898.]

Friday, January 13, 1899
Made our usual trip. Saw one place where I could see the water rushing 4 feet beneath the ice. The ice is very clear in places and from four to ten feet thick. Dreamed last night that I owned a large and beautiful farm, well stocked. Am very tired tonight.

Saturday, January 14, 1899
Hauled everything up to the Cocona [Gulkana] except camp outfit, and that we will move Monday. It snowed about a quarter of an inch in the afternoon and it seemed like so much sand beneath your sled. On top of clear ice, where the ice was rough, it was not so bad.

Sunday, January 15, 1899
Weather: Clear and still
This being the Sabbath, we did not work but went to church, that is, read a part of the book of St. Matthew. Saw a good many sledding by. The boys fixed up their creepers and went out on the ice to try them.

Monday, January 16, 1899

Camp Jan. 16th, about two miles from the Gacona [Gakona] and near where Buckley was drowned. Indian Charley took dinner with us. He was armed for eating "muc-muc," as he had two spoons in his pocket. He lost his "chew" after he left our camp and came back to look for it.

Tuesday, January 17, 1899

Thermometer: 26° below

We all made a trip down, and one upriver. Found the water flowing over the ice near the Gacona. There seems to be more snow on the ice the farther up we go. More Indian visitors to dinner. There were 3 and they were mixed with Russian blood. They said, "Thank God," when through eating.

Wednesday, January 18, 1899

Thermometer: 24° below

Repeated the trip made yesterday. Met two men going back home. They were played out, so they said. Saw a man going after hay with a horse and three sleds. Have got a very bad cold on my lungs. Cough considerably when heated. Opened a sack of flour.

Thursday, January 19, 1899

Thermometer: 22° below

Took our last loads upriver above camp today. Will move camp tomorrow. Understand the water has broken out above the Sanford and is coming down over the ice at the rate of 2½ miles per hour. If so, it will reach us before morning.

Friday, January 20, 1899

Weather: Cloudy and a little snow; Thermometer: 2° below

Camp Jan. 20th, at mouth of Sanford. Left our old camp at 8:30 A.M. and arrived here at 1 P.M. Saw more Indians today than I've seen since being in this country. They had all their dogs packed. One squaw kept way off the trail to avoid meeting the whites. An old buck had on red pants and cap.

Sunday, January 22, 1899
Thermometer: 8°
This has been a very beautiful day. Had a good many Native visitors. Among them were two squaws, one young and quite pretty, too. She had five rings on her fingers and they may have been gold for all I know. They said, "A Clutchman was sick, all same baby." [A "Kloochman" was a female in the Chinook language.]⁶

Monday, January 23, 1899
Weather: Cold north wind; Thermometer: 20°
Started out to work at 7:15. Quite dark but could see the trail. Saw men hauling baled hay. They had a horse. A squaw and her son took dinner with us. She had been to a confinement case and told us all about it. I saw her obstetrical knife and it looked just like one they use for paring horses' hoofs.

Tuesday, January 24, 1899
Made our usual trip downriver but did not go so far up as formerly, as we met water coming over the ice. One would think, as cold as it has been, that water would soon freeze, but [midday temperatures of] 35 and 40 degrees seems to agree with it on Copper River. [In his March 4, 1898, diary entry, Conger indicates that the daily temperatures he records are the readings at daybreak.]

Wednesday, January 25, 1899
Weather: Cloudy, warm and a little snow in the a.m.
Camp Jan. 25th, 10 miles above the Sanford. Had clear, smooth ice for 7 miles. It had frozen over during the night. Met water where camped now. Saw a few Indians. A squaw and her daughter followed us 3 miles, moaning and crying. I could make nothing out of their jargon, but supposed the father was dead and Charley [probably the son] was out hunting. [Conger's supposition was probably based on the Native custom of distributing a family's property among the tribe and burning the family house

upon the death of the husband; subsequently, the oldest son, regardless of age, became the head of the family. This custom left a squaw and her children in a state of destitution; however, they did not fare much better even before this event. According to Lieutenant Allen, Copper River Indian wives were treated with little consideration, being valued in proportion to their ability to pack and do general work. W.C. Mendenhall, the geologist attached to Captain Glenn's 1898 expedition, reported that the men of the Matanuska tribe (dwelling about the southern edge of the Copper River plateau) went to the coast to trade furs twice each winter season, and on these occasions, they left the women and children behind with only a small food supply. The men usually consumed all of the provisions received in trade before returning home, the journey being leisurely performed over a period of several weeks. The Copper River Indian men also traded at the stores on Cook Inlet, and their habits were probably similar to their neighbors, the Matanuskas.][7]

Saturday, January 28, 1899
Thermometer: 10°
This makes the third day we have been pinned in here on account of flooding. Believe it will freeze over tonight, as it is clear now. We are about out of grub. Only two more days' rations, and if it does not freeze by that time, will have to swim the deep places.

Sunday, January 29, 1899
Thermometer: 4° below
Well, we tried to reach our cache but had to give it up after wading through water for a quarter of a mile. Whirley left his sled and went down through the woods and packed back a sack of flour. It may be a week yet before we can move. Quite a push behind us.

Monday, January 30, 1899
Thermometer: 12° below
We finally made it to our cache but had to wade through water

twice. Got my feet wet, but it was not a very cold day. Moved all of our cache one mile farther up and took 200 lbs. apiece home with us (to camp). Went without our dinners. Too busy. One sack flour gone.

Tuesday, January 31, 1899
Thermometer 24° below
There came a time, and it was today, when we got in our work and moved all of cache to camp. There was some water on the ice but we got around it. Tomorrow we start upriver. Two squaws and one dear little baby came to our camp about noon. The poor little papoose, how I pittied it.

Wednesday, February 1, 1899
Thermometer: 22° below
Did a good day's work. Hauled all of our plunder, except camp outfit, 5 miles upriver. Party with a horse broke through the ice. Will call this "Camp Overflow," as everybody gets delayed here on account of water.

Thursday, February 2, 1899
Weather: A little snow; Thermometer: 0°
Camp Feb. 2, about 12 miles from the Christochina [Chistochina]. Had a very hard trail all day. Too much sand, as usual, in the snow. Had to unload part of our loads, and then they got awful heavy. I was nearly done up when camp was struck, but not so much as Corcoran.

Friday, February 3, 1899
Thermometer: 10°
Had a nice day to work and we improved our time. Made 4 miles of trail with snowplow. Have one more load at last cache. The ice is flooded just above us. Don't know how long it is, will know tomorrow. Met a Doctor Winthrop. He says a good many have black leg.

Saturday, February 4, 1899
Thermometer: 12°
Well, here we are, stuck again. Water is over the ice all around us and it will be impossible to move until it freezes. Had to haul our goods back on the trail and cache on higher ground on account of floods. Wet snow falling all day.

Sunday, February 5, 1899
Thermometer: 16°
Lounged around the tent all day. The water is in front of the tent, right handy now to get. Guess we will have several holidays in this place. Saw a rabbit, the first I've seen here. It was almost all white, with tremendous large feet. [Snowshoe hares, also called varying hares, are found in the boreal forests of Canada and Alaska. Their color changes from brown with a white tail in summer to white with black-tipped ears in winter. The soles of their large hind feet are covered with long, coarse hair which grows longer in winter, providing the animal with "snowshoes." The population of these animals fluctuates greatly, following a 10-year cycle influenced by food stress. During periods when they are in great abundance, they deplete their winter food supply, resulting in an inevitable decline in their numbers to a point where it is difficult to locate a single animal. F.C. Schrader reported that the members of his party saw none of these creatures in the Copper River valley in 1898. His statement, together with Conger's observation, suggests that the snowshoe hare population was depressed in that year. According to Allen, in 1885 rabbits ranked second to fish, in the diet of the Copper River Indians.][8]

Monday, February 6, 1899
Thermometer: 14°
Still tied up for want of cold weather. Froze some this afternoon. Saw two men on skates. I longed for mine. Made a watch pocket, put a new seat in my pants, and did some other mending today. Am reading the book of Proverbs and find it very interesting, more so than any other I have read.

Tuesday, February 7, 1899
Thermometer: 10°
We are delayed another day on account of high wind, although the ice is none too strong. We have had but little wind, but when it does blow, it "blows." Cut wood most of the day, as we may be hung up here a week. This is a lonely day and my thoughts are far away.

Wednesday, February 8, 1899
Thermometer: 8°
Well, we finally made a move. Hauled two loads each 3 miles upriver, 500 lbs. to the load. Had clear ice. Tomorrow we move camp. Another sick man went by on his way to Copper Center, and to the States if he lives.

Thursday, February 9, 1899
Thermometer: 10°
Camp Feb. 9th, or camp "Hard Scrabble," as we had to dig into it [the ice] to make any headway. I broke one of my creepers and that not only crippled me but Whirley as well, as he had been hanging onto my sleigh for support in the smooth places. Snow 15 inches deep in some places, others, glare ice. Wind blowing 60 miles an hour. Not so slow.

Saturday, February 11, 1899
Weather: Cloudy and some snow; Thermometer: 0°
Hard work all day. Two trips down and one up. Snow trail most of the way. Three men sick and will have to turn back. One has strained heart, another rheumatic scurvy, and one inflammation of the brain, all brought about by overexertion. Expect to organize a snowplow gang tomorrow.

Sunday, February 12, 1899
Weather: Cloudy and snow in the air; Thermometer: 12°
Funeral today. The man who ruptured his heart, Rob Isert, died last night at 10 o'clock in terrible agony. He leaves a wife and two

little ones in Milwaukee, Wis. He was about 35 years old. Had to thaw the ground to dig the grave. I acted as chaplain and read the XIII [probably the XXIII] Psalm. Three are going back from here. A good many broke camp today. [Charles Brown, the quartermaster's agent, reported that on February 26, W.E. Hendricks and George Hansen arrived in Valdez from Copper Center with news of the death of "Robert Izatt, of Milwaukee, Wis." The two men also reported that 27 men with scurvy were headed for Valdez from the Chistochina and Slana rivers, and that Indians were bringing in two men from the Gakona River.][9]

Tuesday, February 14, 1899
Thermometer: 10° below
Camp Chistochina, 7 miles above last camp. Wood is scarce but squaws plentiful. Had three of them to dinner. Met Mike Beatty and Frank Guyer on their way to Copper Center. They have all their stuff to the Slona [Slana]. The river is wide at this point and full of bars.

Wednesday, February 15, 1899
Weather: Snowed most all day; Thermometer: 14° below
Just one year ago today, dear, I left you and the little ones. God grant that you may be as well now as then. Though I am far away, I hope in another year to be nearer. Had a very hard trail today on account of fresh snow. A young squaw is sitting at my left, eating a biscuit, while I am writing.

Thursday, February 16, 1899
Weather: Clear, still, and very cold
Got all goods up this far and made one trip 3 miles farther upriver. Had so many Native visitors this evening that I had to drive them away. Mr. Drew had a spasm, fell in the snow, and nearly froze to death before [he was] discovered. He will have to go back.

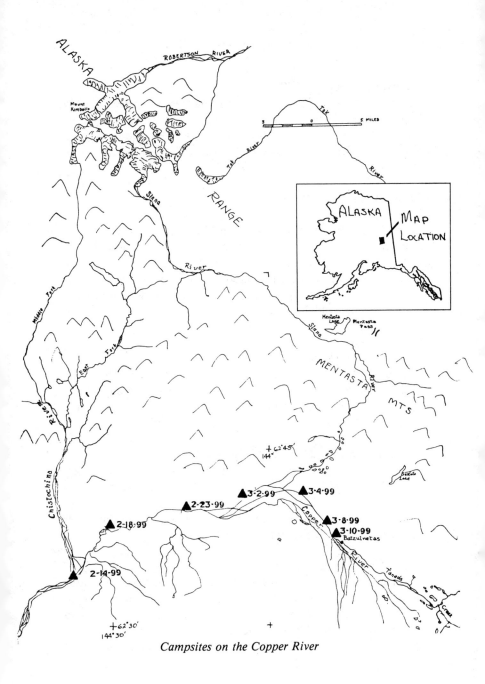

Campsites on the Copper River

Friday, February 17, 1899
This has been one of the coldest days I have ever experienced. My fingers nearly froze at 5 in the morning while dressing my feet. Made a big day's work and tonight I feel well. A good many did not work, for they thought it was too cold. Move camp tomorrow.

Saturday, February 18, 1899
Thermometer: 10° below
Camp Feb. 18th, about 25 miles from the Slona. We are traveling east now. Had an awful bad trail this afternoon. Snowed hard and we did not reach camp till after dark. Then had to wade through 3 feet of snow for wood. Oh, this is mining in Alaska, but never mind. The wind is howling through the pines. God pity the man who is out tonight.

Sunday, February 19, 1899
Thermometer: 14° below
Did not work today. Trail is all drifted full and will be a hard one to break. Wind blew hard all night and part of the day. Some parties have gone back and I understand they are going up the Chittana [Chitina].

Monday, February 20, 1899
Another one of those cold days, but we worked just the same. Had a hard trail downriver but better up. Took loads four miles (and the longest 4 I ever saw) up the Copper. A good many are camped there. The extreme cold seems to have a powerful effect on the lungs. Doesn't seem to bother me much.

Tuesday, February 21, 1899
Oh, the same thing over again. Did the same as yesterday, four miles and repeat. One more load, then comes the camp. Slept cold last night for the first time since starting. What can one expect in a tent when the indicator shows 60° below and on the decline. This is no summer game, no not a bit of it. [When temperatures fell

below the freezing point of mercury, prospectors often determined the reading by observing common substances in their possession such as liquor, kerosene, and patent medicines, whose freezing points had been obtained by comparison with a spirit, or alcohol thermometer.][10]

Wednesday, February 22, 1899
Weather: Clear and beautiful all day; Thermometer: 13° below
Took loads 9 miles upriver. Snow 2 feet deep but trail good. Move camp tomorrow. Saw a man with kid gloves on. Wish I had a pair of silk ones to go inside of yarn, for one's hands perspire so, and I think they would help. [Before the advent of synthetics, silk was widely used as a lining material. In warmth and absorbency it is outranked only by wool; however, its use is limited today by its cost and lack of durability.] Suppose masquerade balls are in vogue this night at home. Will dance mine later on.

Thursday, February 23, 1899
Weather: Cloudy and a little snow; Thermometer: 13° below
Camp Feb. 23, nine miles from last camp and a hard pull it was, too. Arrived here at 1:30. Large clay bank on north side of river opposite camp. River runs from west to east at this point. Met two men from Mentasta Lake. Big push on other side of divide, all headed for 40 Mile and vicinity. [The Copper River route merged with the overland route (Millard trail) from Copper Center at the mouth of the Slana. From this point, the Mentasta Pass trail headed northward, following the eastern bank of the Slana River and crossing Mentasta Pass at an elevation of 2,280 feet, while the Copper River route continued southeastward to the head of the Copper River valley. Most of the gold seekers who headed for the Yukon followed the Mentasta Pass trail and crossed the Tanana River at the present site of Tanacross to reach the headwaters of the Fortymile River.][11]

Sunday, February 26, 1899
Thermometer: 10° below

This has been a terribly windy day. Nobody stirred out of their tents. Snow flying furiously. Trail obliterated. Had to pin down tent on inside with iron pins to hold it. Very cold during the night, but spirits rose before morning. Read the story of Joseph and his reign. Where did Adam's sons get their wives?

Tuesday, February 28, 1899
Thermometer: 6° below
This has been one of the wildest days I ever saw. No man could face this wind and live. Even the dog was nearly scared to death in the tent. This is the third day we have been compelled to lay to on account of wind. Guess old March will come in bristling with rage. This is the last of February, and I am glad of it.

Wednesday, March 1, 1899
Thermometer: 10° below
If this month goes out like it came in, it will have more than the lion's share, for today has been a corker. One good the wind has done: it has swept two feet of snow off the river and left us glare ice, and we hauled a load upriver, even if the wind did blow. Move camp tomorrow. Hope it won't snow for a few days.

Thursday, March 2, 1899
Thermometer: 10° below
Well, my diary, I am almost too tired to pay any attention to you tonight, but as you have not been neglected for more than a year, you shan't be now. Two months today since I left Copper Center and have only lost 12 days during that time. Moved camp today. Only 4 miles from Slona. Clear ice now. Good going. Haul big loads. More sick [men] going back.

Friday, March 3, 1899
Thermometer: 10° below
This has been a fine day and we have all of our stuff moved up to the Slona. Tomorrow we move camp. Received 14 letters and [they] cost me $5.50. Mike Beatty has the scurvy.

Saturday, March 4, 1899
Thermometer: 10° below
Camp Slona, or 2 miles above. River very wide. Big bend to the
S.E. About 20 men will go up this way. All snow and ice to the
south and S.E. [the Wrangell Mountains]. We are camped on top
of ice 6 feet thick. Hard, gloomy looking country.

**Letter dated March 4, 1899, about three miles up Copper River
from the Slona**
Dear Wife,
  I received 14 letters yesterday. Six from you (one as late as
Jan. 9th), three from Len, 2 from Myrtle, 2 from M.J. Hessian,
who is now in Spokane, and one from Mrs. Danforth, who wrote
a splendid letter. It was a surprise to me to get any mail up here so
soon. Had it been 3 days later, the mail carrier would have missed
me, as I turn S.E. from the Slona and go over by Lake Suslota,
while he goes over Mentasta Pass toward 40 Mile to catch those in
advance. The largest push has started for 40 Mile, but doubt if
any get through on snow and ice.
  We left Copper Center Jan. 2nd and have only got this far,
probably not over ⅓ of the way, but have traveled during that
time between 600 and 700 miles in relays. So I concluded to go
over to the headwaters of the Tanana and vicinity. If nothing is
found there, can't say for certain which way I will go. Hessian
wrote me saying, "For God's sake, get out of that country and go
to Lake Atlin, 60 miles from Skagway, where there is
something." But I don't take stock in what he says. Even if I did,
I have not the money now to buy another outfit. When the one I
have is gone, I must go out. "Far away fields look green."
  This has been the biggest fake and humbug I ever heard of so
far. But I am up in here with all I have and mean to push on to the
end if [my] health doesn't give out. Would sell what I have and go
to Dyea and Skagway, but you can't give stuff away. Nobody
wants it. They all have what they can haul, and more, too. There
has been nothing found here on the Copper or its tributaries, nor
on Quartz Creek, nor on the Teikhell and Tonsena as yet. The

report of McClellan, of Princeton, is mostly all false regarding the finds on Quartz Creek and vicinity. [In her letter of November 30, 1898, Conger's wife enclosed a newspaper clipping from the St. Paul *Pioneer Press* in which R.F. McClellan, of Princeton, Minnesota, spoke encouragingly of the Copper River country and of his party's placer prospects on Quartz Creek. The entire text of this article, entitled "Feasible Railroad Route," is included in the appendix.] There are a good many men prospecting this winter all through this section of country, and if there is anything in it, it will come out this season. Don't look for me home before fall. Will come then if I have the price.

I am glad you have got along so well through your sickness and found so many friends. [The mail Conger received on March 3 included several letters written in October of 1898, which informed him of the birth of his third child, Hortense Marie. The letters also contained accounts of the many kind deeds being performed for his family.] God grant that the time will come when we can . . . [reciprocate].[12] The dear little Hortense (the name, how funny), how I would like to see her, also Clifford and Lila. Can't account for those blue eyes though. Got the lock of hair, also the picture and Myrtle's booklet. The candy motto was all broken up and I ate it. Received an account of the Indian trouble [in Minnesota] which Len sent me.[13]

Am going to answer all the letters received in this one in order to save money, as it costs $1.25 for one letter and 25^c for each additional one to get them out from here. Don't stop writing. Will get [the letters] sometime. If not, they will be returned. I will not be able to send another letter out for months, I don't suppose, although there will be a regular monthly mail from Valdes to 40 Mile and Circle City. But I will be off of that line. Understand the government is going to establish a military post at Valdes and Mentasta Pass. What they are doing it for is more than I can understand, for by fall there will not be a man on the line, unless something is found or the boom is continued.

This has not been a very bad winter so far. Have worked all but 12 days during the past 70 and they were lost on account of wind and overflow. Have worked days when it was 65° below zero and did not mind it much either. Our worst days are the windy ones. Last Sunday, Monday, and Tuesday it blew so hard that 2 feet of solid snow was blown off of the ice for 20 miles in length. Last night about ½ inch of snow fell and spoiled it all. Just the least bit of snow on the ice glues a sled fast. Seems as though it is half sand, it pulls so hard.

Many have frozen some member of their body and turned back, while others have gone on, minus a toe. I have met a good many unable to stand on their feet, with rheumatism, scurvy, and black leg. Even my dog has rheumatism at times and howls like fury. Still, I believe this is a healthy country if one has the proper food and doesn't overwork.

So you have bought a piano, have you? Do you think you can meet the payments and pay rent too! Hope you can, for I know the instrument will be lots of company for you.

That Harry T. Smith you spoke of was a conductor on the G.N.R.R. [Great Northern Railroad] and came in here on the same boat we did. He left Copper Center last fall for St. Paul, while the balance of his party have gone on to 40 Mile. I heard of them a few days ago and they were on the Tokio [Tok River]. Smith has Kodak pictures of the entire trip, or knows how to get them, and I told him to write to you and leave his address so I would know where to find him when I return, for I want the views. Mr. Smith is a perfect gentleman. I was called Doc by the Hessian party and am only known by that name here. Some don't know the difference. [This is a response to Lizzie's question about why Smith referred to Conger only as "the doctor" in the letters he wrote to her on November 30 and December 12 of 1898 (see appendix). As a pharmacist living in a small Minnesota town that lacked a doctor, Conger often was called upon to perform the duties of physician, dentist, and veterinarian; thus the nickname.]

I do not take much stock in what Len learned from the fortune teller. He never mentioned it to me in his letter. [In her letter of November 13, 1898, Lizzie gave Conger an account of Len's visit with a clairvoyant in the Twin Cities, where he had gone to purchase holiday goods for his drugstore: "She told him all about you being in a far country, hunting and picking up small particles of something that others trampled over and called worthless. She told him that you were all right and that the particles finally turned out to be gold. It seemed as though it were springtime, and you finally came home very wealthy and moved your family away from the place where they now live. . . . I hope it will come true. She told his past so correctly . . . so there may be something in it. Do you believe in it at all?"] I never will believe in foretelling the future. The past speaks for itself.

Now don't you feel alarmed if you do not hear from me again for six months, for I will be in a place of safety, I hope. Will have to take this letter 6 miles from here tomorrow in order to catch someone who will see the mail carrier on his return trip, in order to get it out. Kiss all the children for me. Kindest regards to my friends and yours, and God grant that we may all meet again soon.

> Lovingly,
> your husband,
> H.S. Conger

Sunday, March 5, 1899
Thermometer: 10° below
Snowed some last night, and today had a strong wind which swept it all off the ice. Took letters up Slona to be sent out. Have a bad pain in my side. Guess it is caused from cold. Read all my letters over again. Did not work. Read the good Book.

Monday, March 6, 1899
Weather: Clear and windy; Thermometer: 6° below
Hauled all [goods] up as far as camp and took 2 loads on upriver. Good ice for 3 miles up. Corcoran was laid up this afternoon with cramps and pain in bowels. Think he took too many C.C.'s [probably compound cathartic pills] last night. Had a chance to sell my share of the grub, but want to sell all or none. Could we do so, would go to Lake Atlin.

Tuesday, March 7, 1899
Thermometer: 6° below
This has been one of those windy days. Hauled 500 lbs. 3 miles upriver in a.m. In p.m. went downriver 2 miles to see a man who they said had been over the Copper River Glacier at its head, but he never had, nor [has] any other man, I guess. Corcoran took the load he missed yesterday upriver this p.m.

Wednesday, March 8, 1899
Thermometer: 10° below
Camp Mar. 8th, about 7 miles up Copper above Slona. Wind blew hard all day, but it is very calm and clear tonight. Snow 2 feet deep from here on. One year ago today steamer *Excelsior* landed me at Valdes. What a fruitless year it has been, too. I am not at the head of the Copper either.

Thursday, March 9, 1899
Thermometer: 12° below
Arose at 4:45 this morning and it was quite light. Could see without a candle. The days are rapidly lengthening. Moved two loads 2 miles upriver to where Bashneta [Batzulnetas] Creek empties into the Copper. [Batzulnetas Creek is present-day Tanada Creek. A Copper River Indian village, called Batzulnetas, was situated on its northern bank, about a mile from its junction with the Copper. The village was named for Batzulneta, a shaman, or witch doctor. Lieutenant Allen wrote that Batzulneta was the chief of the upper Copper River Indians. He was six feet, four inches tall, had hair which hung down his back three feet in a tangled roll, and wore a scarlet flannel blouse obtained from a trading post on the Yukon.][14] Expect to break camp again tomorrow, but it looks like snow now. Saw where some caribou had crossed the river. Millard party camped here January 27.

Friday, March 10, 1899
Thermometer: 4° below

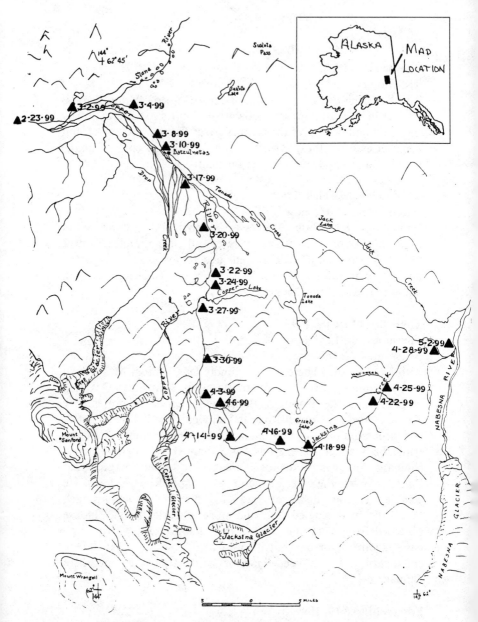

Campsites on the Copper River and Wrangell Mountains

Camp Bashneta, two miles from last camp. We are waiting for some parties behind who say they are going up the Copper to catch up. If we can get crowd enough together, we will go that way too. Party of 13 went up Bashneta Creek yesterday. The ice in front of our tent is 8 feet thick. Can see the different layers. Have water here. River is ½ mile wide and flows west.

Saturday, March 11, 1899
Thermometer: 0°
Washed today and went a ways up the Copper on snowshoes. This has been the warmest day for many months. Whirley was out hunting but got nothing. Party [that went] up Bashneta Creek has to break trail through the woods, as parts of said creek are open. Snow is two feet deep and very soft where not drifted.

Sunday, March 12, 1899
Thermometer: 8°
Walked up the Copper 12 miles. Had to walk on snowshoes most of the way. Saw 3 Indians and one of them had a notion to shoot me, for he was afraid, but a little tobacco gained his confidence. [Lieutenant Allen noted that in 1885 the Copper River Indians were rapidly replacing their bows and arrows with small bore, double-barrel, muzzle-loading shotguns with laminated steel barrels. From these guns they fired pebbles and lead or copper bullets. Evidence suggests that the Copper River Indians obtained these weapons from Yukon trading posts via intermediaries, the Upper Tanana Indians. Close communication between these Natives was maintained through a low pass in the mountains and the valley of Jack Creek — the route of the present-day Nabesna Road. Brooks noted that by 1899, most of the Natives were using breech-loading rifles.][15] Guess there will be 16 who will go this way. Saw two nice fox skins. Could not get the Indian to set a price on them. Corcoran went down to the Slona.

Monday, March 13, 1899
Thermometer: 16°

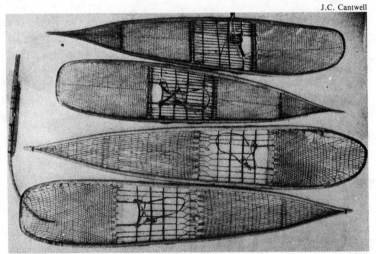

Typical snowshoes used in Alaska in 1899.

Did not work this day, as we thought we would wait for those behind to catch up, but will commence hauling up Copper in the morning. Darned my socks and fixed my snowshoes. Cut wood and lay in camp the balance of the day.

Tuesday, March 14, 1899
Thermometer: 6°
Did not work. Walked up Bashneta Creek 2 miles to where there had been an Indian village. Saw 3 graves. Corpses buried in boxes on top of ground. Saw two huge copper kettles. [According to McKennan, after 1870 the Indians at Batzulnetas buried their dead in crude coffins in shallow graves, over which they erected a low, gabled grave house. Utensils used by the deceased were attached to the grave.][16] A good many have moved up from below. Start up Copper in the morning.

Wednesday, March 15, 1899
Thermometer: 8°

Pulled snowplow 2 miles up Copper in the a.m. In the p.m. hauled all our cache up same distance. Tomorrow we move camp. Traded some flour for caribou meat. Guess it will be tough, for it is black enough to be a year dead, but it will be a change. Thawed a little about noon.

Thursday, March 16, 1899
Thermometer: 28°
Did not move camp on account of storms. Snowed all day. Very wet snow. Almost at the thawing point. Two men went up the Copper to investigate the route. Indian Willie and Thread (his sister) were here all night and part of the day. Have been in my tent all day.

Friday, March 17, 1899
Thermometer: 20°
Camp Mar. 17th, five miles above Bashneta at head of narrows. Pulled snowplow 3 miles and had a hard time of it as the snow was 3 feet deep. There are about 20 men on this trail. Don't know how far we will go on this route. It may end very abruptly.

Saturday, March 18, 1899
Thermometer: 10°
Got everything hauled up this far and 2 miles farther up with two loads. Tried the snowplow but it was drifted and crusted too much to make a good trail, so gave it up. We are still traveling a little south of east. Thawed a little about one o'clock.

Sunday, March 19, 1899
Thermometer: 0°
Had 18 men on snowplow and made 3 miles of fine trail. Two men came down Copper from timber line. They found the Millard party camped there. Two Swedes took the right hand fork and have gone over the glacier, I guess. I am at a standstill. Don't know which way is best.

Monday, March 20, 1899
Thermometer: 4° below
Camp Mar. 20th. Got all our plunder up here and all are camped together. In the morning the snowplow gang will be out. Was taken snow-blind this afternoon and my left eye is very painful now.

Tuesday, March 21, 1899
Thermometer: 10° below
All hands took hold of the snowplow this morning and pulled it upriver 2 miles, when the snow became so deep that the plow was abandoned and snowshoes substituted. Will move camp tomorrow. Have had a bad pain in left breast all day. The auroras are quite brilliant tonight.

Wednesday, March 22, 1899
Thermometer: 18° below
Camp Mar. 22, five miles from last camp in a southerly direction. River is narrow and open in places. Snow is deep. Trail poor. We are rapidly nearing the glacier. Don't think it is more than 15 miles off.

Thursday, March 23, 1899
Thermometer: 19° below
Still tugging away at the sled. Hauled 2 loads upriver and have one more, then comes the camp outfit. The sun has begun to burn my face, and yet it does not seem to melt the snow or settle it one bit.

Friday, March 24, 1899
Thermometer: 22° below
Camp 3 points. I call it by that name because in reaching it you travel in all directions except west. The river is narrow and has high banks on either side. It has been hard sledding today. Trail is very sideling in places.

Saturday, March 25, 1899
Thermometer: 10° below
Hauled most of our grub up as far as Zogneta Creek, a small brooklet putting into the Copper from the S.E.[17] Whirley killed 4 ptarmigans and we ate 3 of them for supper. They are comparatively tasteless. Color, white as the snow.

Sunday, March 26, 1899
Thermometer: 10° below
Did a washing this day and put two new knees in my pantaloons. Whirley went hunting and got nothing. Looks very much like snow tonight. McDonald came up from below. He said there were 8 or 10 more coming this way. We have an even 20 in this push.

Monday, March 27, 1899
Thermometer: 6° below
"Camp Clear Water." This is the first left-hand fork of the Copper, 35 miles above the Slona. The water is clear. It comes in from the S.E. Corcoran and Whirley were sick last night. See a good many marten tracks, also wolverine. Timber is scrubby.

Tuesday, March 28, 1899
Thermometer: 4° below
Worked half day. In the afternoon 3 men started to look for a way out, but did not come to any favorable route. Will move camp once more and then investigate. Am afraid we have come to the end of our rope. McGee came today.

Wednesday, March 29, 1899
Thermometer: 2° below
Hauled 2 loads 5 miles up canyon to where Millard party is camped. They are going to remain where they are till spring. Wilkinson came near drowning. It was one escape in a million. Fields camped near the glacier last night. Don't know our way over yet, but think we will find one.

Thursday, March 30, 1899
Thermometer: 2° below
"Camp Millard." That is the end of their sleighing. Wood is very scarce but water is plentiful. Canyon is wide with high bluffs on either side. Trout in stream. Water clear and pure. There are 21 of us camped here. Trail was quite soft during the middle of the day.

Friday, March 31, 1899
Thermometer: 4°
Hauled all goods one mile above camp Millard. Crossed a plateau and a lake. No wood. Trail very poor. Three of the Millards started this morning to look for an outlet to the Tanana. My knees are giving out. In fact, am all fagged out in general.

Saturday, April 1, 1899
Thermometer: 10°
Dispatched 3 men to the other side of the glacier. Hauled 2 loads to cache above. Corcoran did not work in the p.m. He went hunting. Thawed a good deal.

Monday, April 3, 1899
Thermometer: 6° below
"Camp Dry Gulch," just east of Mt. Sanford [elevation 16,237 feet] and on a level with half its height. Very bad trail over brush and grass. Have to haul wood 1½ miles. Threw away one robe.

Tuesday, April 4, 1899
Thermometer: 16°
Party back from glacier. Can't go that way. Go through canyon on the east [about six miles northeast of the Copper Glacier terminus].[18] Shot some birds. Have one more load below to haul, then through the canyon we go to the Tanana.

Notes—

1. W.R. Abercrombie, "Report of Leroy J. Townsend, M.D., On Scorbutus, or Scurvy," *Copper River Exploring Expedition, 1899* (Washington: Government Printing Office, 1900), p. 45.

2. Abercrombie, "Report of Charles Brown, Quartermaster's Agent," *Copper River . . . 1899,* pp. 38-39.

3. Abercrombie, "Report of Charles Brown, Quartermaster's Agent," *Copper River . . . 1899,* pp. 37, 39.

4. Abercrombie, "Report of Capt. W.R. Abercrombie," *Copper River . . . 1899,* pp. 13-15, 19.

5. Abercrombie, "Report of Capt. W.R. Abercrombie," *Copper River . . . 1899,* p. 19; Charles Remington, *A Golden Cross ? On Trails From The Valdez Glacier* (Los Angeles: White-Thompson, 1939), pp. 137, 149-50.

6. Frederic R. Marvin, "The Chinook Language," in *The Yukon Overland: The Gold-Digger's Handbook* (Cincinnati: Editor Publishing Co., 1898), p. 155.

7. Henry T. Allen, "Report of a Military Reconnaissance in Alaska, Made in 1885," *Compilation of Narratives of Explorations in Alaska* (Washington: Gov. Printing Office, 1900), pp. 475-76; W.C. Mendenhall, "A Reconnaissance from Resurrection Bay to the Tanana River, Alaska, in 1898," *Twentieth Annual Report of the USGS,* Part 7 (Washington: Gov. Printing Office, 1900), pp. 303, 339.

8. Victor H. Cahalane, *Mammals of North America* (New York: Macmillan, 1947), pp. 583, 585, 591; Jerry O. Wolf, "Return of the Snowshoe Hare," *ALASKA®*, April 1977, pp. 60, 96; F.C. Schrader, "A Reconnaissance of a Part of Prince William Sound and the Copper River District, Alaska, in 1898," *Twentieth Annual Report of the USGS,* p. 370; Allen, *Compilation of Narratives,* p. 472.

9. Abercrombie, "Report of Charles Brown," *Copper River . . . 1899,* p. 38.

10. Edwin Tappan Adney, *The Klondike Stampede of 1897-98* (1900; rpt. Fairfield, Washington: Ye Galleon Press, 1968), pp. 203-04.

11. Oscar Rohn, "A Reconnaissance of the Chitina River and the Skolai Mountains, Alaska," *Twenty-First Annual Report of the USGS,* Part 2 (Washington: Gov. Printing Office, 1900), pp. 401-02; Alfred H. Brooks, "A Reconnaissance in the Tanana and White River Basins, Alaska, in 1898," *Twentieth Annual Report of the USGS,* p. 442.

12. "retaliate" omitted from the original.

13. In his letter of October 16, 1898, Conger's brother Len told of an Indian uprising about 75 miles north of Mora, Minnesota: "General Bacon is there with about 700 of the Boys in Blue to look after them. They had one battle — 6 soldiers were killed and 8 wounded and the Peace Commission is there trying to arrange peace with them. If it hadn't been for the promptness of the Gov. in sending

troops to squelch it, all the Indians would have risen up and then God knows who would have had any scalps to call their own."

14. Alfred H. Brooks, *The Geography and Geology of Alaska: A Summary of Existing Knowledge* (Washington: Gov. Printing Office, 1906), p. 55; Donald J. Orth, *Dictionary of Alaska Place Names,* U.S. Geological Survey Professional Paper No. 567 (Washington: Gov. Printing Office, 1967), pp. 111, 946; Allen, *Compilation of Narratives,* pp. 440, 471.

15. Allen, *Compilation of Narratives,* p. 474; Robert A. McKennan, *The Upper Tanana Indians,* in Yale Univ. Publications in Anthropology, No. 55, ed. Irving Rouse (New Haven: Dept. of Anthropology, 1959), pp. 28, 20; Alfred H. Brooks, "A Reconnaissance from Pyramid Harbor to Eagle City, Alaska," *Twenty-First Annual Report of the USGS,* p. 378.

16. A discussion of the early burial practices of Alaskan Natives is contained in McKennan's *The Upper Tanana Indians,* Yale Univ. Publications in Anthropology, No. 55, pp. 146-48.

17. Rohn reported a "Lake Zachnada," which he said was one of several lakes "attaining considerable size" draining into the Copper at the head of its valley. "Report of Oscar Rohn on Exploration in Wrangele Mountain District," *Copper River . . . 1899,* p. 108; Bake lists "Zokneda," two small lakes between Tanana Lake and Copper River and draining into Copper River near latitutde 62°-25′. Marcus Baker, *Geographic Dictionary of Alaska,* 2d ed., USGS Bulletin 299 (Washington: Gov. Printing Office, 1906), p. 690; H. Brian Pearson also mentions "Lake Zocneda" in Abercrombie, "General Sketch of the Upper Tanana and Its Watershed," *Copper River . . . 1899,* p. 153.

18. The route Conger followed into the Wrangells may be the trail roughly described by H. Brian Pearson. See preceding reference.

Chapter 9—

Stalled
in the Wrangells

The Wrangell Mountains are a 100-mile-long volcanic range, separated from the coastal Chugach Mountains by the Copper and Chitina river valleys. They extend from the big bend of the upper Copper River on the northwest to Russell Glacier on the southeast and form the divides between four large rivers. Within this rugged range lie at least nine peaks ranging from 12,000 to over 16,000 feet above sea level. They loom above the surrounding terrain of high ridges and jagged foothills, presenting magnificent vistas in many parts of the Copper River basin. In 1898-99, prospectors and explorers witnessed periodic eruptions of smoke and steam from Mount Wrangell, a 14,163-foot dome near the center of the range.[1]

Because the Chugach Mountains, south of the Wrangells, are not nearly as high as the Saint Elias Range farther east, they are not as effective in precipitating moisture from the warm air currents which move inland from the ocean. Thus, as the moisture-laden air which reaches the interior moves over the Wrangells, it gives rise to heavy precipitation, which falls mainly as snow in the higher elevations. Consequently, a thick ice cap covers the central part of the range. It is the source of the numerous glaciers that radiate down into the valleys and foothills. Oscar Rohn, a civilian topographer who made one of the first government explorations of these mountains in 1899, reported that the south side of the range presented the heaviest glaciation found anywhere in the interior of Alaska. The climate of the upper Tanana basin, to the north of the Wrangells, is characteristic of the great Interior of Alaska, receiving less precipitation and more temperature extremes than regions south of the range.[2]

The Wrangell Mountains were virtually unexplored in April of 1899 when Conger's party ventured into them after reaching

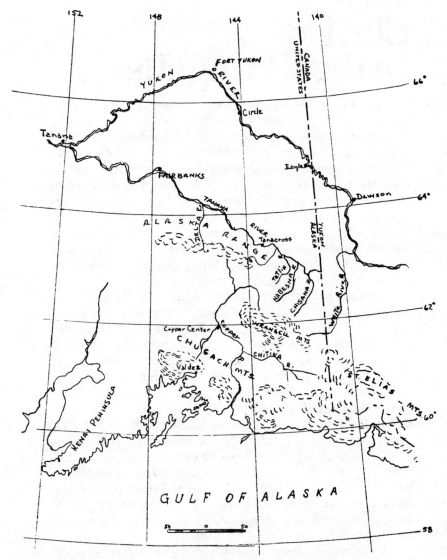

Territory between Valdez and Eagle

the head of the Copper River. Lieutenant Allen ceased his 1885 explorations of the Copper River at Batzulnetas and did not penetrate the range, and in 1891 Dr. C. Willard Hayes, of the Geological Survey, accompanied Lt. Frederick Schwatka on an expedition which crossed Skolai Pass on the southeastern boundary of the range. Beyond the meager information gained about the periphery of the range from these expeditions, nothing definite was known about the region.[3]

The activity of prospectors in the Wrangells prompted the first government investigations of the region in the summer of 1899. A main objective of these explorations was to resolve the vague and conflicting reports about its geography. In mid-August of 1899, a Geological Survey party headed by Alfred H. Brooks and William J. Peters ascended the White River to the Chisana Glacier. They crossed a divide to the Nabesna, descended that stream for 20 miles, then headed overland to the Tanana, reaching the latter stream near the mouth of the Tetlin River on September 1. The same season Oscar Rohn, a member of Captain Abercrombie's Copper River expedition, ascended the Chitina valley along the southern base of the Wrangells, seeking a favorable passage to the headwaters of the Copper. Accompanied by A.H. McNeer, a prospector, he crossed Nizina Glacier to the head of the Chisana, then crossed a divide to the Nabesna, and with the aid of the Natives, succeeded in reaching the Copper River at Batzulnetas by October 2.[4]

Early explorers reported various names for the Nabesna, Chisana, and Tanana rivers. The Nabesna and Chisana rise from glaciers of the same names on the north slope of the Wrangells, and with their tributaries, constitute the headwaters of the Tanana River. On their northward courses they flow through the Nutzotin Range, a southeasterly extension of the Mentasta Mountains, emerging in a broad lowland region where they combine to form the Tanana near Northway Junction. Lieutenant Allen reported that the Indians he encountered on the Tanana River below Bates Rapids (west of the mouth of Delta River) referred to that stream by its present name, but above this point, the Natives

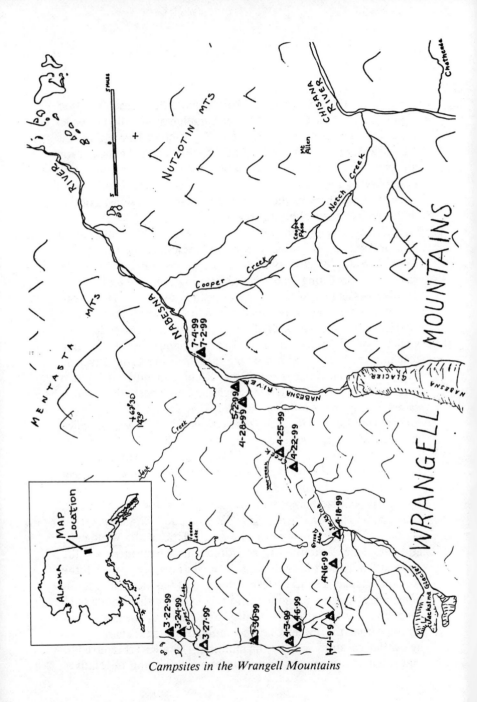

Campsites in the Wrangell Mountains

called the river *Nabesna*. According to Brooks, the Native name for the upper Tanana (Nabesna) had fallen into disuse by 1898, so to preserve the name, he applied it to the upper Tanana's chief tributary, then known as the West Branch of the Tanana. Robert McKennan, who studied the Upper Tanana Indians in 1929, reported that the Natives called the Chisana *tetzan-niu.* The early prospectors in this region heard this as *shushana,* he said, and in 1959 the latter name was still in use locally. However, the first government explorers to visit the Chisana (spelled "Chusana" on Allen's map of explorations) called it the "Tanana." This fact probably can be attributed to the inaccuracies of the first government maps of this area, which do not reflect the true positions of the rivers. (See page 222.)[5]

Allen's map was the basis for all maps made of the Wrangells and upper Tanana basin prior to 1899, but he claimed no accuracy for its topography beyond the immediate route of his travels. He mapped the peaks of the Wrangells during his ascent of the Copper River, but since he did not visit the Nabesna or Chisana rivers, the map in this area probably was drawn from vague information supplied by the Natives, a common cartographic practice in the early days of the territory. Nevertheless, Allen's map was a valuable aid to subsequent explorers, who used the lofty peaks of the Wrangells to determine their own positions. The fact that Allen had mapped a nonexistent peak called "Mount Tillman" was of little consequence and was not discovered until 1899.[6]

Gold was discovered near the heads of both the Nabesna and Chisana rivers after the turn of the century. Placer discoveries along Bonanza Creek resulted in a stampede to the upper Chisana in the summer of 1913, but the placers were relatively small and the rush was short-lived. About 200 gold seekers wintered in the area but the population steadily decreased. McKennan reported only seven persons living in Chisana during the winter of 1929. Between 1913 and 1959, the Chisana district produced 44,760 ounces of gold, all from placers. This amount is insignificant when compared to the more than 12,000,000 ounces produced through the same year in the Yukon region, of which the Chisana

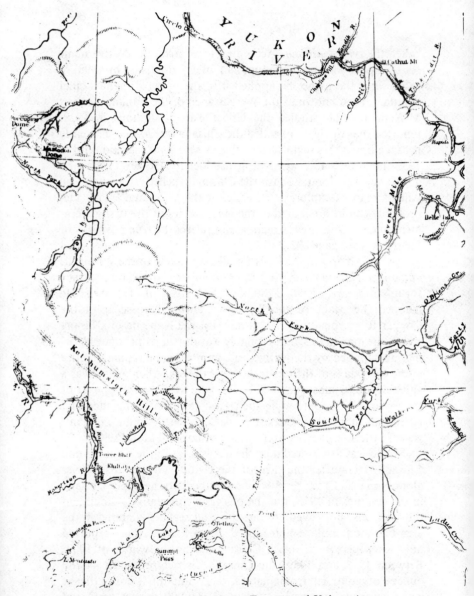

Territory between the Upper Tanana and Yukon rivers,
April 1898, USC&GS

and Nabesna districts are a part. Only two districts in the Yukon region, Fairbanks and Nabesna, have produced any significant amounts of lode gold. Of the 305,560 ounces of lode gold mined in the Yukon region through 1959, 63,300 ounces came from the Nabesna district. The Nabesna Mine was the lone producer in this district. Credit for its discovery is given to a bear who allegedly uncovered a moss-covered outcrop of the principal vein while digging out a gopher. The Nabesna Mining Company began shipping ore from this mine in 1931, but nine years later, the gold was virtually depleted and production halted. In recent years the old mining communities of Nabesna and Chisana have been popular destinations for big game hunters. In the surrounding country range the grizzly and black bear, moose, caribou, and in the higher and less accessible regions, the Dall sheep.[7]

Wednesday, April 5, 1899
Thermometer: 16°
Hauled up east canyon [northeast of the Copper Glacier terminus] 1½ miles. Will move camp tomorrow. Ice clear across canyon one mile up. Millard party sinking a shaft on left-hand side.

Thursday, April 6, 1899
Thermometer: 14°
"Camp Three Forks." We are now where the east canyon forks east, southeast, and north. We are going up the southeast fork. It is 3 miles to the summit. Canyon full of ice. Can haul only 150 lbs. Will have to pack before the summit is reached.

Friday, April 7, 1899
Thermometer: 14°
Worked all day hauling up icy benches which were too steep to coast down. Corcoran laid off in the a.m. Sore eyes.

Saturday, April 8, 1899
Thermometer: 16°
Hard hauling today. Could pull only 100 lbs. Rocks and steep

mountains, high and rough, with little snow on top. All blown into the canyons. Heard rats whistle. [Most likely, these sounds were made by little ground rodents called hoary marmots (*Marmota caligata*). Their warning cry, a long loud whistle, is sometimes mistaken for a human whistle. Audible for over a mile, it alerts all animals to be on their guard. The hoary marmot usually makes its burrows in rocky areas to avoid being excavated by grizzly bears. Alaskan Natives used the pelts of this animal for clothing.][8]

Monday, April 10, 1899
Weather: Clear; Thermometer: 10°
All packing done by noon. In p.m. hauled one load to summit. While coasting back, struck a rock with my right heel and had to be hauled to camp. Am a cripple now.

Tuesday, April 11, 1899
Weather: Cloudy; Thermometer: 10°
Could not stand on my right foot. Stayed in tent all day and applied hot water. Corcoran and Whirley have gone to the summit to work. Expect to be hauled up on sled tomorrow.

Wednesday, April 12, 1899
Weather: Stormy; Thermometer: 0°
Hobble around on crutches. Andrew and Jack went after wood in the a.m. In the p.m. stayed in tent. Too rough to be out. Have got to move camp tomorrow.

Thursday, April 13, 1899
Weather: Clear and warm; Thermometer: 6°
The boys made a trip to the summit in the a.m. with part of the camp. In the p.m. they hauled me up. Oh, how I hate to be pulled along. It is awful.

Friday, April 14, 1899
Weather: Clear and bright; Thermometer: 20° below

"Camp Summit," between headwaters of Copper and Tanana rivers, east of glacier. Can't stand on my foot yet. There are 32 men going over this divide. We are about 12,000 feet above sea level. [The summit here is little more than half this height.]

Saturday, April 15, 1899
Weather: Strong wind; Thermometer: 15° below
The boys are hauling down the summit a short distance and will move me and camp tomorrow. Tried to get dinner but knocked the frying pan off the stove, then quit. Can't use the crutches very well.

Sunday, April 16, 1899
Weather: Clear and beautiful; Thermometer: 4° below
"Camp Willows," over summit on Tanana side. The boys hauled me down. Am able to stand on my foot. Expect to walk in 2 days. It is warm here. Little snow on north side of canyon. Walls very high.

Monday, April 17, 1899
Weather: Clear and warm; Thermometer: 10°
Just a week since I sprained my ankle and can't walk yet. McDonald is helping the boys haul our stuff down. Am all alone in tent. Everybody has moved to timber 3 miles lower down.

Tuesday, April 18, 1899
Weather: Warm and bright; Thermometer: 6°
"Camp Tanana," or a branch of it. We are 8 miles from the summit leading to Copper River. [This location is about one and a half miles southeast of Grizzly Lake on Jacksina Creek, a southwest tributary of the Nabesna.] Mountains are high and formed of lava rock. Little snow on the north side. Plenty on the south. Timber is very scrubby. Skinner killed a mountain sheep. He gave us a piece. Some are going to remain here. This is a large basin with 5 canyons leading into it. My foot is better but can't walk yet.

Thursday, April 20, 1899
Weather: Cloudy and warm; Thermometer: 15°
The boys are hauling down the West Fork of the Tanana
[Jacksina Creek] about 3 miles. We must get through on ice and
snow, for it is too dangerous for boating. Won't go more than 10
miles from here.

Friday, April 21, 1899
Weather: Clear and springlike; Thermometer: 10°
The boys have all [goods] hauled down three miles except camp.
Will move it tomorrow. There have been 4 sheep killed here. This
ought to be called Sheep Camp.

Saturday, April 22, 1899
Thermometer: 32°
"Camp Box Canyon," down West Fork of Tanana, about 15
miles from its head. Walls on either side very high and rough. We
are trying to get through [to] where it will be safe boating. The
boys took the camp down in the morning and Andrew came up
after me in the p.m. He had to put snowshoes on before we got
through, or else he would have fallen through to his waist in
snow. Wind blowing a gale from the south. Snow melts like a
candle burning. The tent I was in fell down.

Monday, April 24, 1899
Thermometer: 28°
Just two weeks since I hurt my ankle and it is but little better.
Can't walk. Very lonely in tent all day and nothing to read. Will
be crazy soon if no change for the better occurs. Snow going fast.

Tuesday, April 25, 1899
Thermometer: 16°
"Camp Tanana," just below first tributary on N.W. side and 12
miles from where we first struck it (Tanana). [On Jacksina Creek
near the mouth of Wait Creek.] The snow was quite hard today.
Could travel without snowshoes. Skinner and Reonalds came up

and took two loads down. There are twelve of us here. Twenty stayed at headwaters. Saw a fox and it was the first wild animal I've seen in this country. River is very wide at this point, but shallow. The country looks favorable for prospecting. Don't think we will sled much farther.

Wednesday, April 26, 1899
Thermometer: 20°
This has been dear little Clifford's birthday. How I long to see him. Have all goods at this point. Andrew and Jack slept all day and I nursed my ankle. It is turning black and I am getting discouraged.

Friday, April 28, 1899
Thermometer: 24°
Folded our tents and silently stole away downstream amidst a blinding snowstorm at 5 this morning. Now camped 3 miles above junction of Shushana and West Fork. [In reality, their position was near the junction of the Nabesna and Jacksina Creek. The inaccuracies of the maps depicting this unexplored country were responsible for their erroneous assumption.] Water is bad and think we will move.

Saturday, April 29, 1899
Weather: Clear; Thermometer: 12°
Have all of our cache together once more. Skinner went downriver and has not got back yet. Party which went up Bashneta [Tanada] Creek passed here 12th instrument [April 12].

Sunday, April 30, 1899
Weather: Clear and cold; Thermometer: 10°
Much pain in my leg today. Andrew went hunting but saw nothing. Am reading *Romance of Two Worlds* [by Marie Corelli]. Have become somewhat of a believer in the occult myself.

Tuesday, May 2, 1899
Thermometer: 16°
"Camp Junction," . . . [on][9] Shushana, where West Fork come in. Here is where our sleighing ends for 1899, although good ice extends on down. Very little snow on west side. River very wide. Mountains abrupt on east side, flat and receding on west. Moore, McDonald, and Ludwig have gone on down, leaving 11 of us. Sold one sack of flour for $10. Country looks none too good.

Wednesday, May 3, 1899
Thermometer: 15°
Just 4 months yesterday since I left Copper Center and have traveled during that time 1,260 miles [in multiple trips over the same ground] and pulled a load. Have eaten 150 lbs. flour and other food in proportion. Have 300 lbs. flour left. Was hauled on a sled the last 30 miles by Andrew Whirley of Belle Plaine, Minnesota. Am still unable to walk.

Thursday, May 4, 1899
Thermometer: 20°
Held meeting to decide about hauling some grub down East Fork 10 or 15 miles. Corcoran and Croop start tomorrow. The balance of the party are to cut logs for boats. Most everyone has the blues.

Friday, May 5, 1899
Weather: Clear and cool; Thermometer: 10°
Logs are all cut and sawmill built. Commence sawing tomorrow. Have lost my appetite and feel generally depressed. Nearly 4 weeks unable to walk.

Saturday, May 6, 1899
Thermometer: 22°
Three geese flew over the tent but no one saw them till too late to bag one. Nobody worked. Am drinking a mixture of cottonwood bark and spruce bows made into a decoction. [Spruce tea was a popular antiscorbutic among the gold seekers.]

Sunday, May 7, 1899
Weather: Clear and windy; Thermometer: 40°
Sleepy day, as everyone lay abed. Made a linament of tablets and essence Jamaica ginger. Am getting alarmed about my ankle.

Monday, May 8, 1899
Weather: Snowed all day
Nobody worked on account of the weather. The days seem terribly long. Skinner gave me a bottle of pain killer. Now I will get well. A drowning man grasps at a straw.

Tuesday, May 9, 1899
Weather: Damp snow falling all day
Dear me, but these are weary days. Nothing to read. Sit up a while then lie down. The ice has not budged an inch yet, but when it goes out it will all go at once.

Wednesday, May 10, 1899
Weather: Cloudy and damp
Lay around all day. Too nasty to get out. Snow hanging to trees till late in p.m. Some loons flew over and they made an awful cry.

Thursday, May 11, 1899
Weather: Clear
The boys hauled 2 loads of wood in a.m. In p.m. started the sawmill. Took my temperature: 99.7°. Hobbled out and gathered a little gum. A year ago today we were sawing.

Friday, May 12, 1899
Weather: Clear and windy
All are sawing lumber except two. Can't reduce the swelling in my leg. Swollen now to the knee. Has a yellow and blackish appearance. It may be erysipelas [a blood infection which produces fever, rash, and local inflammation and swelling of the skin and subcutaneous tissues].

Sunday, May 14, 1899
Weather: Bright, beautiful day
Whirley and Reonalds have gone hunting. Whirley got a duck. John Mackin and Fields were here. They are camped 3 miles above us.

Monday, May 15, 1899
The boys sawed nearly all day. George Mahler was here. Ice has commenced moving in the river. It is 5 weeks today since I met with misfortune and can't walk yet.

Tuesday, May 16, 1899
Weather: Clear and warm
All the lumber is sawed for our boats. Will let it season for a while. Ice has melted rapidly today. Too much snow yet for prospecting.

Wednesday, May 17, 1899
Weather: Cloudy and cool
The boys are edging lumber. Water is getting higher and swifter. Can see the anchor ice in the bottom [of the stream]. I hobbled out to the bank and watched the chunks of ice go by.

Friday, May 19, 1899
Loitered around all day. Nobody did much work. Skinner tapped some birch trees and is making sugar.

Saturday, May 20, 1899
Another long, lonesome day has nearly gone and I am glad of it. To be stretched upon your back during 18 hours of sun makes one weary and long for the "flesh pots" [luxuries of civilization].

Sunday, May 21, 1899
Weather: Cloudy, cool, and windy
The roaring of the river sounds like the surf at a distance. It's

soothing and quieting to the nerves. Vegetation has sprung up quite rank around my stove.

Monday, May 22, 1899
Started to build one boat, 4 ft. on bottom, 22 ft. long. Six weeks since I got hurt. Am still using the crutch. Rapidly improving.

Tuesday, May 23, 1899
Weather: Cloudy and cool
One boat is done, all but calking and pitching. Some are out gathering pitch now. We mix the soft gum from spruce trees with sperm candles. Candles alone are good.

Wednesday, May 24, 1899
Commenced raining in the middle of the night and continued till 7 in the morning, when it turned to snow. Flakes 2 inches square came down. Damp, bad day. No work.

Thursday, May 25, 1899
Weather: Cloudy, cold and damp
Started another boat, 22 feet long, 40 inches across bottom in widest place. Water fell a foot in the river. There is a bird here that whistles like a man calling a dog.

Friday, May 26, 1899
Weather: Cloudy and more rain
Whirley went gunning and got a spoonbill duck. Reonalds waded across the river. Water very low.

Saturday, May 27, 1899
Another damp and dismal day. It is enough to drive one afflicted distracted. Am helpless as yet. Hopes are strong though. The boys worked on the boat a little. It is nearly done.

Sunday, May 28, 1899
Well, it is Sunday once more and I am no better than a week ago.

Some have gone hunting. Whirley is baking yeast bread in the Dutch oven for the first time.

Monday, May 29, 1899
Weather: Cloudy and cold
The boats are all done except calking and pitching. Seven weeks since my accident and am getting worse, I believe. Discoloration and pains above knee to groin.

Tuesday, May 30, 1899
Weather: Cloudy, cold
Decoration day. It would be hard, indeed, to find flowers enough here for one grave. There are a few lonely graves, though, down the Copper and up the Klutena. The boys are building a small boat to cross the river in. The ice falling in sounds like the booming of a cannon.

Wednesday, May 31, 1899
Weather: A little sun
Some are pitching boats, others making packsaddles. Leg worse again. Still I am calm.

Thursday, June 1, 1899
The boats (3) are all pitched and in the water ready for embarking. Ice is not all out yet. It would be dangerous to attempt a descent now. Have a rosebush growing at the foot of my bed.

Friday, June 2, 1899
Weather: Cold rain all day
My God! What a country. Even the Indians do not inhabit this section. Mahler was here. Nobody worked. Lots of pain inside of leg above knee.

Saturday, June 3, 1899
Had my hair cut. It hung down on my shoulders and was coming

out fast. Jack went hunting and got 2 ducks. Andrew picked me some mossberries. Am doctoring now for rheumatic scurvy.

Sunday, June 4, 1899
Weather: Cold rain
I will be alone tomorrow, as all except McGee go prospecting. McGee will be back at noon. God only knows how I will get along alone.

Monday, June 5, 1899
Weather: Cloudy and damp
The fiends incarnate, every last one of them, have gone out for a 3 weeks' prospect and left me alone, helpless, with my leg black to the knee. It is help yourself or die now. Skinner and Park Griswold are the only two who bade me good-by. My two partners never said a word. Oh well, thank God there's a day of retribution coming. Two months ago I got hurt and can hardly get around with crutch and cane now.

Tuesday, June 6, 1899
Weather: Rain
Oh, what a lonely life. Not a sound, only the rippling of the water. My leg is no better. It looks like a mortified member. Have faith still.

Wednesday, June 7, 1899
Weather: Cold and windy
A repetition of yesterday. Nothing new, nor strange. What an insignificant figure is man. A mere speck on the Great Canvas. A sweep of the brush and he is blotted out, and where is he.

Thursday, June 8, 1899
Two men were here from above. They are having an awful time boating. Swamped one boat. Here is my daily bill of fare: eggs (crys.), potatoes, cocoa, dried fruit, bread (yeast), citric acid, and a tea made from spruce bows and poplar bark.

Saturday, June 10, 1899
Weather: A summer day
It is getting warmer, still there is ice 6 feet thick on the river. Big John[10] was here to dinner. Don't feel very well tonight. Appetite all gone.

Sunday, June 11, 1899
Finished reading the Bible through from Genesis to Revelations. McGee gave me 2 jars of beef extract. My leg pains above the knee.

Monday, June 12, 1899
Weather: Cloudy and some rain
Five men were here and they gave me some sheep meat and said they would get me a whole one (sheep). God bless them. Have been using hot water freely on leg. The pain and blackness still goes on.

Tuesday, June 13, 1899
Weather: Cloudy, cold
Whirley and Croop came back last night. Found nothing. We are expecting the others in tomorrow.

Wednesday, June 14, 1899
Andrew went hunting and brought two nice fish. They resemble pike and [are] as boneless as trout. Believe my leg is improving, but slowly.

Thursday, June 15, 1899
Weather: Cloudy and very windy
Whirley and Croop went fishing. Whirley caught 30 beauties with his hands. They would not bite a hook. Plucked the rosebud that was growing at the foot of my bed. Great excitement. Bear in camp.

Friday, June 16, 1899
Weather: Cold rain
The balance of the prospectors came back. Did not find a color. [The Nabesna Gold Mine was subsequently discovered about five miles from this location.] Reonalds gave me 1 lb. beef extract and a grouse. Can hear my heart beating loudly in right ear. Byjorum brought in a large string of grayling.

Saturday, June 17, 1899
Weather: Windy
Andrew went fishing and handed out 17. McGee went to camps above. Andrew gave me some lime juice capsules. Hot water on leg all day.

Sunday, June 18, 1899
Weather: Windy and warm
Bill Tiner sent me 10 lbs. sheep meat. The blackness is leaving my leg but swelling and stiffness at knee still remain. Some are going out prospecting tomorrow.

Monday, June 19, 1899
Weather: Cloudy and sultry
Four have gone for one week's prospect. Two went fishing in the p.m. My leg is rapidly improving, thank God. Mosquitoes are getting thick.

Tuesday, June 20, 1899
Weather: Cloudy, very strong S. wind
Thirty-six summers ago today I first saw light. What rejoicings then. What now?-----. Jack a fishing went and caught one fish. I ate it like a man for dinner. Fresh meat and everything antiscorbutic is all gone.

Wednesday, June 21, 1899
Weather: Cloudy but warm
Skinner and Griswold returned. Found colors. Lots of men at

Mantasta [Mentasta]. Millard party has 16 claims (quartz) on the Tanana. Country well peopled.

Thursday, June 22, 1899
Weather: Cloudy with wind
Mahler and Tiner were here for dinner. They are camped 3 miles above us. Most everybody is smoking a new brand of tobacco, "Mocha and Java."

Friday, June 23, 1899
Weather: Cloudy and sultry
The other four of our party returned ragged and hungry. Found no colors. My knee is badly swollen and stiff. Am very poor. Won't weigh over 130 lbs.

Saturday, June 24, 1899
Weather: Cloudy and some rain
Whirley, Skinner, and two more started out to prospect a gulch 10 miles from here in which Skinner found good colors.

Sunday, June 25, 1899
Weather: Very cool
Great excitement! Bear seen on bar. At 4 o'clock P.M., while lying on my bed, I happened to look across the river and saw a large black bear coming towards camp. I gave the alarm and every man got his rifle. I crawled out of the tent on my hands and one leg and managed to get 5 shots in. He was knocked down 3 times but finally got across the river and crawled into the brush. Four men are after him now. They have returned empty.

Monday, June 26, 1899
Weather: Clear and hot
Well, we got the bear after all and I had liver and heart for breakfast. Three men went after bruin after 10 o'clock last night. Returned at 1 with him.

Tuesday, June 27, 1899
Weather: Strong north wind all day
Rapid firing of guns across the river early this morning. There are three tents there and I think it is the Millard party. The prospectors returned. Same result.

Wednesday, June 28, 1899
Weather: Clear and hot
Eight men and two boats came downriver. Had sheep and greens for dinner and supper. Got a few scurvy berries and some tincture iron chloride. Knee stiff, black, and swollen. [A severe vitamin C deficiency (scurvy) hinders the body's healing processes and its ability to absorb iron from food.][11]

Thursday, June 29, 1899
Weather: Cloudy and cool
We are preparing our boats for descending the river. Heard two men go by about midnight.

Friday, June 30, 1899
Weather: Clear and cool
Whirley and Reonalds have gone 10 miles upriver for sack of flour. Makiesport party came down. They knocked a hole in boat and are fixing it here. We leave here tomorrow night. Just finished reading "Science of Being," by Mrs. Eddy.

Saturday, July 1, 1899
Weather: Cloudy, cold
Two Indians here. Loaded them down with clothes. Cooper here with eight horses. He is going to head of White River.[12] Water too low. Can't boat yet.

Notes—

1. Alfred H. Brooks, *The Geography and Geology of Alaska: A Summary of Existing Knowledge* (Washington: Gov. Printing Office, 1906), pp. 31-32, 250; E.F. Glenn and W.R. Abercrombie, "Report of Guide J.J. Rafferty," *Reports of Explorations in the Territory of Alaska, 1898* (Washington: Gov. Printing Office, 1899), p. 447; Basil Austin, *The Diary of a Ninety-Eighter* (Mount Pleasant, Michigan: John Cumming, 1968), p. 96; C.H. Remington, *A Golden Cross ? On the Trails from the Valdez Glacier* (Los Angeles: White-Thompson, 1939), pp. 111, 155; Oscar Rohn, "A Reconnaissance of the Chitina River and the Skolai Mountains, Alaska," *Twenty-First Annual Report of the USGS,* Part 2 (Washington: Gov. Printing Office, 1900), pp. 403, 410; Mount Wrangell was also active in 1884, 1885, and 1891. See F.C. Schrader, "A Reconnaissance of a Part of Prince William Sound and the Copper River District, Alaska, in 1898," *Twentieth Annual Report of the USGS,* Part 7 (Washington: Gov. Printing Office, 1900), p. 404.

2. Rohn, "A Reconnaissance . . . Skolai Mountains," *Twenty-First Annual Report of the USGS,* p. 412.

3. Schrader, "A Reconnaissance . . . 1898," *Twentieth Annual Report of the USGS,* p. 377; According to McKennan, no fur traders had penetrated this mountainous region in the nineteenth century and not until the Chisana gold rush of 1913 did gold seekers in any numbers find their way into the Chisana and Nabesna basins. Robert A. McKennan, *The Upper Tanana Indians,* in Yale Univ. Publications in Anthropology, No. 55, ed. Irving Rouse (New Haven: Dept. of Anthropology, 1959), p. 3; Rohn, "A Reconnaissance . . . Skolai Mountains," *Twenty-First Annual Report of the USGS,* pp. 403-04; Lt. Henry T. Allen, "Report of a Military Reconnaissance in Alaska, Made in 1885," *Compilation of Narratives of Explorations in Alaska* (Washington: Gov. Printing Office, 1900), p. 441; Also see C.W. Hayes, "An Expedition Through the Yukon District," *National Geographic,* May 15, 1892, pp. 117-62.

4. Rohn, "A Reconnaissance . . . Skolai Mountains," *Twenty-First Annual Report of the USGS,* pp. 404, 406-08; Alfred H. Brooks, "A Reconnaissance from Pyramid Harbor to Eagle City, Alaska," *Twenty-First Annual Report of the USGS,* pp. 339, 351.

5. Allen, *Compilation of Narratives,* pp. 441, 450, 476; Alfred H. Brooks, "A Reconnaissance in the Tanana and White River Basins, Alaska, in 1898," *Twentieth Annual Report of the USGS,* pp. 436, 449-50; McKennan, *The Upper Tanana Indians,* Yale Univ. Publications in Anthropology, No. 55, p. 176 (note); Brooks, *Geography and Geology,* p. 82; Brooks, "A Reconnaissance from Pyramid Harbor," *Twenty-First Annual Report of the USGS,* pp. 339, 352, maps: pp. 338, 346; Rohn, "A Reconnaissance . . . Skolai Mountains," *Twenty-First Annual Report of the USGS,* pp. 407-08, 411; also see General Chart of Alaska, published by the U.S. Coast & Geodetic Survey in June 1897 (first published in 1890) and U.S. Coast & Geodetic Survey map No. 3094, published April 1898

(map reference Nos. G4370 and G4371, Gov. Documents, Shields Library, Univ. of California, Davis).

6. Walter C. Mendenhall, "A Reconnaissance from Resurrection Bay to the Tanana River, Alaska, in 1898," *Twentieth Annual Report of the USGS,* p. 294; Allen, *Compilation of Narratives,* p. 435; Glenn and Abercrombie, "Report of Lt. P.G. Lowe," *Reports of Explorations . . . 1898,* p. 372; Brooks, *Geography and Geology,* p. 297; In 1899 Oscar Rohn concluded that Allen mistook Mt. Sanford for the nonexistent Mt. Tillman due to "an error in observing bearings," or to the "deceptive position of Mt. Sanford," which he said "might easily be considered south of Drum and between it and Wrangell" when viewed from points along the Copper River south of Copper Center. W.R. Abercrombie, "Report of Oscar Rohn on Exploration in Wrangele Mountain District," *Copper River Exploring Expedition, 1899* (Washington: Gov. Printing Office, 1900), pp. 109-10.

7. A.H. Koschmann and M.H. Bergendahl, *Principal Gold-Producing Districts of the U.S.,* USGS Professional Paper No. 610 (Washington: Gov. Printing Office, 1968), pp. 23-25, 30; McKennan, *The Upper Tanana Indians,* Yale Univ. Publications in Anthropology, No. 55, pp. 21, 26, 32, 34, 47.

8. Adolph Murie, *Mammals of Mount McKinley National Park, Alaska* (n.p.: Mt. McKinley Natural History Association in cooperation with the National Park Service, 1962), p. 38; A.L. Rand, *Mammals of Yukon,* Biological Series No. 29, Bulletin No. 100 (Ottawa: National Museum of Canada, 1945), pp. 45-46; Stewart W. Aitchison, "Marmots," *Summit,* 23 (Oct.-Nov. 1977), 42.

9. "at mouth of" has been deleted.

10. Perhaps this was "Suslota John, an unusually large native," who had a salmon cache on the "Batzulnetas" (Tanada Creek). Abercrombie, "Report of Oscar Rohn," *Copper River . . . 1899,* p. 128.

11. *The Merck Manual of Diagnosis and Therapy,* ed. David N. Holvey, M.D., and John H. Talbott, M.D., 12th ed. (Rahway, N.J.: Merck, 1972), pp. 1056-57.

12. Oscar Rohn noted that "a prospecting party in charge of Mr. Cooper went through the pass from the Nabesna to the Tanana earlier in the season on its way from Copper Center to the Upper Yukon." Cooper Creek and Cooper Pass in the Wrangells were probably named for this man. Rohn, "A Reconnaissance . . . Skolai Mountains," *Twenty-First Annual Report of the USGS,* pp. 407-08.

Chapter 10

Boating Down the Nabesna and Tanana Rivers

From its glacial source in the Wrangell Mountains, the Nabesna River flows in a northeasterly direction about 80 miles to the Tanana River. For the first 20 miles of its course, the Nabesna flows in a comparatively wide valley in the Wrangell Mountains, where it receives several other glacial streams, including Jacksina Creek, which rises from the glacier of the same name heading on 13,421-foot Mount Jarvis. Leaving the Wrangells, the Nabesna enters another valley separating the Nutzotin and Mentasta mountains, and within 20 miles it emerges onto a broad gravel plain which is covered by spruce forests interspersed with low hills and numerous lakes. The northward slope of this lowland imparts a swift current to the Nabesna as it crosses to the base of the low hills bordering the north side of the valley. Here it merges with the Chisana flowing from the east to form the Tanana River. From this confluence, the Tanana flows northwesterly more than 500 miles to its mouth on the Yukon River, near the village of Tanana. It is the longest tributary of the Yukon.[1]

Lieutenant Allen called the Athabascan Indians he met in the upper Tanana valley in 1885 "Nabesnatanas," after the Native name for the upper Tanana River. McKennan later termed these people "Upper Tanana," because their territory extended well beyond the drainage of the Nabesna River, named by Brooks in 1898. The Upper Tanana Indians were nomadic hunters with only semipermanent settlements. This lifestyle was necessitated by the absence of salmon in the upper Tanana, the result of a series of rapids located below Tanacross. Dependent mainly on moose and

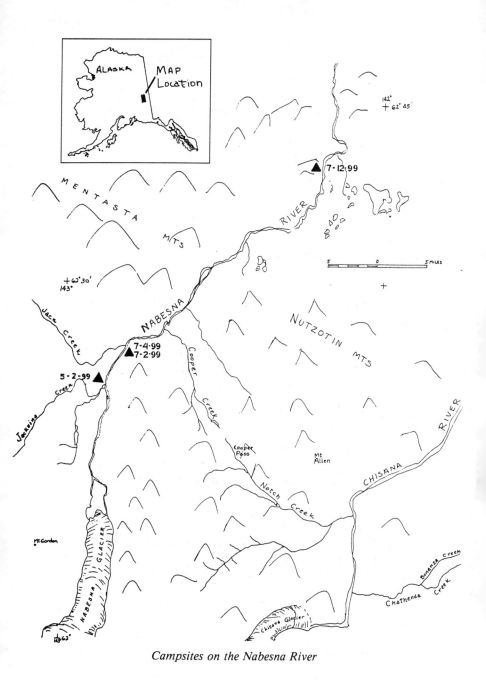

Campsites on the Nabesna River

caribou for subsistence, they roamed the territory in small bands, stopping at various caches, cabins, and tents, where they remained for only a few weeks. Fish was not a significant part of their diet, those caught being used for dog food or by themselves when other food sources were depleted. The hunting range of the Upper Tanana Indians included the Nabesna and Chisana River basins, the Tanana and its tributaries down to the Tok River, and a portion of the headwaters of the White River.[2]

Sunday, July 2, 1899
Weather: Cloudy, cool
Left "Bear Camp" [at the junction of the Nabesna River and Jacksina Creek] 11:00 P.M. with 4 boats, 16 men for downriver. 12:15 boat sprung a leak. Had to unload. 2:15 knocked a hole in side when in middle of stream. Had to pack stuff 6 rods to a narrow bar. Took 2 men to bail out to keep goods from ruin. I am sitting on a narrow bar at this writing with rushing water all around me. It is nearly 3 in the morning. Pitched camp on point "Hard Scrabble" at 5 in the morning. I nearly froze.

Monday, July 3, 1899
Weather: Wind and rain
Went to bed at 8 in the morning. Slept till 4 P.M. when I was awakened by the wind and rain. It took 4 men to keep the tent from blowing down. One tent blew down over a man while asleep.

Tuesday, July 4, 1899
Weather: Nice and warm
Camp "Graves End," ¼ mile from last camp. Nice clear water here. John Stehn was buried here June 28th. He was in our party coming up Copper. Age 38. We are going to take a couple days' hunt, then move.

Wednesday, July 5, 1899
Weather: Cloudy, cool
Eight men have gone hunting. The balance sawing lumber for

extra bottoms in the boats. Four men came down on raft part way. Lost some stuff. Walked in here.

Thursday, July 6, 1899
This has been a summer's day. My leg is getting a good deal better. I walked (with crutch) quite a good ways up the creek.

Friday, July 7, 1899
Weather: Strong N.E. wind, rain
This has been a rough day. [Wind] blew our tent down and two others but did not catch me under it. Oh, but this is a dirty place. Had a duck for dinner.

Saturday, July 8, 1899
Weather: Sultry and hot
Hunters returned at noon. No game. Got to live on rancid bacon a while longer. Lumber is ready for bottoms of boats. Whew, the mosquitoes.

Sunday, July 9, 1899
It thundered and lightened and rained in regular Minnesota style today. I am terribly disgusted with this kind of life. Grub is stale and only one kind at that.

Monday, July 10, 1899
Weather: Cool and windy
Skinner, Jacobson, and Nelson left for Lake Luslota [Suslota] to have another hunt for Cpt. West gold banks. [In 1898 one Captain I.N. West, a 72-year-old adventurer, told of a year-long solo journey he supposedly made in the Copper River region during the 1880s. He allegedly crossed many miles of snow and ice fields in the Saint Elias Mountains to gain access to the region, and after blazing a trail across the Wrangells, he eventually exited the country by way of Valdez Glacier. Prospector Luther Guiteau, who was camped in the Klutina River valley on May 1, 1898, wrote: "Philo . . . informed us that the Capt. West trail had

been abandoned as absolutely impossible. This Capt. West is a kind of visionary fellow and we imagine he is an old timber cruiser and thinks he knows everything about establishing a trail, but he surely got fooled in this Alaskan country which is full of lakes, swift dangerous streams and quick surprises and we now have to be on the alert every minute."]³ We will wait for them at mouth of Shushana. [Conger believed he was on the Chisana but was actually on the Nabesna.]

Tuesday, July 11, 1899
Weather: Cold, windy
Three Indians came looking for cache left by parties ahead. Lots of white men and gold on Chicken Creek [in the Fortymile River country], so says the "Siwash." We leave tomorrow. Indians go with us.

Wednesday, July 12, 1899
Weather: Cloudy, cool
Decamped this morning. Three Indians with us. Now camped on bars 30 miles below. Hurt my leg in the mix-up. Bad river. Full of bars, snags [roots of trees], and sweepers [trees overhanging the river from undercut banks]. Knocked a hole in boat and broke oarlocks off.

Thursday, July 13, 1899
Weather: Cloudy, rain
Three white men have gone upriver to look for cache. We get half if found. We are out of meat, beans, rice, and sugar. See a good many moose tracks but no moose.

Friday, July 14, 1899
Weather: Cool, windy
The Indians found cache containing 10 sacks flour, 5 tents and stoves, clothing, and tools of all descriptions, but the bears had eaten up the bacon. White men returned. Indians remain.

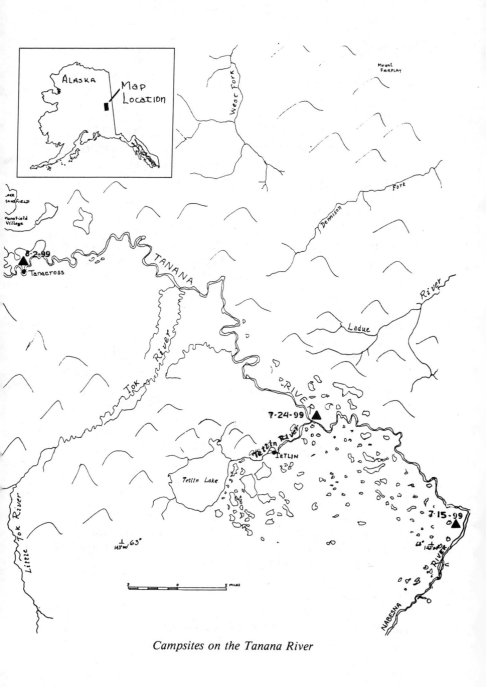

Campsites on the Tanana River

Saturday, July 15, 1899
Weather: Smoky, warm
"Camp Shushana" [at the mouth of the Nabesna], 100 [about 70] miles from where boats were built. Low flat country. Hills on north side of river. River flows west from this point. Water runs slow [not over two to three miles per hour].⁴ Broad and deep. The last 20 miles has been fine boating. Saw a fox.

Sunday, July 16, 1899
Weather: Cloudy and damp
McKeesport party and H. Croop left for Mansfield [a Tanana Indian village south of Lake Mansfield]. We will wait here for Skinner. We wallow in the sand like a chicken. Oh, but it is disgusting.

Monday, July 17, 1899
Weather: Beautiful
Sawed off my crutch and made a cane of it. Am using two canes now and I hope to discard one of them in a few days. There are fish in this river, but they won't bite.

Tuesday, July 18, 1899
Weather: Cloudy and warm
The Indians we left upriver came down today. They had a kind of boat and a raft. Water rose one foot.

Wednesday, July 19, 1899
Weather: Cool and cloudy
Four Indians came down the Shushana with birchbark canoes. I traded some flour for 2 young geese and moose meat. Three of us went upriver looking for fish but found none.

Thursday, July 20, 1899
Weather: Rain all day
Traded flour for fish. At night 7 Indians came down from the Shushana. They stayed all day and all night. One could talk fairly

Page in Horace S. Conger's diary.

good English. [Lieutenant Allen noted that many of the Upper Tanana Indian men had visited the Yukon for trading purposes, but some of the men and most of the women and children had never seen a white man.][5]

Friday, July 21, 1899
Weather: Clear and warm
I walk up and down the bar 2 hours a day to exercise my leg. Use two canes.

Sunday, July 23, 1899
Weather: Clear, warm, and a little windy
Discarded one of my canes. Mosquitoes nearly all gone. Gnats and moose flies take their place. Leave this camp tomorrow.

Monday, July 24, 1899
Weather: Cloudy and cool
"Camp 40 Mile Trail," or where trail comes across from Mentasta. [One of the trails from the Copper River crossed the Tanana here, at the mouth of the Tetlin River. Lieutenant Allen reached the Tanana at this point in 1885 after crossing Suslota Pass. Several Indian trails headed north to the Yukon from the Tanana. The most generally used were those descending one of the many branches of the Fortymile or the Ladue River. See map, page 245.][6] One Indian has just returned from packing over to Chicken Creek. Saw some young geese but could not get any. Killed a duck. River wide and banks low.

Tuesday, July 25, 1899
Weather: Rain
Sold flour and tea to Indians. Two sacks flour, $7.50; ten lbs. tea, $2. Bought some whitefish. No game. [The Indians caught great numbers of whitefish in July, when the fish migrated from the lakes into streams draining into the Tanana.][7]

some image of the page

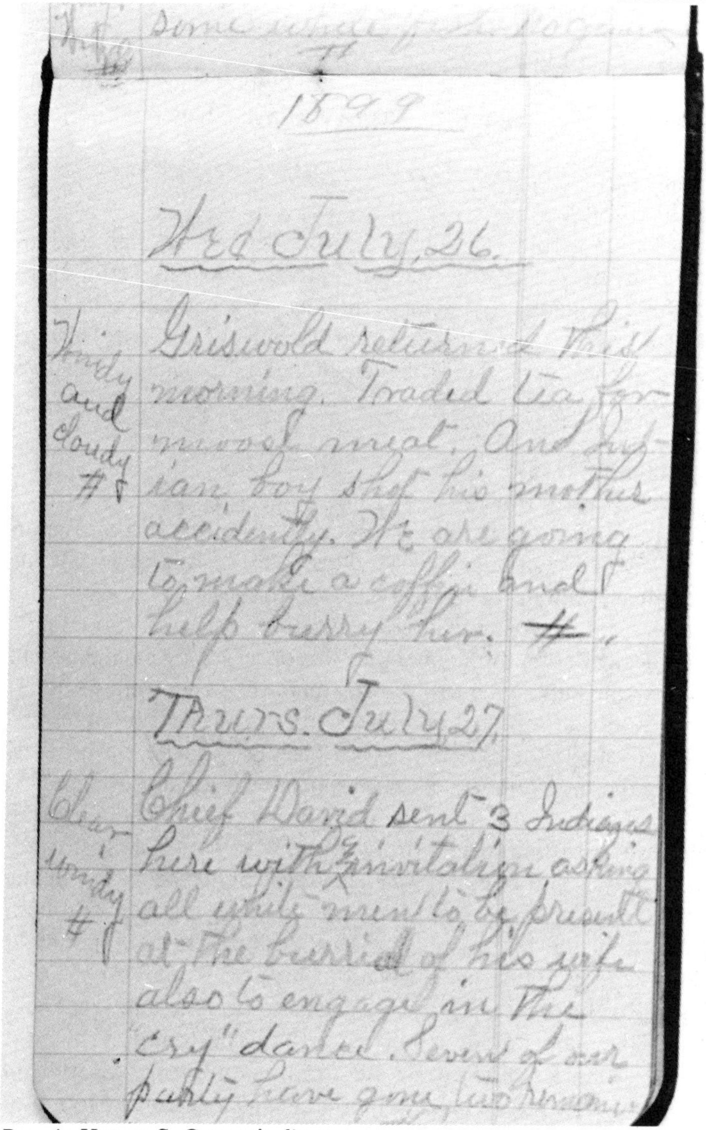

1899

Wed July, 26.

Windy and Cloudy # Griswold returned this morning. Traded tea for moose meat. And Indian boy shot his mother accidently. We are going to make a coffin and help bury her. #

Thurs. July 27,

Clear windy # Chief David sent 3 Indians here with invitation asking all white men to be present at the burrial of his wife also to engage in the "cry" dance. Seven of our party have gone two remain

Page in Horace S. Conger's diary.

Wednesday, July 26, 1899
Weather: Windy and cloudy
Traded tea for moose meat. An Indian boy shot his mother accidentally. We are going to make a coffin and help bury her.

Thursday, July 27, 1899
Weather: Clear, windy
Chief David [from "Tetling's" (now Tetlin), a small Indian village on the Tetlin River, about halfway between Tetlin Lake and the Tanana River][8] sent 3 Indians here with an invitation asking all white men to be present at the burial of his wife, also to engage in the "cry" dance. Seven of our party have gone; two remain.

Friday, July 28, 1899
Weather: Fearful wind all day
Fires raging in all directions. Reonalds returned from Indian camp. Dance continues for 15 days. Chief gives away all his belongings, then burns his house down. Makes a new start in life. [The custom of giving a large celebration, called a "potlatch," after the death of a family member was observed by most Alaskan Indians and some Eskimos. A feast and gift giving were common features of all potlatches. The Upper Tanana potlatch also included singing and dancing, ostensibly for the purpose of helping the survivors forget their grief; however, the potlatch also provided an occasion for these nomadic people to meet in a group and to socialize with neighboring tribes, who were usually invited. The duration of a potlatch was dependent upon the wealth of the sponsor, or "potlatch-man," usually a close relative, and continued until the food supply was exhausted. Then the potlatch-man was required to give away all of his possessions. At the conclusion of the event, he was considered to be spiritually renewed. One of the many taboos associated with this custom prevented the potlatch-man from accepting aid from anyone for the period of one year. Though the original potlatch was a ceremony to honor the dead, it later evolved into a means of achieving prestige, with

1899

Fri. July 28

Fires raging in all directions. Redonalds returned from Ind. camp. Dance continues for 15 days. Chief gives away all his belongings, then burns his house down. Makes a new start in life.

Sat. July 29

Quiet all day. White men are still at the Indian village. Chief David won't let them go till it suits his pleasure. 100 bucks in the dance.

Page in Horace S. Conger's diary.

aspiring leaders trying to outdo each other in giving a large number of these celebrations for distant relatives or other tribesmen.][9]

Saturday, July 29, 1899
Weather: Smoky, warm
Quiet all day. White men are still at the Indian village. Chief David won't let them go till it suits his pleasure. 100 buck Indians in the dance.

Monday, July 31, 1899
Weather: Warm and windy
Skinner and party returned. Bad reports from all directions. Making packsaddles for our dogs. Will leave tomorrow. Some go by way of Mentasta and Copper River. Others [go] down Tanana to Lake Mansfield and on over trail to Dawson. Post at Mentasta. All mail that way for American territory. [In the summer of 1899, Brooks met some Indians who told him "the United States Army had established a post at Mentasta Pass."][10]

Tuesday, August 1, 1899
Weather: Very smoky and bad navigating
Left camp "Tatlin" [Tetlin], or 40 Mile Trail, at 8:30 A.M. Boated down Tanana bound for Mansfield. Made a run of 12 hours. [Near the mouth of the Tetlin River, the Tanana valley constricts and the current of the river usually becomes very swift.][11] Camped on Mosquito Point. River very crooked. Seven men have gone out via Copper. McGee, Nelson, Byorum, Andrews, and I constitute this party.

Wednesday, August 2, 1899
Weather: Cloudy, smoky
Left camp at 7:30 and reached where [Mentasta] trail crosses to Mansfield [present-day Tanacross, formerly called Tanana Crossing]. Met Exploring Party No. 2 from Cooks Inlet. They are on their way to Eagle City. [Party] consists of A.G. Able, A. Fels,

Page in Horace S. Conger's diary.

Frank Lee, John Dillon, William Dittnack, Billie (Indian), and C.E. Griffith, in charge. Latitude 63°-24'-21" N. Longitude 143°-13'-00" W. Altitude 2,375 feet. Magnetic variation 33°. They have 16 head of stock. Swam them across the river this morning. Have engaged transportation with this party to Eagle City. McGee is going also. [Charles Griffith, a civilian topographer, led one of the four detachments comprising Captain E.F. Glenn's 1899 army expedition, which was sent to Cook Inlet to continue explorations begun the previous season. Captain Glenn instructed Griffith to proceed to Eagle City via the Matanuska River valley and the most practicable pass available in the Alaska Range. On June 9, Griffith left Knik Arm accompanied by a hospital steward, 1 soldier, 3 packers, an Indian guide, and 17 pack animals. The party headed north by way of the Chickaloon, Talkeetna, and Susitna rivers. Then, paralleling the Alaska Range in search of a pass to the Tanana, they passed into the Copper River drainage. Crossing from the upper Slana to the Tok, they descended the latter stream to the mouth of the Little Tok and proceeded north to the Tanana over the well-traveled Mentasta trail. The following paragraph is an excerpt from Griffith's report.

"Soon after crossing the Tanana, we met a party of prospectors from the extreme head of the Tanana, who had come down the river. They had not tasted sugar for a long time. In this party was Mr. H.S. Conger, of Mora, Minn., who had been afflicted with scurvy and was still quite lame and unable to walk much, and Mr. W.J. McGee, of Pueblo, Colo. These gentlemen accompanied us to Eagle City."][12]

Notes—

1. Alfred H. Brooks, *The Geography and Geology of Alaska: A Summary of Existing Knowledge* (Washington: Gov. Printing Office, 1906), pp. 82-83.

2. Robert A. McKennan, *The Upper Tanana Indians,* in Yale Univ. Publications in Anthropology, No. 55, ed. Irving Rouse (New Haven: Dept. of Anthropology, 1959), pp. 15-19, 21, 35, 46-47.

3. William S. Hanable, *The Copper River, Alaska in the 18th and 19th*

Centuries (Anchorage: Alaska Historical Commission, 1982), p. 58; quote in "Alaska Gold Rush Diary," serialized 1928 in the Freeport, Illinois, *Journal-Standard* (manuscript in Alaska Historical Library, Juneau).

4. Alfred H. Brooks, "A Reconnaissance in the Tanana and White River Basins, Alaska, in 1898," *Twentieth Annual Report of the USGS,* Part 7 (Washington: Gov. Printing Office, 1900), p. 451.

5. Lt. Henry T. Allen, "Report of a Military Reconnaissance in Alaska, Made in 1885," *Compilation of Narratives of Explorations in Alaska* (Washington: Gov. Printing Office, 1900), pp. 444-45. Belle Isle and Fort Reliance, near the present sites of Eagle and Dawson, were the only trading posts in existence on the upper Yukon in 1885. McKennan, *The Upper Tanana Indians,* pp. 24, 28-30.

6. Brooks, *Geography and Geology,* p. 83; McKennan, *The Upper Tanana Indians,* p. 30.

7. McKennan, *The Upper Tanana Indians,* pp. 21, 35, 46.

8. E.F. Glenn and W.R. Abercrombie, "Report of Lt. P.G. Lowe," *Reports of Explorations in the Territory of Alaska, 1898* (Washington: Gov. Printing Office, 1899), p. 370; McKennan, *The Upper Tanana Indians,* p. 18.

9. McKennan, *The Upper Tanana Indians,* pp. 130, 134-39, 144-45.

10. Alfred H. Brooks, "A Reconnaissance from Pyramid Harbor to Eagle City, Alaska," *Twenty-First Annual Report of the USGS,* Part 2 (Washington: Gov. Printing Office, 1900), p. 391.

11. Brooks, "A Reconnaissance . . . 1898," *Twentieth Annual Report of the USGS,* p. 451.

12. C.E. Griffith, "From Knik Station to Eagle City," *Compilation of Narratives,* pp. 724-26; Capt. E.F. Glenn to the Asst. Sec. of War, Tyoonok, Alaska, June 5, 1899, in *Annual Reports of the War Dept. 1899,* House Doc. 2 [3901], 56th Congress, 1st sess., Vol. 1, Part 3 (Washington: Gov. Printing Office, 1899), pp. 89-90.

Chapter 11

Overland to Eagle

Less than 120 miles of rolling hills and low mountains separate Tanacross, on the upper Tanana River, from Eagle, on the Yukon. For the most part, this terrain is drained by the many branches of the Fortymile River, a large tributary of the upper Yukon. The so-called Fortymile country was well traveled by the Indians, and their trails facilitated the journey of prospectors and explorers heading north to Eagle or the Fortymile gold fields in 1898-99.

The southern tributaries of the Fortymile gave the Upper Tanana Indians easy access to the Yukon River. The North and South forks of the Fortymile join about 40 miles southwest of Eagle to form the main river, which descends from the highland in stretches of rapids and smooth water on its northeasterly course to the Yukon. The mouth of the river is 20 miles inside Canadian territory but its headwaters include meandering streams extending far to the southwest toward the Tanana. The Upper Tanana Indians descended these streams in skin boats or rafts to trade with the Yukon Indians and, later, with American traders, who established posts on the upper Yukon in the 1870s and 1880s. They returned by land, traveling along the hard, flat ridges joining the hills to avoid the marshes and brush of the river valleys.[1]

Prospectors began ascending the Fortymile from the Yukon in the 1880s, and in 1886 they made the first discovery of paying gold in Interior Alaska within 30 miles of the Canadian border. By the end of 1899 most of the gold-bearing streams in the Fortymile drainage system had been located. Extensive dredging and hydraulic mining methods have been used in this district, and today, with the increased value of gold, modern-day prospectors are sifting the tailings of these operations, searching for nuggets that may have been overlooked.[2]

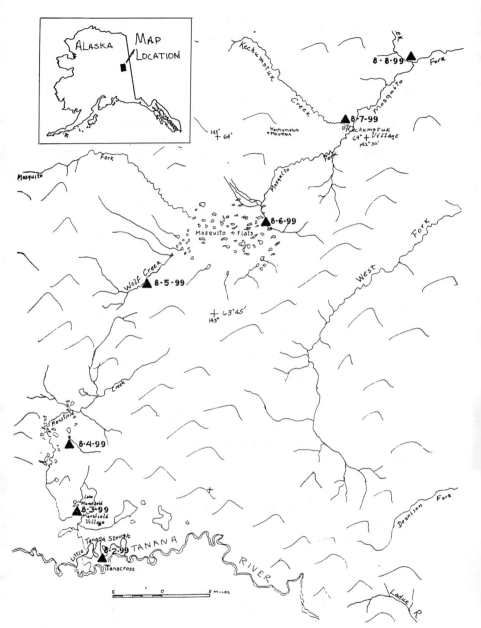

Campsites from the Tanana River to Gold Creek

Thursday, August 3, 1899
Weather: Clear and hot; gnats thick
Left Tanana at 8:30 with Griffith's party. Rode a horse all day.
Traveled north over a fine trail. Three miles out came to a branch
of Tanana [Little Tanana Slough] where we swam horses across.
Took grub over in boat. Camped now at Mansfield Lake. Distance 6 miles from Tanana over trail. Fine looking country. Best
grass I've seen. Lots of Indians. A good many died last winter.
Abundance of fish here. A good many caribou in early winter,
also moose. [The abundance of fish and game in this district per-
mitted the Lake Mansfield Indians to lead a semisedentary lifestyle which contrasted with that of their nomadic neighbors, the
Upper Tanana Indians. Though these two groups of Natives were
often at war, Robert McKennan concluded that, when con-
sidering the Tanana as a whole, the Mansfield Indians should be
"lumped together" with the Upper Tanana Indians, because both
groups shared a similar culture and both were geographically
separated from the lower Tanana Indians and the range of the
salmon by stretches of rapids located between Tanacross and
Fairbanks. These rapids were exceedingly dangerous to navigate
in their frail canoes and practically prevented communication
with the Indians of the lower river. The fear that the Mansfield
Indians had for the rapids was revealed to Lieutenant Allen in
1885 when his efforts to get them to accompany him downriver
ended with the Natives "pointing to the canoes and making
gestures indicative of capsizing and imitating, with their voices,
the roaring sound of the water."[3]
    The following account of the Mansfield Indians is from the
report of C.E. Griffith, with whom Conger was traveling.

Lake Mansfield was reached . . . on August 3.
Here we found a Tanana Indian village of about 65
inhabitants. All the men and boys were out to meet us.
These Indians were very friendly, and wanted to buy
tobacco before everything else. They would, however,
buy tea, sugar, guns, and ammunition. They all

*seemed to be supplied with money and offered big
prices for anything they wanted. They were very intel-
ligent, and all the young men spoke good English. A
very noticeable feature was the healthy appearance of
these Indians, which was in striking contrast to so
many Alaska Indians. . . . They told us, however, a
great tale of woe of how many Indians had died, from
which we understood that some epidemic had afflicted
them.*[4]]

Friday, August 4, 1899
Weather: Rain, hot
Did not break camp till 10 A.M. Traveled 7 miles to next water. Met
two men who had lost their horses. They were going back to the
Tanana.

Saturday, August 5, 1899
Weather: Smoky, cloudy, and sultry
Camp "Wool [Wolf] Creek," 18 miles from "Side Hill" camp.
Good trail but a good many hills to climb. Scrubby timber and
scarce. Good grass. Water, very little. Saw 3 miles of fence built
by Indians for corralling game. [The Indians constructed these
barriers of small trees and brush to trap caribou. While the
animals could easily cross these makeshift fences, they were more
inclined to follow them to one of the narrow openings left for the
purpose of snaring or killing them as they emerged.][5] Gnats, the
thickest and largest I ever saw.

Sunday, August 6, 1899
Weather: Rain
Left Wool Creek at 10 and reached Mosquito Creek at 3 P.M.
where we will camp tonight. The country between here and Wool
Creek [Mosquito Flats] is the finest grazing ground I have ever
seen, but think the mosquitoes and gnats would torment stock to
death. My neck is raw from their bites. Received 3 letters from
Lizzie.

Monday, August 7, 1899
Weather: Cloudy, sultry
Camp "Ketchumstock [Kechumstuk] Creek," 15 miles from Mosquito Creek [camp]. Fine grass country all the way. Rolling hills. Shot 2 ducks and caught a mess of fish. Life is miserable on account of the mosquitoes. [Griffith gave the following description of the country between Kechumstuk Creek and Gold Creek, which they crossed the next day.

> In due time we crossed Ketchumstock Creek, where there is another Indian village. After traversing a distance of 12 miles we struck Gold Creek. The country from Gold Creek to Ketchumstock Creek contained very extra-fine high grass. It had a long head of yellowish seed, stood very thick, was from 2 to 3 feet high, and looked like a big grain field. It was rich in seeds and proved to be excellent feed for stock. The country hereabouts possesses plenty of game and is a favorite hunting ground for the Indians. We saw many old camps and great numbers of caribou horns, bones, and skin, and some fine specimens of antlers that were hung in trees along the trail.][6]

Tuesday, August 8, 1899
Weather: Clear and warm
Camp "Gold Creek," near where it flows into Mosquito Creek. This camp is 11 miles from Ketchumstock village, a deserted Indian town. The Indians all died last winter with grippe. [John Rice, a quartermaster's clerk with Captain Abercrombie's 1899 army expedition, preceded Conger on the trail to Eagle by approximately two weeks. He reported that he found a band of about 50 Kechumstuk Indians at Lake Mansfield, and that they hunted and fished in that region in the summer, returning to their village on Kechumstuk Creek for the winter. He also reported that three Upper Tanana Indians he found camped at Lake Mentasta told him that all but two of the Mentasta Lake Indians had died

the previous winter and that the two survivors had joined the Kechumstuk tribe.][7] There are 4 men who came up the Copper last winter prospecting on this creek. They think they have found platinum. Four more men passed on down the river in boats. Water is too low for boating. Burr and his wife went down yesterday, bound for Dawson.

Wednesday, August 9, 1899
Weather: Clear and cool
We lay over today. Griffith takes observations. Latitude 64°-11 '. Went fishing and caught one fish. This is a good country to prospect in for placer mines.

Thursday, August 10, 1899
Weather: Cloudy, rain
Camp "Franklyn Gulch," at the mouth. We struck this gulch at its head and followed down [the canyon six miles to the mining camp at the junction of Franklin Creek and South Fork Fortymile River]. It is very narrow and rough. Saw the first mining here. There are about 15 miners at work. The gulch is practically worked out. It was mined 12 years ago.

Friday, August 11, 1899
Weather: Cloudy, cool
We lay over here today. Bought a hind quarter of moose. Paid 50¢ per pound. Tobacco is $2.50 per lb. Flour $14 per C [hundredweight]. Sugar, bacon, and rice 35¢. Some of the boys bought gold nuggets. The miners tell me that they are only making wages in this gulch, $10 per day. This is a sort of grubstake claim. Most of the miners have been in here 3 years and have not made a stake yet. [Griffith wrote: "We saw a number of men at work with sluice boxes, although water for sluicing was very scarce. The miners were 'sniping' on deserted claims, simply trying to make a stake. . . . En route we heard of a 'strike' on Jack Wade Creek, which is a short stream heading a little east of South Fork, and flowing in a southerly direction into Walkers Fork. We met a

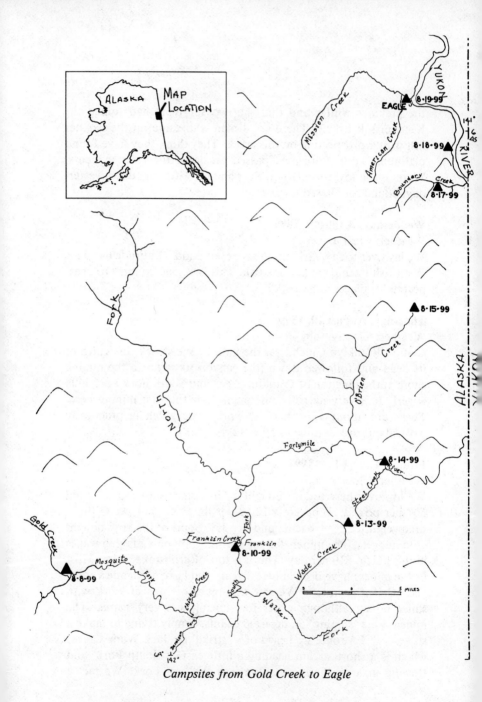

Campsites from Gold Creek to Eagle

number of miners who were going to Jack Wade." John Rice reported that on August 9, 1899, 700 men were located along the nine-mile length of Wade Creek and that more than $800 of gold had been panned from a single wheelbarrow of dirt.][8]

Saturday, August 12, 1899
Weather: Clear
Layed over on account of sickness. Nearly every man is sick. Too much fresh meat. There is a big excitement on Jack Wade Creek. If I had money enough to grubstake a man, I could get half interest in a claim. But I am broke and a cripple besides. Most of the men working here are poor. There is a thirty thousand dollar flume here that was built 16 years ago. [The Fortymile district is one of the oldest placer areas in the Yukon region, with a small amount of production reported as early as 1883.][9]

Sunday, August 13, 1899
Weather: Cloudy
Left Franklyn Gulch at 8:30 A.M. Crossed the [South Fork Fortymile] river and took to the high ridges. Crossed the head of Wade Creek. Met 5 men from the forks [junction of the North and South forks of the Fortymile] going to Wade to buy claims. Camped for the night 12 miles from Franklyn. Nothing but hills and mountains as far as one can see.

Monday, August 14, 1899
Weather: Cloudy
Left camp at 8:30. Met Holman and part of the government mail party going to Valdes. [Holman, assisted by Jackson, was a subcontractor carrying mail for Capt. Richard Chilcott of San Francisco, who had the contract for carrying the mail from Valdez to Eagle. At this time, Holman was leading a pack train loaded with winter supplies to cache at several mail stations he was establishing along the trail. John Rice, the quartermaster's clerk, had escorted Post Office Inspector C.L. Wayland to Eagle so that Wayland could establish post offices at several mining

Cabin and cache, Fort Egbert, Alaska.

camps along the route. Wayland established a post office at
Valdez on May 9, 1899.][10] Also met several packers on their way
to Wade. Reached mouth of Steel [Steele] Creek, which empties
into 40 Mile, about noon. Swam our horses across 40 Mile, then
got dinner. In the p.m. we boated our stuff over. Seventeen [less
than nine] miles from the boundary line and 42 miles from the
post [at Eagle]. Panned out a little dust.

Tuesday, August 15, 1899
Weather: Cloudy
Left 40 Mile River at an early hour and traveled in a northerly
direction up very steep hills. Did not stop for dinner. Camped at
five o'clock at the head of O'Brien Creek. We are traveling now
without a trail. Left 40 Mile trail to our right about 3:30 P.M. Am
very tired and my leg aches terribly.

Wednesday, August 16, 1899
Weather: Cloudy
Did not leave camp very early. Got off our course and haven't

found it yet, either, although we were in sight of the Youcon [Yukon] once. Camped at 7:30 P.M. high up in the hills. We do not know whether Eagle City is below or above us. [Their maps were of little value in guiding them through this country, as the region between the Tanana and Yukon had been drawn by imaginative cartographers using information obtained from the Indians.][11]

Thursday, August 17, 1899
Got up this morning in a rain. Ate breakfast, packed up, and decamped in a downpour. Went down some of the steepest hills I ever saw. We finally drew up in a box canyon where we had to wade in the middle of the creek for over a mile. [This waterway was Boundary Creek, which flows north and east 12 miles to the Yukon at the Alaska-Yukon boundary. Rice followed the same route, thinking he was on American Creek, which flows north nine miles to Mission Creek, one mile northwest of Eagle.][12] Camped for the night only 3 miles from the Youcon. Guess we will retrace our steps, for we are above [upriver of] Eagle City.

Friday, August 18, 1899
Weather: Cloudy
Three men have gone up the canyon to see if they can get up over the hills. Can't go down this way, for rocks project out into the Youcon, making it impossible to pass them without rafting and swimming horses. Climbed hill one mile long. On top found 3 bears. Killed two. Went down a long, swampy hill to the Youcon. We are still 9 miles above Eagle City. Lee quit. [Probably Frank Lee, of Griffith's party.]

Saturday, August 19, 1899
Weather: Clear
Left camp on Youcon at an early hour and went downriver 8 miles to Eagle City, or Fort Egbert. The government is erecting some fine buildings. City has a population of 1,000, including soldiers. A good deal of work is being done, but there are 3 [men] for one job. No drugstore. Think one would pay now. Town on west side

Completed barracks at Fort Egbert, Alaska, August 15, 1899.

of river. [Gold was first discovered in the Eagle district in 1895 on American Creek, a tributary of Mission Creek. Three years later, the mining camp which had developed on the Yukon at the mouth of Mission Creek was platted and named Eagle City for the American eagles nesting on a nearby bluff. In earlier years a trading post called Belle Isle existed at this location. The Alaska Commercial Company, North American Transportation and Trading Company, and Alaska Exploration Company established general supply stores at Eagle in 1898, and the population grew to 1,700 before decreasing with the stampede to Nome, which began with the opening of navigation in 1899. In late May of 1899, Captain W.P. Richardson received orders at Circle City to establish a military post and reservation at Eagle. The orders were the result of reports made in 1897-98 by (then lieutenant) Richardson and Captain P.H. Ray, Eighth Infantry. They had been sent to Alaska in August of 1897 to investigate conflicting reports of lawlessness on the Yukon and determine whether troops were needed to keep order. A scarcity of food led to mob violence at Circle and Fort Yukon in the fall of 1897. Large numbers of lawless men, who

The Hannah, *1899-1901*

had been attracted north by the Klondike excitement, were being forced downriver, out of Dawson, by the Canadian North West Mounted Police. The lack of law enforcement officials on the American side of the boundary prompted Ray to return to the States to personally report the rapidly changing conditions along the river. To protect life and property, he recommended that three military posts be established — at Saint Michael, near the mouth of the Yukon, and at the mouths of the Tanana River and Mission Creek. On July 31, 1899, Ray, who had been promoted to the rank of major, arrived in Eagle with soldiers and officers of the Seventh Infantry to garrison Fort Egbert and establish his headquarters as commander of the newly created District of North Alaska. By that time, Eagle was boasting a sawmill, restaurants, saloons, and the stores of the aforementioned companies, and Captain Richardson had already begun construction of the military post.][13]

Sunday, August 20, 1899
Weather: Clear
Had an interview with Major Ray and he has given me transportation to St. Michaels. [Saint Michael is on the east coast of the island of the same name in Norton Sound.] I leave tonight at 8:30

on steamer *Hannah,* a fine boat. [Three large, elegant stern-wheelers, the *Hannah, Susie,* and *Sarah,* were built in the winter of 1897-98 and put into service on the Yukon the following summer by the Alaska Commercial Company. They were styled after the Mississippi River steamers and were named for the wives and daughters of the company's directors. The number of river steamers operating on the Yukon rose from 7 in 1897 to 30 by 1899.][14] McGee got full, spent all of his money, and lost transportation. Poor old man. I feel sorry for him. Wish I was well and strong. I would remain here.

Notes—

1. Alfred H. Brooks, *The Geography and Geology of Alaska: A Summary of Existing Knowledge* (Washington: Gov. Printing Office, 1906), pp. 73-74; Robert A. McKennan, *The Upper Tanana Indians,* in Yale Univ. Publications in Anthropology, No. 55, ed. Irving Rouse (New Haven: Dept. of Anthropology, 1959), pp. 22, 24, 28-30.

2. Alfred H. Brooks, "A Reconnaissance from Pyramid Harbor to Eagle City, Alaska," *Twenty-First Annual Report of the USGS,* Part 2 (Washington: Gov. Printing Office, 1900), pp. 376-77; A.H. Koschmann and M.H. Bergendahl, *Principal Gold-Producing Districts of the United States,* Geological Survey Professional Paper 610 (Washington: Gov. Printing Office, 1968), pp. 23, 27.

3. Henry T. Allen, "Report of a Military Reconnaissance in Alaska, Made in 1885," in *Compilation of Narratives of Explorations in Alaska* (Washington: Gov. Printing Office, 1900), p. 445, quote on p. 448; McKennan, *The Upper Tanana Indians,* p. 23; Alfred H. Brooks, "A Reconnaissance in the Tanana and White River Basins, Alaska, in 1898," *Twentieth Annual Report of the USGS,* Part 7 (Washington: Gov. Printing Office, 1900), pp. 490-92, 439; Brooks, *Geography and Geology,* p. 88.

4. C.E. Griffith, "From Knik Station to Eagle City," in *Compilation of Narratives,* p. 726.

5. Alfred H. Brooks, *Blazing Alaska's Trails,* 2d ed. (1953; rpt. Fairbanks: Univ. of Alaska Press, 1973), pp. 78-79.

6. Griffith, *Compilation of Narratives,* p. 727.

7. W.R. Abercrombie, "Report of John F. Rice," *Copper River Exploring Expedition, 1899* (Washington: Gov. Printing Office, 1900), pp. 98-99.

8. Griffith, *Compilation of Narratives,* p. 727; Abercrombie, "Report of John F. Rice," *Copper River . . . 1899,* p. 101.

9. Koschmann and Bergendahl, *Principal Gold-Producing Districts,* p. 27.

10. "Building a Long Alaska Trail," *San Francisco Chronicle,* Oct. 30, 1899,

p. 5; "New Alaska Mail Route," *Seattle Post-Intelligencer,* Aug. 21, 1899, p. 5; Abercrombie, "Report of John F. Rice," *Copper River . . . 1899,* pp. 95, 102; C.H. Remington, *A Golden Cross ? On the Trails from the Valdez Glacier* (Los Angeles: White-Thompson, 1939), p. 23.

11. E.F. Glenn and W.R. Abercrombie, "Report of Lt. P.G. Lowe," *Reports of Explorations in the Territory of Alaska, 1898* (Washington: Gov. Printing Office, 1899), p. 372; The watersheds between the Yukon and Tanana were unmapped from actual observation until E.C. Barnard surveyed 2,000 square miles of the Fortymile River basin in 1898. His map and report were published by the USGS in 1899. E.C. Barnard, "Report of the Fortymile Expedition," *Maps and Descriptions of Routes of Exploration in Alaska in 1898, with General Information Concerning the Territory* (Washington: Gov. Printing Office, 1899), [3737], pp. 76-84. Brooks, *Geography and Geology,* p. 129; Brooks, "A Reconnaissance in the Tanana . . . 1898," *Twentieth Annual Report of the USGS,* p. 445.

12. Abercrombie, "Report of John F. Rice," *Copper River . . . 1899,* p. 100.

13. Koschmann and Bergendahl, *Principal Gold-Producing Districts,* p. 26; Donald Orth, *Dictionary of Alaska Place Names,* U.S. Geological Survey Professional Paper 567 (Washington: Gov. Printing Office, 1967), p. 291; Barnard, "Report of the Fortymile Expedition," *Maps and Descriptions of Routes,* p. 80; Brooks, "A Reconnaissance from Pyramid Harbor," *Twenty-First Annual Report of the USGS,* p. 391; Abercrombie, "Report of John F. Rice," *Copper River . . . 1899,* pp. 100-101; *Annual Reports of the War Department, 1899,* House Doc. 2 [3901], 56th Congress, 1st sess., Vol. 1, Part 3 (Washington: Gov. Printing Office, 1899), pp. 77, 93, 115; P.H. Ray, "Alaska — 1897, Relief of the Destitute in Gold Fields," *Compilation of Narratives,* pp. 530-32, 535-37, 542-44, 547, 558; also see *San Francisco Chronicle* for June 24, 1899, p. 7, and June 26, 1899, p. 9.

14. Clarence L. Andrews, *The Story of Alaska* (Caldwell, Idaho: Caxton Printers, 1938), p. 191; Pierre Berton, *The Klondike Fever* (New York: Knopf, 1958), p. 307; William R. Siddall, "The Yukon Waterway in the Development of Interior Alaska," *Pacific Historical Review,* 28 (Nov. 1959), 374.

Chapter 12—

Homeward Bound

Conger returned to the States from Eagle in 24 days by way of the Saint Michael (all-water) route. The 1,460-mile river boat journey down the Yukon and up the coast to Saint Michael took eight days; and the transfer to ocean steamer, a short stopover in Nome, and the subsequent 3,000-mile voyage back to Seattle consumed the remaining 16 days.

The Yukon, Alaska's longest river, heads in the Yukon Territory of Canada in Marsh Lake, one of a series of navigable lakes stretching across the British Columbia-Yukon border. A portion of the upper Yukon, south of its junction with the Pelly, is sometimes referred to as the "Lewes." On its 1,900-mile course to the Bering Sea, the Yukon flows in a northwesterly direction as far as the Arctic Circle, then makes a marked change of direction to the southwest. Though it is navigable for its entire 1,400-mile length in Alaska, ocean-going vessels can not ascend the Yukon because of its shallowness. Thus passengers and freight were transferred to shallow-draft sternwheelers at Saint Michael, the nearest port to the mouth of the Yukon. Even these flat-bottomed river boats had difficulty navigating the river in the fall, when the river is at its lowest level. The last of the large steamboats stopped plying the Yukon on a regular basis about 1960.[1]

Monday, August 21, 1899
Weather: Cloudy
Reached Circle City at 2 P.M. The town is nearly depopulated [because of the stampede to Nome]. Low ground. No mountains in sight. River between here and Fort Youcon is full of bars, 40 miles wide, with thousands of islands. Passed Ft. Youcon [originally the site of an isolated fur trading post established by the Hudson's Bay Company in 1847] at 8:30 P.M. It is 90 miles from Circle City. Saw two steamers stuck on sand bars. [Between

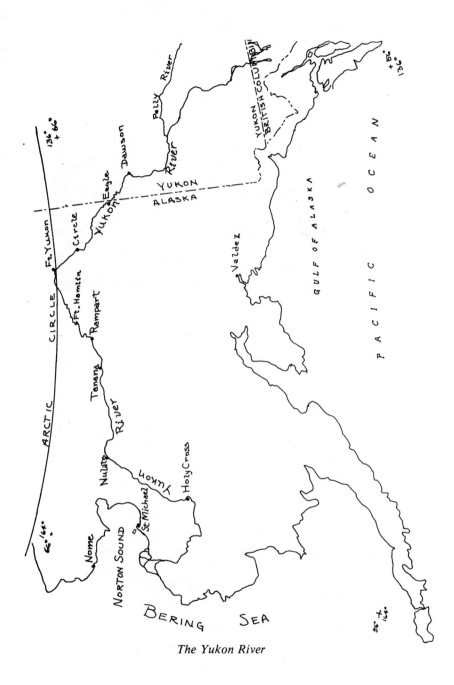

The Yukon River

The steamer Sarah *at Fort Egbert, August 1899.*

Eagle and Circle the Yukon winds through hilly plateau country in a comparatively narrow, steep-sided valley. But below Circle the river spreads out in the Yukon Flats, a lowland region 180 miles long and 70 miles wide, where it meanders in numerous, ever-shifting channels. During the Klondike rush, river boat captains hired Indians living along the river to guide them through these uncharted waters. Alfred H. Brooks wrote the following description of the Yukon Flats in 1906.

> *From the steamer deck the Yukon Flats present a monotonous expanse of sand bars and low, densely forested spruce islands, through which the boat follows a tortuous channel among a bewildering maze of tributary and distributary watercourses, with an occasional glimpse of the distant rim of the plateau which surrounds the lowland. The presence of man in this dreary tract is made manifest only in the clearings from which the spruce has been cut for fuel, or in the occasional small Indian settlement, or wood-chopper huts. At low water 10 or 15 feet of frozen silt bank is*

exposed, while during floods the river is almost even with the surface of the islands.][2]

Tuesday, August 22, 1899
Weather: Cold, cloudy
Met steamer *Sarah* going upriver. Major Ray [traveling aboard the *Hannah*] stopped her and kept both boats waiting for 6 hours. Am feeling badly today. Rheumatic pains in both knees. Passed Hamlin in the evening. Got a quarter of moose meat. From here down, the shores are terraced and very beautiful. [Fort Hamlin was a small Yukon trading station located about 40 miles northeast of Rampart. Below Fort Hamlin, the Yukon leaves the flats and flows through a narrow valley in low mountainous country. At the mouth of the Tanana the river again broadens.][3]

Wednesday, August 23, 1899
Weather: Cloudy, cold
Stopped running about midnight. Reached Weare [a trading post operated by the North American Transportation and Trading Company, and named for either the director, Portus B., and/or the president, Ely E., of that company] at mouth of Tanana about 9 A.M. The government is building a post here called Fort Gibbon. They have a sawmill running in full blast. It is a nice, high and dry place for a town. [About one-half mile above Weare was Tanana, a trading post operated by the Alaska Commercial Company, and just below Weare was the U.S. Army post, commanded by Major C.A. Booth.][4]

Thursday, August 24, 1899
Weather: Cloudy
Saw an ocean steamer high and dry on a sand bar. Met the U.S. Revenue Cutter [*Nunivak* just below Nulato].[5] They boarded us and took pictures of *Hannah*. [In 1897 Captain P.H. Ray recommended that a small, armed government steamer be placed in operation on the Yukon to patrol the river and to provide mobility for the military in dealing with the shifting population along

Alaska Commercial Company post at Rampart City, Alaska, July 1899.

Typical trading post of the Yukon valley, 1899-1901.

the river. The *Nunivak*, a wooden vessel, was especially designed for this purpose. She was completed in San Francisco in the spring of 1899 and was commanded by First Lieutenant J.C. Cantwell, of the Revenue Cutter Service (now called Coast Guard). Her duties included enforcing the customs and navigation laws along the Yukon, extending assistance to destitute miners, and aiding the civil or military authorities in the enforcement of the law. Her cruising ground was limited to the lower 1,000 miles of the river.][6] Passed by several small missionary towns. Stopped at several of them. Stopped for wood and coal. Coal mine right on riverbank. [The Alaska Commercial Company had a coal mine on the Yukon about 50 miles below Nulato, while a Mr. Frank Pickarts operated another just above Nulato. Both of these mines produced coal of the lignite variety.][7]

Friday, August 25, 1899
Weather: Foggy
Had to stop 3 hours on account of fog. Have got a cold on lungs. Bad weather for colds. Stopped at Holy Cross Mission. They have a fine garden there. Saw some magnificent cauliflower and radishes. The natives came aboard our boat to sell curios and they had some beauties. [The Roman Catholic Mission of Holy Cross was established in 1886 near the Ingalik Indian village called Koserefski by the Russians. In August of 1899 the mission school had 25 Native pupils. The school and six-acre garden were the responsibilty of three Sisters of the Canadian Order of Saint Anne, with headquarters in Quebec.][8]

Saturday, August 26, 1899
Weather: Rain, cold
5:10 P.M. Stuck on a sand bar 3 miles from the mouth of the river. Will wait for high tide, 4 in the morning. This channel is not more than 100 yards wide. Saw lots of geese and swan. [In the delta, the Yukon divides into a number of divergent channels which flow to the Bering Sea. Steamboats heading for Saint Michael usually took the northernmost waterway, called Apoon Pass, and they

U.S. revenue steamer Nunivak *at Rampart, 1899-1901.*

frequently went aground in its narrow, intricate channels. From the Apoon mouth to Saint Michael, the river boats crossed 60 miles of open sea, a dangerous voyage for these shallow-draft craft in stormy weather.][9]

Sunday, August 27, 1899
Weather: Cloudy
Weighed anchor about midnight but did not go far till daylight. Came out of the mouth of the river into Norton Sound at an early hour. Arrived at St. Michael at 12:30. Anchored 200 yards off wharf. Strong wind. [The shores of Saint Michael Bay are fringed with rocks and reefs, and during strong northerly winds, which

cause a low stage of water and high seas in the harbor, river boats anchored in deeper water to the east of Saint Michael.][10]

Monday, August 28, 1899
Weather: Windy
Loaded 150 tons of coal on boat off barge in bay. About 5 in the evening we pulled up at the wharf. Went ashore and took in the town. Saw lots of fur and ivory. Town is dead. Everybody has gone to Nome. [The discovery of gold on Anvil Creek, a tributary of the Snake River, on September 22, 1898, led to the formation of the Cape Nome Mining district the following month. Rumors of the discovery were heard in the fall and winter of 1898, but by that time most people were skeptical of such reports. With the opening of navigation in 1899, confirmation of the strike was brought to Dawson, and by mid-summer the news reached Seattle with the season's first returning steamers. The stampede to Nome from Outside began early the following summer. The Nome district has produced more gold than any other district in Alaska except Fairbanks (discovered in 1902).][11]

Tuesday, August 29, 1899
Weather: Cloudy
They are loading the *Hannah* for her return trip. Am still on board. Hotel is full. No room for me. Expect to leave for Seattle on steamer *Charles Nelson* Thursday, the 31st. Will stop off at Nome if possible. Have to pay $1.00 a meal. Will eat only two meals a day. Could do on less, as appetite is poor.

Wednesday, August 30, 1899
Weather: Cloudy
Left A.C. Co. dock at 7:30 this morning and pulled over to NAT&T Co.'s. [All of the companies doing business on the Yukon had warehouses, stores, hotels, and offices at Saint Michael.][12] Got stuck on the rocks and had to be pulled off. Am stopping at Healy Hotel [probably named for John J. Healy, the manager of the NAT&T Co.]. Heard a piano today for the first

Saint Michael, 1902

time in 1½ years. Those returning from Nome tell fabulous stories of the wealth there.

Thursday, August 31, 1899
Weather: Sunshine
Bought ticket for Seattle. Went aboard the Klondyke [a NAT&T Co. river steamer] at 3 P.M. It took me out to the *Charles Nelson*. [The *Charles Nelson* was built for the gold trade at the Union Iron Works shipyard in San Francisco and completed in June of 1898. After a short period in the Alaska trade, she served in the transport service, returning from the Philippines in June of 1899. At that time she was a vessel of the Alaska Exploration Company, but by September she was sailing under the banner of the Kruse Steamship Line.][13] Supper time and the *Nelson* is still at anchor. [The harbor at Saint Michael was too shallow for ocean-going vessels, which had to anchor at least one and a half miles offshore. Their cargoes were transferred to shore with lighters.][14] Don't think we will get out before tomorrow afternoon. There are 3 cripples on board. One poor fellow has inflammatory rheumatism badly.

Friday, September 1, 1899
Saw two boxes of gold dust of one hundred thousand [dollars]

Street in Anvil City, Alaska, 1899.

each put aboard this morning. [The *Seattle Post-Intelligencer* for September 14, 1899, reported the *Nelson*'s arrival in Seattle and said she carried between $500,000 and $600,000 in gold dust.][15] We are crowded into a stinking place where cattle were stored coming up. Had to eat standing up this morning. The fare is awful for the price paid, $60. Left St. Michaels at 9:30 P.M.

Saturday, September 2, 1899
Weather: Foggy
8 A.M. Stuck on bar near Cape Nome. Arrived at Anvil City, 3 miles above Cape Nome, at 12 M [noon]. Left Anvil at 4 P.M. [The town of Anvil City, now called Nome, is located at the mouth of the Snake River, about 12 miles west of the point of land called Cape Nome. It was built on the beach just above high tide and its name was derived from an anvil-shaped rock which stood on the top of a hill several miles inland. At an election held at Anvil City in mid-September of 1899, the miners voted to change the town's name to Nome so a post office could be located there. It seems the

government had designated "Nome" as the post office, and Cape Nome was a long hike from the business district of Anvil City.][16]

Sunday, September 3, 1899
Rough sea. Sick all day. Such grub as we have would kill a dog. Can't eat it. It is far worse than any I had in the Klondyke. [The term "Klondike" was commonly applied to the gold fields of Interior Alaska as well as those in the adjacent Yukon Territory.] A good many are sick now. Will have 8 days more of it before Seattle is reached.

Monday, September 4, 1899
Water very rough. Stuck to my berth. Did not eat anything all day.

Tuesday, September 5, 1899
Reached Dutch Harbor [on the north coast of Unalaska Island in the Aleutian chain] at 3:30. Found two American Revenue Cutters [the *Rush* and *McCulloch*] and one English [gunboat, the *Pheasant*] in harbor.[17] The iron clad *Athenian* was coaling up. She is on her way to Manila loaded with cavalrymen and 400 horses.

Wednesday, September 6, 1899
Weather: Cloudy
Went to Baranoff Inn and got breakfast. We are taking on coal. [Vessels traveling to or from the Bering Sea and Arctic Ocean usually stopped at the trading stations on Unalaska Island to renew their supplies of coal and water.][18] This is a fine, beautiful harbor. It is nice and warm. Lots of grass. Left Udakta or Dutch Harbor at 2:30 P.M. [*Udakhta* was the Aleut name for Dutch Harbor.][19] Stopped outside for half hour to fish but only 2 were caught.

Thursday, September 7, 1899
This is a lovely day. A man died this morning of typhoid fever.

He was buried at sea at 2:30 P.M. Nobody knew him. [According to the purser of the *Nelson*, his name was E.C. Hindman, of Whidbey Island in the state of Washington.][20]

Friday, September 8, 1899
Weather: Cloudy
Sea very rough all day with strong head wind. Stuck to my bunk pretty closely all day.

Saturday, September 9, 1899
Storm continues. Am on deck. Have to hang on to rail for support. Stern wind. Sails set. Speeding rapidly before the wind.

Sunday, September 10, 1899
Clear part of the day, rough in p.m. Am sick as usual. Had boiled hog's head with hair on for dinner. Enough to sicken a dog.

Monday, September 11, 1899
Cloudy and a quartering wind blowing. Sea is mighty rough. Ship is tossed about like a chip. A man is a liar who says he travels the sea for pleasure. When I reach land, will stay on it. No more ship for me.

Tuesday, September 12, 1899
Favorable wind all day and night. Made 270 miles in the last 24 hours. Sighted land about 4 P.M. Passed Flattery at midnight. [Cape Flattery is on the northwest tip of the Olympic Peninsula in the state of Washington. It marks the entrance to the Strait of Juan De Fuca.]

Wednesday, September 13, 1899
Calm after passing Flattery. Reached Seattle at 3 P.M. Never was so glad to put foot on land before.

[Conger began the following letter to his wife in Eagle on August 20 and finished it in Seattle on September 13, 1899.]

Dutch Harbor, Unalaska Island, 1899-1901.

Dear Lizzie,

It is by the will and grace of God that I am able to write to you. Since last writing you (in March while on the Copper), I have passed through death's valley and have returned haggard and worn. At the present moment I am able to move around (slowly) by the aid of a cane. Below is a synopsis of what happened.

On April 10, while crossing a rough and precipitous divide between headwaters of Copper and Tanana rivers, I sprained my right ankle. Fearing I might have broken it in my fall, I endeavored to walk, to see if I could. I managed to hobble about a quarter of a mile, when I became weak and exhausted and fell by the wayside. A man by the name of Jacobson came along and picked me up, placed me on a sled, and hauled me into camp nearly frozen to death. After a good deal of rubbing, I thawed out and found that my ankle was badly swollen and inflammed. I at once applied a hot water compress and continued that treatment for weeks. I had no linament, so did the best I could.

We were moving camp every three days and I had to be hauled on a sled every 3rd day, with mercury 20° below at that time of year. But we were some 12,000 [6,000] feet above sea level. I was pulled over a distance of fifty miles to last forks on headwaters of Tanana [Nabesna], where on May 2nd we quit sledding.

On account of improper treatment, exposure, and anxiety, scurvy set in and for 3 months I battled with the grim monster. Not on account of remedies, kindness, and good care (for I had none) do I attribute my recovery, but to my prayers and faith in Christ Jesus. He alone carried me over the yawning chasm of death and preserved my life. I managed to move around the tent with the use of a cane and crutch. Had to wait on myself. When my leg was black and swollen to bursting above the knee, and shooting pains in abdomen and back, the most critical stage, my two partners went off prospecting for a week and left me alone, knowing I might die any hour. Such is life in the interior of Alaska. Man loses kindness, honor, self-respect, and becomes a fiend and a wild beast in his base endeavors to grab on to the filthy lucre.

On July 2nd we started down the Tanana [Nabesna] with our boat. The first 60 miles was swift and dangerous. Knocked two holes in our boat but lost nothing. After reaching the Shushana [Tanana] we had beautiful water to navigate and it continued so for as far as I boated on that river [about 75 miles]. When we reached the trail crossing the Tanana from Lake Mentasta, my partners decided to go back that way, down the Copper to Valdes and out. That meant a pack on your back and a tramp of some 150 [250] miles. As I was unable to walk, let alone carry a pack, my only hope for escape was down the Tanana in the boat to the Youcon, thinking when I reached Mansfield I could hire some Indians to help me through the rapids. But upon reaching there,

View of the wooded section of the Yukon River valley, 1899-1901.

they would not venture down at any price. As it was impossible for me to handle the boat I had in my condition, I concluded to live with the Indians this winter, or until able to walk across country.

Providence once more stepped in and aided me. A party of government explorers from Cook Inlet was making its way through to Eagle City. So I joined them. They gave me a horse to ride. We were 16 days coming across. Saw lots of mining in Franklyn Gulch, also all along 40 Mile.

Eagle City (or Fort Egbert, named after Col. Egbert who was killed in the Cuban war)[21] is destined to become quite a camp. Six [three] weeks ago Major Ray, with 200 men, came here and is building a post.[22] [By way of the river] the town is 105 miles from

Dawson and 20 [about 10] miles from the boundary line, making it the last American town up the Youcon.

I could have gotten work there for $50 per month, everything furnished, but was unable to do outside work. Carpenters are getting $10 a day but have to board themselves. Board is high. I paid $1.50 for a meal at the restaurant. A good stand for a drugstore. None there now. There were some last winter, but they left in the spring for Cape Nome.

Big excitement at Nome, 60 [125] miles above St. Michaels. It is destined to rival Dawson, I do believe. A man coming here now needs to bring $1,000 or $1,500 along. Then he can do something.

On August 20th I left Eagle City for St. Michaels on board steamer *Hannah,* one of the finest boats on the Youcon. The distance is about 1,700 [1,460] miles and its takes from 6 to 8 days to make the run. It takes 1,000 cords of wood, besides several tons of coal for one trip — $8,000 for wood, and I don't know how much for coal. [Large vessels consumed about $15,000 worth of wood on a round trip from Saint Michael to Dawson. The transportation companies had contracts with woodchoppers living along the wooded portions of the Yukon for cordwood, but along the lower 200 miles of the river, where trees are lacking, the steamers were sometimes compelled to burn coal. In the spring the Eskimos in the delta gathered driftwood to sell to passing steamers; this was limited, expensive, and of poor quality.][23]

We passed two steamers stuck in the sand. One, an ocean propeller, was a good 6 feet high and dry and at least 100 yards from water. She will probably go to wreck in the spring during the breakup. [The violent movement of the ice during the spring breakup caused serious damage or total destruction to most vessels stranded in the main channel of the Yukon.][24] The river is very low now, and they tell me it will not rise again this fall. It is very shallow and wide between Ft. Youcon and Circle City, requiring very cautious navigation to avoid sand bars.

There was a man and his wife, with a little boy 4 years old, on the boat down the Youcon. The little fellow was born in Circle City. The father and mother were there 5 years and now they are returning with one hundred thousand, besides their claims. I had lots of fun with the little fellow, for he reminded me of Clifford. I find that those who stay here 5 or 6 years manage to make a stake. It takes 2 years to locate yourself. Had I come directly up the river from the coast, or down from Skagway, I would have landed in the heart of the gold bearing district. At the same time, I did Copper Center, where there is nothing. The trip from Valdes to the Youcon took from me my money and health but not ambition and hopes. Only for you and the little ones my bones would bleach in the midnight sun of the far north before I would say I am done, give up defeated, and return a pauper. You plead in every letter to return, no matter if I have failed in my attempt to gain wealth. So I will return and we will battle together to keep the wolf from the door.

How the news ever reached the States that I had made several thousand dollars is more than I know. I have not taken $20 from the ground since I came here, nor have I seen anyone else do so on the Copper side. [Conger's wife had sent him a newspaper article which quoted from a letter written to the *Times* (probably the Kanabec County *Times* of Mora, Minnesota) by Geo. E. Clark. It said: "I came across a person on my travels who has seen H.S. Conger quite recently, and I am informed that Mr. Conger has two claims, from which he has taken a few thousand dollars since Nov. 1, 1898."] Saw men take out from 50 to 100 dollars a day on 40 Mile, but they were old claims and were working at the time on bedrock. I talked with a good many miners who have been in there 2 or more years, and they have only managed to make a grubstake. But they hang on, thinking they will hit it by and by. And so they will if they stay long enough. There is plenty of work for those who are able and chances to make money otherwise than mining. Wood is worth 8 and 9 dollars a cord anywhere on the river. Logs are $40 per thousand [board feet] at mill.

Dawson is a lively town and lots of it. One can obtain almost anything the market affords, if you have but got the price. Lots of style. Even the Indians wear broadcloth and silk.

I saw garden truck of all kinds growing in small patches

along the Youcon. Corn and potatoes do not thrive. Potatoes are worth 50ᶜ per lb. in Eagle City, but that is the dearest town on the river.

We shot two bears the day before we arrived in Eagle City, a mother and her cub. We ate the cub and sold the old one for $30. She was not very large. There was another one with them (a big fellow) but he made good his escape. I sold my rifle and ammunition. Got more for the ammunition than for the gun. Sold my fur robe and a few other things. There are three companies which operate in all the towns on this river and coast, and they monopolize everything. Sell provisions and clothing at their own price.

Arrived at St. Michaels August 27th. It is situated on an island and is the bleakest and most desolate place I ever saw. Not a stick of wood grows within 60 miles of the shore. All the wood they have is driftwood, collected by the Indians. [Eskimos inhabited the Bering Sea coast as well as the lower 300 miles of the Yukon River. Living immediately above the Eskimos along the Yukon were the Ingalik Indians, Athabascan speaking people.][25] Those who can afford it burn coal. Last winter, coal sold as high as $40 per ton.

Nome, up the coast from here, is the most remarkable mining district in the known world. The gravel all along the beach for 60 miles pays from $10 to $200 per day per man. The government owns all the ground for 60 feet back from high tide but allows anyone to work who can. The country back from the beach has been staked by power of attorney for 40 miles square. Some staked as many as 60 claims. The law allows only 8 claims for one person under that power. [According to other sources, the district laws put no restriction on the number of power of attorney claims.][26] The claims are under litigation now. They will probably be thrown open for relocation. If they are, there will be a tremendous stampede, and those who are near at hand will stand the best chance of securing choice claims. It is hard to determine just when this dispute will be settled. Some think this fall, others, not till spring. The judge and governor are at Nome now.

[When the first wave of gold seekers from Dawson reached Anvil City, late in the spring of 1899, they found that the original discoverers and early arrivals from nearby areas in Alaska had staked scores of claims on Anvil and the adjacent creeks. Many of these claims were held by forged powers of attorney and by foreigners, and their ownership was disputed by the newcomers. Although there was no limit to the number of power of attorney claims a man could hold, the staking of hundreds of claims which had not been prospected was contested by the newcomers on the grounds that the law required a gold discovery on each claim before it could be staked. The dissatisfaction of the idle men in Anvil City led to claim jumping and general lawlessness, but the situation was somewhat alleviated in late June or early July by the discovery of rich beach placers. This large new area for prospecting accommodated hundreds of men, for the miners contended that the beach was public property and could not be staked. But in August, a conflict developed between the beach miners and a company holding a group of tundra claims stretching inland from the sea. The company claimed ownership of the beach placers in its area, and when it complained to the commander of the small group of troops stationed there, several hundred beach miners were arrested. The miners were not prisoners long, however. The revenue cutter *Bear* arrived and her captain, siding with the miners, promptly revoked the order of the arresting officer. In the late summer of 1899, the lone judge in Alaska, C.S. Johnson, arrived in Anvil City after completing his circuit down the Yukon River. In his brief court session at Anvil City, he ruled that the validity of a claim staked by an alien could not be contested by private persons and could only be disputed by the government upon the alien's request for patent. This decision was later upheld by a higher court. The miners' contention — that a 60-foot strip of beach was reserved for public use and could not be disposed of to individuals — was upheld by the commissioner of the General Land Office in December of 1899.][27]

Bought ticket for Seattle [at Saint Michael, Aug. 31] and went on board steamer *Charles Nelson* but did not sail till

Sept. 1st. Arrived at Anvil City, Cape Nome, next day. I tell you, that town is a live place. Men are as thick as mosquitoes along the beach for 10 miles. [When Major P.H. Ray arrived at Anvil City from his headquarters at Fort Egbert in late August of 1899, he estimated the town's population to be between 3,000 and 3,500. He reported that 600 to 1,000 people were at work mining the beach placers. C.E. Griffith (with whom Conger traveled to Eagle) arrived at Anvil City September 12, 1899. His report contained the following description of the beach operations.

Some work was being done below high tide, although it was principally carried on above that mark. The tools used were simply a shovel and rocker. The modus operandi being to clean off a space of 20 to 25 feet square, removing the coarse sand and gravel until the "pay streak" was reached. This was carefully scraped up and piled separately, to be washed later. The "pay streak" was very thin, in some places being only a fraction of an inch thick, while at others it was several inches thick. The rockers used were of various models and many of them very crude affairs. Water was obtained by small hand pumps in a few instances, but in the main by carrying it in buckets from the sea or by constructing small dams that filled up when the tide flooded. There were a few sluice boxes in operation, water being secured by pumping from Snake River. However, this process was not common, as it was difficult to obtain the water necessary. We saw one dredger at work in Snake River, taking the sand from the river bottom and catching the gold by a sluicing operation. Sample of "pay streak" sand was obtained from one of the miner's dumps. This is called "ruby" sand, because so many of its particles resemble the ruby in appearance. . . . It was learned that men who would work had taken out not less than $10 per day, and the average had been much more, some fabulous sums having been taken out.][28]

Oh, how I wish I were able to work. I would be there now, rocking out my 30 or 40 dollars a day, the same as the rest are doing. It is really too bad, after 18 months of "mushing" through this forsaken land, that I should reach the goal at last, powerless to do myself any good. It is enough to discourage the bravest of the brave. But no matter, I ought to be thankful that I am alive.

Bhering [Bering] Sea was very rough all the way to Dutch Harbor. Left one sick man there who had typhoid fever. After one day out from Dutch Harbor, one poor unknown man died and was buried at sea. It was a sad sight. Nearly everybody on board was sick. The grub we had was enough to sicken a strong man to look at it, let alone eat it. However, had I the means, I would go back to Nome in the spring, for I am sure if one reaches there with the rush he can't help but make money. Dawson won't be in it next summer with that town. There is no hope for me now, as money and health is nearly all gone.

Seattle, Sept. 13, 1899: Reached this port at 3 P.M. I never was so glad to walk ashore before. Two had to be carried, as they had not strength enough to support their own weight. I am just able to walk and will remain here three days to gain strength, then come on [home]. I have just money enough to take me through if nothing serious happens. I have been thinking that I would go down to Frisco and see if I could get a position there through my friend Newton. But I have given up that idea now, not knowing what you might think of it. And besides, Newton might not be there. Then I would be lacking funds to carry me homeward. So look for me in about 8 days. Prepare yourself to see a changed man. Kiss the dear little ones and tell them papa is coming.

Horace

Notes—

1. Alfred H. Brooks, *The Geography and Geology of Alaska: A Summary of Existing Knowledge* (Washington: Gov. Printing Office, 1906), p. 92; Donald J. Orth, *Dictionary of Alaska Place Names,* U.S. Geological Survey Professional Paper 567 (Washington: Gov. Printing Office, 1967), p. 1068; J.C. Cantwell, *Report of the Operations of the U.S. Revenue Steamer Nunivak on the Yukon*

River Station, Alaska, 1899-1901 (Washington: Gov. Printing Office, 1902), pp. 115, 131; *Alaska's Great Interior, ALASKA GEOGRAPHIC®* 7, no. 1 (1980): 53, 56.

2. Brooks, Geography and Geology, pp. 74-75, 92, quote on p. 75; Orth, *Dictionary,* p. 1068.

3. Josiah E. Spurr, "Through the Yukon Gold Diggings," Part 8, *ALASKA®*, Sept. 1977, p. 31; Brooks, *Geography and Geology,* p. 92.

4. Cantwell, *Report of the . . . Nunivak,* pp. 42, 148, 127.

5. Cantwell, *Report of the . . . Nunivak,* p. 40.

6. P.H. Ray and W.P. Richardson, "Relief of the Destitute in the Yukon Region," *Compilation of Narratives of Explorations in Alaska* (Washington: Gov. Printing Office, 1900), p. 544; Cantwell, *Report of the . . . Nunivak,* pp. 9, 20, 38-39.

7. Cantwell, *Report of the . . . Nunivak,* pp. 144-46.

8. Cantwell, *Report of the . . . Nunivak,* pp. 40, 142, 215.

9. Brooks, *Geography and Geology,* pp. 79, 81-82; Cantwell, *Report of the . . . Nunivak,* p. 36.

10. Cantwell, *Report of the . . . Nunivak,* p. 112; William R. Siddall, "The Yukon Waterway in the Development of Interior Alaska," *Pacific Historical Review* 28 (Nov. 1959): 368.

11. Alfred H. Brooks, *Blazing Alaska's Trails,* 2d ed. (1953; rpt. Fairbanks: Univ. of Alaska Press, 1973), pp. 375, 385, 387; Through 1959, the Fairbanks district produced 7,464,167 ounces of gold, while the Nome district produced 3,606,000 ounces. However, production figures for the period between 1931 and 1946 are lacking for Nome, so the figure given is a minimum. A.H. Koschmann and M.H. Bergendahl, *Principal Gold-Producing Districts of the United States,* Geological Survey Professional Paper 610 (Washington: Gov. Printing Office, 1968), pp. 18, 26; If rough estimates of production from 1960 to 1979 are included, Nome's total would stand at 4,051,155 ounces. See M.S. Robinson and T.K. Bundtzen, "Historic Gold Production in Alaska," *Mines and Geology Bulletin,* 28 (Sept. 1979), 3.

12. Cantwell, *Report of the . . . Nunivak,* p. 111.

13. Clarence L. Andrews, *The Story of Alaska* (Caldwell, Idaho: Caxton Printers, Ltd. 1938), p. 191; *San Francisco Chronicle* for June 3, 1898, p. 10, Aug. 1, 1898, p. 10, and June 6, 1899, p. 10; "Advertisement," *Seattle Post-Intelligencer,* Sept. 14, 1899, p. 9.

14. Siddall, *Pacific Historical Review,* p. 368; Ray and Richardson, *Compilation of Narratives,* p. 520.

15. "More Rich Tales of Nome: The Charles Nelson Arrives Direct from New Diggings," p. 12. Conger's name was included in the passenger list in this article.

16. Charles E. Griffith, "From Knik Station to Eagle City," *Compilation of Narratives,* p. 727; "All Can Mine Nome Beach," *San Francisco Chronicle,* Sept. 27, 1899, p. 3.

17. "More Rich Tales of Nome," *Seattle Post-Intelligencer,* Sept. 14, 1899, p. 12.

18. Cantwell, *Report of the . . . Nunivak,* pp. 30-31.

19. Orth, *Dictionary,* p. 290.

20. "More Rich Tales of Nome," *Seattle Post-Intelligencer,* Sept. 14, 1899, p. 12.

21. On June 7, 1899, Fort Egbert was officially named for "Lieutenant" Harry C. Egbert, killed in Manila. *Fort Egbert and the Eagle Historic District, Summer 1977,* BLM-AK Technical Report 2, Prepared for the U.S. Dept. of Interior, Bureau of Land Management, Fortymile Resource Area, Tok, Alaska, p. 37.

22. Ray arrived in Eagle on July 31, 1899. See W.R. Abercrombie, Report of John F. Rice," *Copper River Exploring Expedition, 1899* (Washington: Gov. Printing Office, 1900), pp. 100-101; According to "Eagle—Fort Egbert," a 1977 booklet distributed by the U.S. Dept. of Interior, Bureau of Land Management, "In July Major Ray, accompanied by Captain Wright, 99 enlisted men and a detachment of the Hospital Corps, arrived at Fort Egbert." (quote on p. 13). A plaque on the grounds of newly restored Fort Egbert reads: "At the height of Fort Egbert's development, 10 officers and 147 enlisted men were stationed here, along with 21 horses, 60 mules, and 30 dogs."

23. Cantwell, *Report of the . . . Nunivak,* pp. 132-33.

24. Cantwell, *Report of the . . . Nunivak,* p. 133.

25. Cantwell, *Report of the . . . Nunivak,* pp. 209, 103, 141.

26. "Truth About Cape Nome," *San Francisco Chronicle,* July 26, 1899, p. 7; Cantwell, *Report of the . . . Nunivak,* p. 195.

27. Brooks, *Blazing Alaska's Trails,* pp. 375-76, 379-80, 384; The beach placers were discovered before July 5, because on that date a *San Francisco Chronicle* correspondent wrote that "the beach claims are paying handsomely." "Truth About Cape Nome," July 26, 1899, p. 7. Also see the following articles from the *San Francisco Chronicle:* "Miners Stampede to Cape Nome Placers," July 1, 1899, p. 3; "More Rosy Tales of the Golden Sands on Beaches at Cape Nome," Sept. 12, 1899, p. 5; "Cape Nome Said to be Very Rich," July 15, 1899, p. 3; "All Can Mine Nome Beach," Sept. 27, 1899, p. 3; "Department Decision Important to Miners," Dec. 16, 1899, p. 7. Cantwell, *Report of the . . . Nunivak,* p. 186; For a detailed account of the early history of the Cape Nome district see Leland H. Carlson, "The Discovery of Gold at Nome, Alaska," *Alaska and Its History,* ed. Morgan B. Sherwood (Seattle: Univ. of Washington Press, 1967), pp. 353-80.

28. Maj. P.H. Ray to the adjutant general, St. Michael, Aug 31, 1899, in *Annual Reports of the War Department, 1899,* House Doc. 2 [3901], 56th Congress, 1st sess., Vol. 1, Part 3 (Washington: Gov. Printing Office, 1899), p. 120; C.E. Griffith, "From Knik Station to Eagle City," *Compilation of Narratives,* p. 728.

292 — *In Search of Gold*

Epilogue

The Klondike strike lured more than 50,000 persons to Alaska and the adjacent parts of Canada in 1897-98. Alfred H. Brooks, an Alaskan geologist from 1898-1923, estimated that if the gold produced by both the Klondike and Alaska in 1898 had been equally divided among all of the gold seekers, each man's share would have amounted to about $250 — not enough to have paid for his expenditures for equipment, let alone his months of toil and hardship. "As a financial venture," wrote Brooks, "the world was a loser by the Klondike gold rush. Yet measured by the building of character and physical strength, the world was better off. Who can measure the good done by the broadening influence of the frontier life, by the development of self-reliance and strengthening of character, by the facing of hardships and

Conger family portrait, circa 1916; from left to right: Myrtle and Leonard Conger, Elizabeth and Horace Conger.

dangers? Measured by standards of good citizenship, the influence of the Klondike rush was not a loss but a great gain."[1]

Though Conger failed to find gold in Alaska, he achieved success later in Minnesota as a businessman and civic leader. He returned to Minnesota on September 19, 1899, in broken health and nearly penniless and found employment in his brother's drugstore in Mora. His fourth child, Newton, was born there on August 10, 1900. Conger worked for his brother until 1902, when he opened a drugstore of his own in nearby Ogilvie, Minnesota. He played a prominent part in the upbuilding of that community and held many positions of trust. He was treasurer of the village for 16 consecutive years and served as the community's only registered pharmacist until his death on January 17, 1941, at the age of 77.

Notes—

1. Alfred H. Brooks, *Blazing Alaska's Trails,* 2d ed. (1953; rpt. Fairbanks: Univ. of Alaska Press, 1973), pp. 369-70; also see Alfred H. Brooks, *The Geography and Geology of Alaska: A Summary of Existing Knowledge* (Washington: Gov. Printing Office, 1906), p. 126.

Appendix

Harry T. Smith's letters to Lizzie Conger

Letter dated November 30, 1898, Fergus Falls, Minnesota

Dear Madam,

I left your husband at Copper Centre, Alaska about Sept. 14th. He was well and expected to stay in that country this winter and probably next summer. He had plenty of provisions and clothing and was well provided for, for the winter. He and his party expected to go up the Copper River and possibly over into the Yukon country, somewhere in the neighborhood of "Forty Mile" Creek. He was somewhat undecided as to his destination. He desired me to let you know how he was and what my future address would be, as he wanted to communicate with me. When you write him again you may say that for the present my address will be "Flat 42, The Albion," St. Paul, Minn.

Hoping this will find you and your family quite well and that you have received later news from the Doc other than I can give you.

> I remain yours
> to command,
> Harry T. Smith

Letter dated December 12, 1898, St. Paul, Minnesota

Dear Madam,

Your favor of 2nd inst. came to hand some days ago. You must pardon me for not writing sooner but I have been out of town, more or less, and could not find time to write you.

Now as to your questions. I went to Alaska last February. The Doctor and his party and my own party sailed from Seattle at the same time and on the same boat, the *Excelsior*. We were together going over the glacier. The Doctor's party was delayed by a snowstorm (their goods were on the summit of the glacier and ours were all over) and we went ahead of them and did not see them again for almost 2 months. We got our outfit in as far as the junction of the Klutena and Copper Rivers. From there we prospected up the Copper, the Slana, over the Mentasta Pass, down the Little Tokio, the Big Tokio, the Tanana River, and over as far as the head of Forty Mile Creek. We met with no success but the boys of my party that remained in the country (there are five of them) think they can do something on Forty Mile and that is where they are going this winter. I do not intend to go back there myself. From what I saw and from all I can learn from others, I am satisfied that there is no gold in the Copper River country. But one might strike it if he went into the Yukon country.

I do not consider it a particularly hazardous undertaking, if a person uses a proper amount of common horse sense and caution. The streams are all swift-running, full of rocks, snags, and bars, but they can be navigated with safety if one does not get in too big a hurry. The country is rough, of course. There is plenty of wood and water everywhere, some game and fish, and if a person can stand the cold in winter and the heat and mosquitoes in summer, I know of no reason why they should not get along all right. But as to making a fortune out of it, that I cannot answer for.

I heard a few days ago that a Mr. Fred McClellan of Princeton, Minnesota had just returned from Copper River. He was along with our crowd and I understand he has struck something somewhere up there. I think he knows the Doctor and can perhaps give you some late news of him. It would do no harm to communicate with him at any rate.

Hoping that I have made myself sufficiently clear to you and that you understand the situation, I remain

Yours very truly,
Harry T. Smith

P.S. If I can be of any service to you at any time, do not hesitate to call upon me.

Memoranda at the end of Horace S. Conger's diaries.

Memoranda

R.R. fare from St. Paul to Tacoma	$ 35.00
Steamship fare from Seattle to Port Valdes	70.00
Hardware bill	23.00
Groceries	63.40
Tobacco	5.10
	196.50
Total clothing [see below]	96.10
	292.60
1/12 interest in drill	2.10
Freight and drayage	6.50
Extra fare on boat	10.00
	$312.12

1 Pr. boots	6.50
1 Pr. miner's shoes	4.50
1 Pr. moccasins	2.50
1/2 Doz. Handkerchiefs	.35
2 Pr. gloves	2.00
1 wire mask	1.25
1 Parraffin bag	1.00
1 Pr. blankets	9.00
[Total clothing bought at F.W. Merrick's]	$27.10

1 Chamois suit	$ 8.00
1 Pr. mackinaw pants	3.50
1 fur robe	20.00
1 hunting knife	1.00
1 hunting ax	1.00
1 belt and holster	1.00
Bill [clothing] bought from Sommer's (St. Paul)	34.50
	$96.10

Cash Account—1898

Date			Rec'd	Paid
March	4	Cash on hand	250.00	
March	15	Cash in purse	17.28	
		Extra Boat fare		10.00
		Balance expenses on outfit		10.00
March	15	Cash now	247.28	
March	21	Dog food		.10
March	21	Postage		.10
March	25	Chewing tobacco		1.00
March	30	Mattress		2.00
		Pie		.15
April	2	1 Pr. Creepers		2.50
April	2	1 Pr. Shoes		4.00
April	2	Ts. Arnica		.50
April	3	Dr. bill for Roy		5.60
April	5	Pipe		.75
April	5	M.J. Hessian		.05
April	22	Letter carrying		1.00
May	24	Rec'd Mail		.25
May	27	Cardigan Jacket		3.00
		Suspenders		.75
		Plug Tobacco		1.25
June	4	Paid Reigel		1.25
,,	,,	Paid for grub		2.25
June	10	Paid for Murfin		11.35
,,	,,	Cr. Cash for dog	1.85	
June	23	Bought Rub. boots		2.50
,,	,,	Brought forward	249.13	
,,	,,	Brought forward		37.85
June	25	Safety pins		.25
,,	,,	Paid for bacon and coffee		7.75
June	29	Undershirt		1.50
June	30	Sent Lizzie		20.00
,,	,,	Paid for mail		1.00
,,	,,	Rec'd from Beatty	2.25	
,,	,,	Rec'd from M.J. Hessian	.35	
,,	,,	Paid for shirt		1.00
,,	,,	Paid for sending mail		.50
,,	,,	Paid for tobacco		2.50
,,	,,	Paid for outfit		50.00
July	1	Paid Whirley		10.00

Date			Rec'd	Paid
July	1	Rec'd from Buckley	16.66	
,,	,,	Rec'd from Corcoran	20.00	
,,	,,	Rec'd from Whirley	1.90	
July	17	Paid Corcoran		1.00
,,	,,	Paid for fish		.75
			.23	
			290.52	136.40
July	25	Cash on hand		154.12
			290.52	290.52
July	25	Cash on hand	154.12	
July	25	Cash for Buckley	11.75	
July	27	Cash for Buckley	1.00	
Sept.	7	1 Pr. Boots		2.00
,,	,,	One Rub. blanket		1.00
,,	,,	One Clothes bag		.25
,,	,,	10 lbs. coffee		.75
,,	,,	Weighing 157#		.05
,,	,,	Mail		2.50
Sept.	9	4# baking powder		2.00
,,	,,	Supper for two		1.00
Sept.	10	Pipe		.25
Sept.	13	Clothing		4.00
Sept.	14	Cap		.60
,,	,,	1/4 interest stove		2.00
,,	,,	Rec'd from M.J. Hessian	25.00	
,,	,,	Paid		26.50
,,	,,	Picture		.50
,,	,,	Hunting knife		1.00
,,	,,	Mending shoes		.75
			191.87	45.15
Sept.	14	Cash on hand		146.72
			191.87	191.87
Sept.	14	Bal. cash on hand	146.72	
Sept.	16	2# moose meat		.50
Sept.	18	Rec'd cash	14.25	
,,	,,	Hand rope		.25
,,	,,	Bal.	160.97	.75
Sept.	18	Bal. Cash on hand	160.22	
Sept.	19	Bought hammer		.25
Sept.	24	Rec'd mail		1.00

Date			Rec'd	Paid
Sept.	27	Snowshoes		2.90
"	"	2 Pr. socks		1.00
Sept.	28	10# coffee		.80
"	"	pack sack		.40
"	"	2 boxes cocoa		.40
"	"	1 towel		.15
"	"	Castile soap		.10
"	"	37# O. Meal		2.95
Sept.	29	Plug tobacco		1.00
Oct.	3	Paid Corcoran		5.15
"	"	Pictures		2.00
Oct.	4	Rec'd Wherley	.65	
Oct.	5	Rec'd Corcoran	.67	
Oct.	6	Cash balance		143.44
			161.54	161.54
Oct.	6	Cash on hand	143.44	
Oct.	16	Sold P.O. stamp	.02	
Oct.	19	Interest in bake oven		.50
Oct.	20	Bought books	.50	
Nov.	2	Mail		1.10
"	"	Sent Lila		1.00
Nov.	3	Shoe packs		.65
Nov.	5	Tobacco		.45
Nov.	24	Squaw		.05
Nov.	26	Record claim		4.00
			143.46	8.25
Nov.	26	Cash on hand		135.21
			143.46	143.46
Nov.	26	Cash on hand	135.21	
Nov.	26	2# tobacco		2.50
Nov.	29	Paid Corcoran		1.15
"	"	Paid for book		.05
Dec.	1	Cash bal.		131.61
		Rec'd for books	.10	
			135.31	135.31
Dec.	1	Cash on hand	131.61	
"	"	1 Oz. acid Sal.		.50
Dec.	3	Mending shoes		.20
Dec.	10	Rec'd from Rope	.25	
Dec.	24	Tobacco		1.50

Date			Rec'd	Paid
Dec.	24	Honey bread		.40
"	"	For 25# tea	2.50	
"	"	For 2 sleds	2.00	
Dec.	26	Rec'd for tobacco	1.50	
"	"	Paid Wherley		1.50
"	"	Paid Corcoran		1.50
"	"	Rec'd for goods	.10	
Dec.	31	Rec'd for goods	.80	
Jan.	1	Cash balance		133.16
			138.76	138.76

Cash Account—1899

Date			Rec'd	Paid
Jan.	1	Cash	133.16	
Aug.	1	Cash on hand	136.45	
Aug.	2	For rifle	7.00	
"	"	1 Pr. shoes	3.50	
"	"	Shotgun	5.00	
Aug.	3	One pipe	1.00	
Aug.	19	Paid for dinner		1.50
"	"	Paid for tobacco		1.00
Aug.	21	Sold robe	10.00	
Aug.	24	Paid for Med.		1.00
Aug.	28	Paid for sundries		.30
Aug.	29	Paid for pipe		.50
"	"	Sold syringe	1.50	
Aug.	30	Sold forceps	8.00	
"	"	Paid for tobacco		.50
Aug.	31	Paid for board		6.00
"	"	Paid for ticket		60.00
"	"	Paid for tobacco		.50
Aug.	31	Cash balance		101.15
			172.45	172.45
Sept.	7	Cash on hand	101.15	
Sept.	5	Paid for tobacco pouch		1.00
Sept.	6	Meals		1.00
		Figs, tobacco		.35
		Dinner		.75
Sept.	11	Meals on ship		.75
Sept.	16	[Great Northern R.R. (2nd class ticket)]		40.00

Buckley Account
(Deceased)

Date			Rec'd	Paid
July	17	2 Pr. shoes	6.00	
,,	,,	1 coat	1.00	
,,	,,	1 compass and glass	1.00	
,,	,,	1 knife	1.00	
,,	,,	1 hatchet	1.00	
,,	,,	1 Pr. mits	.25	
,,	,,	1 Pr. Buck. mits	.50	
July	20	1 Pr. overalls	1.00	
July	27	1 Pr. gloves	1.00	
Sept.	5	Money on body	153.87	
,,	,,	Clothing	22.90	
,,	,,	Share of provisions	34.78	
,,	,,	Funeral expense		92.00
Sept.	13	Clothing	15.20	
Sept.	14	Interest in stove	2.00	
,,	,,	Bal. and cash delivered to M.J. Hessian		149.50
			241.50	241.50

Distance from Port Valdes to Copper River

Valdes to first camp	5 miles
First to second camp	12 miles
Second to third camp	4½ miles
Third to fourth camp, over [summit of] glacier	12 miles
Fourth to fifth camp	2 miles
Fifth to sixth camp	2½ miles
Sixth to seventh camp, the Lake	6 miles
Seventh to eighth camp, Head of the [lake] to the Klutena	30 miles
Eighth to ninth camp, Copper River	25 miles
Total	99 miles

Distance up Copper River [July 2, 1898, to July 25, 1898]

First camp on Copper River	7 miles
Second camp on Taslena [Tazlina] River	3 miles
Third camp on Copper	7 miles
Fourth camp on Copper	4 miles
Fifth camp on Copper	4 miles
Sixth camp on Copper	4 miles
Seventh camp on Copper	3 miles
Eighth camp on Copper	7 miles
Copper Center to mouth of the Gacona [Gakona]	39 miles
Ninth camp on Copper	1 mile
Tenth camp on Copper	4 miles
Eleventh camp on the Sanford	3 miles
Twelfth camp on Copper	5 miles
Thirteenth camp on Copper	4 miles
Fourteenth camp on Copper	3 miles
Fifteenth camp on Copper	2 miles
Sixteenth camp on Copper	4 miles
Seventeenth camp on Copper	3 miles
Eighteenth camp on Christochina [Chistochina]	5 miles
Total	79 miles

Three Months' Provisions Taken up Copper River July 2, 1898, for Four Men

Flour	450 lbs.
Bacon	90½ lbs.
Dried beef	13 lbs.
Salt	24 lbs.
Beans	25 lbs.
Peaches	23 lbs.
Dried apples	10 lbs.
Sugar	12 lbs.
Oatmeal	10 lbs.
Potatoes	5 lbs.
Potatoes (our own)	5 lbs.
Rice	18 lbs.
Cornmeal	9 lbs.
Onions	3 lbs.
Coffee	12 lbs.
Total	709½ lbs.

September 9, 1898
Amount of Provisions etc. Found in Cache at Head of Rapids

3 Sleds
10 cans tea (5# cans), 50 lbs.
4 cans onions (5# cans), 20 lbs.
4 cans tea (5# cans), 20 lbs.
3 cans matches
4 boxes candles
3 bottles Jac. Ginger
1 bevel square
1 soldering iron
4 cans mustard
3 cans pepper
2 cans ginger
37 bars laundry soap
17 bars hand soap
1 lb. citric acid
51½ lbs. coffee
4 pick handles
1 pick (no handle)
30 cans milk
2 bottles vinegar
15 cans eggs (15 lbs.)
7 sacks bacon (205½ lbs.)
peaches (63½ lbs.)
apples (53 lbs.)
sack salt (50 lbs.)
sugar (60 lbs.)
19½ sacks flour (975 lbs.)
1 sack oatmeal (50 lbs.)
4 sacks beans (272 lbs.)
1 sack rice (65 lbs.)
5 sacks potatoes (150 lbs.)
1 sack cornmeal (50 lbs.)
2 shovels
1 ax and extra handle
1 grindstone
1 saw
1 water bucket

Letters Received

February 25, 1898	One from Lizzie
April 22, 1898	Two from Lizzie
„ „	One from Len
May 24, 1898	One from Len
„ „	One from Lizzie
„ „	One from A.W. Crusoe
May 30, 1898	One from Len
„ „	One from Mrs. Eldred
June 29, 1898	Two from Lizzie
Sept. 7, 1898	Four from Lizzie
„ „	Two from Len
„ „	One from Crusoe
„ „	One from Myrtle
„ „	One from Mrs. Eldred
Sept. 12, 1898	Three from Lizzie
Sept. 24, 1898	One from Len and Myrtle
Nov. 2, 1898	Two from Lizzie
March 3, 1899	Six from Lizzie
„ „	Two from Len
„ „	Two from Myrtle
March 3, 1899	Two from M.J. Hessian
„ „	One from Mrs. Danforth
August 6, 1899	Three from Lizzie

Letters Dispatched

March 4, 1898	Lizzie and Len
[March 8, 1898]	Lizzie
March 13, 1898	Lizzie
March 27, 1898	Lizzie
April 3, 1898	Len
April 23, 1898	Len
April 25, 1898	Lizzie
June 2, 1898	Lizzie
„ „	Mrs. Eldred
„ „	A.W. Crusoe
June 30, 1898	Lizzie
July 29, 1898	Lizzie
„ „	Mrs. Buckley
„ „	Kasota *Times*
September 12, 1898	Lizzie

September 12, 1898	Len and Myrtle
September 13, 1898	A.W. Crusoe
September 14, 1898	Lizzie with picture
September 25, 1898	Lizzie with picture
,, ,,	Len and Myrtle
October 4, 1898	Lizzie with photo
November 2, 1898	Lizzie
January 1, 1899	Lizzie
March 5, 1899	Lizzie
September 14, 1899	Lizzie

Text of 1898 newspaper article from the Saint Paul *Pioneer Press*
(Referred to by Conger in his letter dated March 4, 1899)

"Feasible Railroad Route: To the Yukon Via Valdes Basin;
Mr. McClellan's Report on the Copper River Country —
Princeton Party's Success"

R.F. McClellan insists that the Copper river route is the best way into Alaska, and he ought to know, for he is the only man who has been over that route both ways. "It is the all-American route," he says, "and it's not only the shortest but the easiest for a railroad. The divides between the Copper and the Tanana and between the Tanana and the Forty-mile, which flows into the Yukon, are low and gradual. A wagon road or a railroad could get over them without any trouble."

Mr. McClellan was head cruiser for the state auditor. He left for Alaska last March with six others. . . . He was at the capitol yesterday with a pocket full of nuggets, some of which were Dawson gold and some picked up on the party's claims. The rest of them are there digging. Mr. McClellan came home to see about things and is going back next March.

Thousands of men have tried to get to the Yukon by way of Copper river, and terrible tales have been told of suffering, hardship and absolute failure. No man could possibly go that way, the story ran, and there was nothing to be had in that country.

This party did get through, and it is pretty sure the two claims on Quartz creek, a branch of Copper river, sixty miles from the ocean, are valuable. When Mr. McClellan left they had only prospects, but the prospects ran 30 cents to $1 a pan. Placer mining can't be done in summer because the frozen ground can only be treated by thawing and in summer the water puts out the fires. In winter there is nothing to hinder.

He has a bottle full of prospects, as big as pin heads of assorted sizes, and another set of bigger nuggets that came from the bed rock, flakes of gold as large as a man's finger nail. Where the stream runs through a canyon every bar bears gold.

The initial difficulty of the Copper river route is the Valdes glacier. Mr. McClellan admits it is something like work to haul 1,500 pounds of supplies over the icy steep. There are several benches from 100 to 5,000 feet high. No, not a precipice. The angle is about forty-five degrees and a man with creepers can walk up the face of the steep. At the top a tackle is rigged to haul the stuff. Going in March one finds on the coast the same climate as in Minnesota in March, and follows the March weather inland. It has thawed all the way. Once over the glacier horses can graze themselves all the way. He saw one train of horses that looked sleek and well favored. He says it is a fine grazing country. The mosquitoes did not seem to bother the horses much.

It is hard work under any circumstances, but not dangerous or specially difficult for men who have had the advantage of an education in the north woods of Minnesota. That was the trouble with the men who failed. They were city men, wholly unaccustomed to that sort of life. "As nice a set of men as you would find anywhere," Mr. McClellan says, "but they don't know how to manage in that country. They say they had a hard time and I suppose it was hard for them," this said gently without any imputation of weakness to the men who can't make a picnic of camping in the snow with the temperature forty below and living on hardtack and beans.

But hardened men ought to stand it. His party hadn't suffered a touch of sickness and he left them all well, two on a claim on a branch of Forty-mile and the others on Quartz creek. Going up the Copper river they had their hardest work, towing their stuff up stream against a twelve-mile current, walking on the bank or in the water and dragging the three batteaux through the rapids and over the rocks for 150 miles. Coming out, Mr. McClellan made the 425 miles from Forty-mile to the coast in eighteen days. Next year there will be something like trails, and it will be easier going.

Bibliography

BOOKS

Adney, Edwin Tappan. *The Klondike Stampede of 1897-1898*. 1900 reprint, Fairfield, Washington: Ye Galleon Press, 1968.

Andrews, Clarence L. *The Story of Alaska*. Caldwell, Idaho: Caxton Printers, 1938.

Austin, Basil. *The Diary of a Ninety-Eighter*. Mount Pleasant, Michigan: John Cumming, 1968.

Bancroft, Hubert Howe. *History of the Pacific States of North America: Alaska 1730-1885* (Vol. 28). San Francisco: A.L. Bancroft and Co., 1886.

Becker, Ethel Anderson. *Klondike '98: Hegg's Album of the 1898 Gold Rush*. Portland, Oregon: Binfords and Mort, 1949.

Berton, Pierre. *The Klondike Fever*. New York: Alfred A. Knopf, 1958.

Brooks, Alfred Hulse. *Blazing Alaska's Trails,* 2d ed. 1953 reprint, Fairbanks: University of Alaska Press, 1973.

Cahalane, Victor H. *Mammals of North America*. New York: Macmillan, 1947.

Carlson, Leland H. "The Discovery of Gold at Nome, Alaska," in *Alaska and Its History*, edited by Morgan B. Sherwood. Seattle: University of Washington Press, 1967.

Chicago Record. *Klondike: The Chicago Record's Book for Gold Seekers*. Chicago: Monarch Book Co., 1897.

Dictionary of American Biography, Vol. 1. Edited by Allen Johnson. New York: Charles Scribner's Sons, 1927-36.

Gabrielson, Ira N. and Lincoln, Frederick C. *The Birds of Alaska*. Harrisburg, Pa.: Stackpole Co., and Washington, D.C.: Wildlife Management Inst., 1959.

Golder, Frank A. "Mining in Alaska before 1867," in *Alaska and Its History,* edited by Morgan B. Sherwood. Seattle: University of Washington Press, 1967.

Harris, A.C. *Alaska and the Klondike Gold Fields*. Chicago: n.p., 1897.

Holvey, David N., M.D. and Talbott, John H., M.D., editors. *The Merck Manual of Diagnosis and Therapy,* 12th ed. Rahway, New Jersey: Merck, 1972.

Margeson, Charles A. *Experiences of Gold Hunters in Alaska*. Hornellsville, New York: Charles Margeson, 1899.

Marvin, Frederic R. *The Yukon Overland: The Gold-Digger's Hand-Book*. Cincinnati: Editor Publishing Co., 1898.

McKennan, Robert A. *The Upper Tanana Indians,* Yale University Publications in Anthropology, No. 55, edited by Irving Rouse. New Haven: Department of Anthropology, Yale University, 1959.

Morgan, Murray. *One Man's Gold Rush: A Klondike Album.* Seattle: University of Washington Press, 1967.

Murie, Adolph. *Mammals of Mount McKinley National Park, Alaska.* Published by the Mount McKinley Natural History Association in cooperation with the National Park Service, 1962.

Newel, Gordon. *Pacific Steamboats.* New York: Bonanza, 1958.

_____. *SOS North Pacific: Tales of Shipwrecks off the Washington, British Columbia, and Alaskan Coasts.* Portland, Oregon: Binfords and Mort, 1955.

Osgood, Cornelius. *The Distribution of the Northern Athapaskan Indians,* Yale University Publications in Anthropology, No. 7. New Haven: Yale University Press, 1936.

_____. *The Ethnography of the Tanaina,* Yale University Publications in Anthropology, No. 16. 1937 reprint, New Haven: Human Relations Area Files Press, 1966.

Remington, C.H. (Copper River Joe). *A Golden Cross (?) on the Trails from the Valdez Glacier.* Los Angeles: White-Thompson, 1939.

Sherwood, Morgan B. *Exploration of Alaska, 1865-1900.* New Haven: Yale University Press, 1965.

_____. "George Davidson and the Acquisition of Alaka," in *Alaska and Its History,* edited by Morgan B. Sherwood. Seattle: University of Washington Press, 1967.

Wharton, David. *The Alaska Gold Rush.* Bloomington: Indiana University Press, 1972.

GOVERNMENT PUBLICATIONS — United States

Abercrombie, Capt. W.R. *Copper River Exploring Expedition, 1899.* Senate Document No. 306, Vol. 32, U.S. 56th Congress, 1st session, 1899-1900. Washington: Government Printing Office, 1900. (Includes reports of W. Babcock, C. Brown, E. Cashman, E. Gillette, H.B. Pearson, A. Powell, J. Rice, O. Rohn, and L.J. Townsend, M.D.)

Annual Reports of the War Department for the Fiscal Year Ended June 30, 1899. Vol. 1, Part 3, House Document No. 2, U.S. 56th Congress, 1st session. Washington: Government Printing Office, 1899.

Baker, Marcus. *Geographic Dictionary of Alaska,* 2d ed. House Documents, Vol. 78, U.S. Geological Survey Bulletin 299. Washington: Government Printing Office, 1906.

Brooks, Alfred Hulse. *The Geography and Geology of Alaska: A Summary of Existing Knowledge.* U.S. Geological Survey Professional Paper 45. Washington: Government Printing Office, 1906.

Cantwell, 1st Lt. J.C. *Report of the Operations of the U.S. Revenue Steamer 'Nunivak' on the Yukon River Station, Alaska 1899-1901.* Treasury Department Document 2276, Division of Revenue-Cutter Service. Washington: Government Printing Office, 1902.

Compilation of Narratives of Explorations in Alaska. U.S. 56th Congress, 1st session, Senate Committee on Military Affairs, Senate Report No. 1023. Washington: Government Printing Office, 1900. (Includes reports by W.R. Abercrombie, H.T. Allen, C.E. Griffith, P.H. Ray, and W.P. Richardson)

Eagle — Fort Egbert. U.S. Department of the Interior, Bureau of Land Management, 1977.

Fort Egbert and the Eagle Historic District, Summer 1977. BLM — AK Technical Report 2, prepared for the U.S. Department of the Interior, Bureau of Land Management, Fortymile Resource Area, Tok, Alaska, December 1978.

Glenn, Capt. Edwin F., and Abercrombie, Capt. W.R. *Reports of Explorations in the Territory of Alaska, 1898.* U.S. Adjutant General's Office, Military Information Division, Publication No. 25, War Department Document 102. Washington: Government Printing Office, 1899. (Includes reports by R.M. Brookfield, C. Brown, P.G. Lowe, G.H. Preston, and J.J. Rafferty)

Koschmann, A.H., and Bergendahl, M.H. *Principal Gold-Producing Districts of the United States.* U.S. Geological Survey Professional Paper 610. Washington: Government Printing Office, 1968.

Maps and Descriptions of Routes of Exploration in Alaska in 1898, with General Information Concerning the Territory. Senate Documents, Vol. 13, U.S. 55th Congress, 3d session. Washington: Government Printing Office, 1899. (Includes reports by E.C. Barnard, A.H. Brooks, W.J. Peters, and F.C. Schrader)

Orth, Donald J. *Dictionary of Alaska Place Names.* U.S. Geological Survey Professional Paper 567. Washington: Government Printing Office, 1967 (reprinted with minor revisions in 1971).

Swanton, John R. *Indian Tribes of North America.* Smithsonian Institution, Bureau of American Ethnology, Bulletin 145. Washington: Government Printing Office, 1953.

Twentieth Annual Report of the U.S. Geological Survey, Part 7 (Explorations in Alaska in 1898). Washington: Government Printing Office, 1900. (Includes reports by A.H. Brooks, W.C. Mendenhall, F.C. Schrader, and J.E. Spurr)

Twenty-First Annual Report of the U.S. Geological Survey, Part 2 (General Geology, Economic Geology, Alaska). Washington: Government Printing Office, 1900.

GOVERNMENT PUBLICATIONS — Canada

Rand. A.L. *Mammals of Yukon.* Bulletin 100, Biological Series No. 29, Canada Department of Mines and Resources, Mines and Geology Branch. Ottawa: National Museum of Canada, 1945.

ARCHIVAL SOURCES

Benedict, Neil Dow. "The Valdes and Copper River Trail, Alaska, with 158 Photographic Views." 1899. Manuscript in Alaska Historical Library, Juneau.

Hanable, William S. *The Copper River, Alaska in the 18th and 19th Centuries.* Anchorage: Alaska Historical Commission, 1982.

Reid, Shad. Alaska diary from 1898-1903. Copy in Alaska Historical Library, Juneau.

"Vessels Wrecked in Alaskan Waters." Map with supplementary information. Compiled by the Alaska Bureau, Seattle Chamber of Commerce and Commercial Club, 1918. Map No. G4371, P 57, located in the Government Documents Section, Peter Shields Library, University of California, Davis.

PERIODICALS

Aitchison, Stewart W. "Marmots," *Summit.* Vol. 23, October-November 1977, pp. 6, 40-43.

The Alaska Geographic Society. *Alaska's Great Interior.* Vol. 7, No. 1, 1980, 128 pp.

Andrews, Clarence L. "Alaska Under the Russians: Industry, Trade, and Social Life," *Washington Historical Quarterly.* Vol. 7, No. 4, October 1916, pp. 278-295.

_____. "Marine Disasters of the Alaska Route," *Washington Historical Quarterly.* Vol. 7, No. 1, January 1916, pp. 21-37.

Beerman, Eric. "Spanish Admiral Antonio Valdez and Valdez, Alaska." *The ALASKA JOURNAL®.* Vol. 9, No. 2, Spring 1979, pp. 38-43.

Golder, Frank A. "Mining Before 1867," *Washington Historical Quarterly.* Vol. 7, No. 3, July 1916, pp. 233-38.

Hayes, C.W. "An Expedition Through the Yukon District," *National Geographic.* Vol. 4, May 15, 1892, pp. 117-62.

Robinson, M.S., and Bundtzen, T.K. "Historic Gold Production in Alaska: A 'Minisummary'," *Mines and Geology Bulletin.* Vol. 28, September 1979, pp. 1-4. (Published quarterly at College, Alaska: State of Alaska, Department of Natural Resources, Division of Geological and Geophysical Surveys)

Siddall, William R. "The Yukon Waterway in the Development of Interior Alaska," *Pacific Historical Review.* 28 (Nov. 1959): 374.

Spurr, Josiah E. "Through the Yukon Gold Diggings," Part 8 of 10 part serialization from a 1900 book in *ALASKA®*, September 1977, pp. 30-31, 90.

Wolf, Jerry O. "Return of the Snowshoe Hare," *ALASKA®*, April 1977, pp. 60, 96.

NEWSPAPERS

The Daily Ledger. Tacoma, Washington, February 21, 1898.

The Freeport, Illinois, *Journal-Standard.* 1928 issues. Contains serialization of Luther Guiteau's Alaska Gold Rush Diary for 1898 (clippings in Alaska Historical Library, Juneau).

San Francisco Chronicle, 1896-1899 issues.

Seattle Post-Intelligencer, 1896-1899 issues.